Abdulrazaq:
Nigerian Revenue Law

Malthouse Law titles

Adah C. E., *The Nigerian Law of Evidence*
Bambale, Y. Y., *Crimes and Punishments under Islamic Law*
Fogam, P., *Law of Contract*
Igweike, K., *Nigerian Commercial Law: Agency*
Igweike, K., *Nigerian Commercial Law: Contract*
Igweike, K., *Nigerian Commercial Law: Hire Purchase*
Ladan, M. T., *Introduction to Jurisprudence: Classical and Islamic*
Omorogbe, Yinka, *Oil and Gas Law in Nigeria*
Sagay, I., *Nigerian Family Law: Principles, Cases, Statutes and Commentaries*
Sagay, I., *Nigerian Law of Succession: Principles, Cases, Statutes and Commentaries*
Shoyele O., *Principles and Practice of Administrative Law in Nigeria*
Udombana, N., *Human Rights Issues in Africa*
Utuama, A. A., *Nigerian Law of Real Property: An Introduction*
Utuama, A. A., *Nigerian Planning Law*
Utuama, A. A., *The Law of Trusts and their Uses in Nigeria*
Uvieghara E. E., *Labour Law in Nigeria*
Uvieghara E. E., *Sale of Goods*
Yakubu J. A. and Oyewo A. T., *Criminal Law and Procedure in Nigeria*
Yakubu J. A., *Administration of Justice in Nigeria*
Yakubu J. A., *Harmonisation of Laws in Africa*
Yakubu J. A., *International Contracts: Evolution and Theory*
Yakubu J. A., *Law of Contract in Nigeria*
Yakubu J. A., *Limits to the Application of Foreign Laws*
Yakubu J. A., *Press Law in Nigeria*

Abdulrazaq: Nigerian Revenue Law

by

M. T. Abdulrazaq
LL.B; PhD (ABU), LL.M (Lond) BL, FCIB, FCTL
Professor of the Law of Taxation;
Executive Consultant-Tax, Ernst & Young;
formerly Dean, Faculty of Law, University of Ilorin

malthouse MP

Malthouse Press Limited

Lagos, Benin, Ibadan, Jos, Oxford, Port-Harcourt, Zaria

Malthouse Press Limited
11B Goriola Street, Off Adeola Odeku
Victoria Island, Lagos
E-mail: malthouse_press@yahoo.com
malthouse_lagos@yahoo.co.uk
Tel: +234 (01) -773 53 44; 613 957; 0802 364 2402

First Published 2005
ISBN 978 023 190 0

Distributors:
African Books Collective Ltd
Unit 13, Kings Meadow, Ferry Hinksey Road
Oxford OX2 0DP, United Kingdom
Tel: +44 - (0) 1865 -726686
Fax: +44 - (0) 1865 -793298
Email: abc@africanbookscollective.com
Website: http://www.africanbookscollective.com

Dedication

This work is dedicated to my brother and sisters:

Mr. Ahmed Abdulrazaq
Mrs. Taiwo Ayoola
Mrs. Kehinde Gbelee
Mrs. Idowu Laro
Mrs. Risi Oyetola
and to the memory of Kudirat

"This story shall the good man/woman teach his/her son/daughter;
We few, we happy few, we band of brothers and sisters."

– Adapted from Shakespeare, Henry V, Act IV, Scene 3, Line

Preface

This work was originally compiled as lecture notes for Revenue Law students of the University of Ilorin and therefore does not pretend to be comprehensive. It is offered as a statement of the fundamental principles of revenue law and it aims to state those principles in as readable and intelligible a form as the subject-matter and the need for conciseness allow.

The principles it states are those which practitioners in the field, whether lawyers, accountants or tax administrators, will need to have at their fingertips. The text will not reveal the solution to every problem but it is hoped that it will provide a useful starting point which will lead on to consideration of the statutes and cases and, where necessary more detailed reference books.

This book is directed primarily towards the university law student and those studying for the professional examinations of the Chartered Institute of Taxation of Nigeria. It is also hoped that it may assist the student of accountancy, banking and economics to appreciate the role of law in taxation. The selection of topics also aims to meet the needs of those who practise, or hope to practice, and who have to consider the impact of taxation on ordinary transactions.

I owe many debts of gratitude. My thanks are due to all my colleagues and former students at the University of Ilorin, my colleagues in the Nigerian Bar Association, Ilorin Branch, my former colleagues at Trade Bank Plc, President of The Chartered Institute of Taxation of Nigeria, Mrs Adebimpe Balogun, my colleagues at the Institute's secretariat, Mr. Eddie Osakwe, Managing Partner, and my colleagues in the tax department of Ernst and Young, Lagos,

I am also grateful for the magnificent clerical and administrative assistance provided by Gbolahan Bilewu of the Chartered Institute of Taxation and Ebenezer Agboola of Ernst & Young, and to the publishers who encouraged me to undertake the task.

Finally, I would like sincerely to acknowledge the support of the Abdulrazaq, Oshodi and Kamorudeen families, 'Tayo Quaye, 'Tola Owolabi, Latif Buari, 'Lara Coker, Isiaq Salman, Adebayo Adelodun, Ismaila Oyelude, Shadiat Akinsemoyin, Kola Salman, Ade Ipaye, Abiola Sanni, Helen Ijewere, Latifat Kamorudeen, 'Sola Oyetayo, 'Bayo Ojo, Dada Ajetunmobi, Nimota Kamorudeen, 'Funsho Mustapha, A.T. Ahmed, Latif Okandeji, and of course Falilat and the children for their love and affection.

Contents

Chapter 6: Companies income tax

Chapter 7: Settlements, trusts and estates

Chapter 8: International taxation

Cases

Table of statutes

Chapter 1

General principles

Definitions

The Oxford English Dictionary defines a tax as "a compulsory contribution to the support of government levied on persons, property, income, commodities, transactions etc., now at a fixed rate mostly proportionate to the amount on which the contribution is levied."[1] Thus, when stripped of its limited view as to the purpose of taxation, its irrelevant description of tax base and its undue stress on proportionate as opposed to progressive taxation, tells us very little, beyond that taxes are compulsory. To this criterion one may add that taxes are imposed under the authority of the legislature, that they are levied by a public body and that they are intended for public purpose.[2]

These criteria become clearer when distinguishing a tax from a charge for a government service as the Canadian courts have had to do. In the first place if the payment is a charge for a government service, some service must be provided directly to the individual.[3] There is a substantial difference between paying a bridge toll and paying a tax to be used for the defence of one's country. Secondly, the charge must be related to the service given, and not varied according to the person's ability to pay or to some other criterion such as the value of his property.[4] Thirdly, it is no objection that a charge may result in a profit provided only that the profit is a reasonable one.[5] On this basis the steep increase in energy prices or in Post Office charge not to keep the books balanced but as a fiscal device to restrain domestic consumption, as has been practised by various governments, gives those charges some of the characteristics of a tax.[6]

---

[1] See generally Tiley (1981) *Revenue Law* (Butterworths) pp 3-36; See also generally Willoughby. P.G. & Harvey Brian W. (1969) *A Guide to Income Tax and Capital Gains Tax in Nigeria* (Sweet & Maxwell)

[2] Duff J, in *Lawson* v. *Interior Tree Fruit and Vegetable Committee of Direction* (1931) SCR 357 (CAN)

[3] Duff CJ in *Reference Tax on Foreign Legations and High Commissioners' Residences* (1943) SCR 208 (CAN). Note the refusal of Lord Cairns to use the presumption of a strict interpretation of tax when considering tolls: *Pryce* v *Monmouthshire Canal and Rly Companies* (1879) 4 App Cas 197 at 202: See *Congreve* v *Home Office* (1976) 629 (1976) 1 All ER 697

[4] Montgomery J. in *Societe Centrale D'Hypotheques* v *Cite de Quebec* (1961) All ER 697; *Daymond* v *South West Water Authority* (1976), AC 609 (1976) All ER 39

[5] *Minister of Justice* v. *Levis* (1919) AC 505 (PC Can)

[6] See Sabine, *British Budgets in Peace and War* 163 and R.C. 1966 Study 24 pp 1-10

On these tests a purchase at fair market price of some goods from a nationalized industry would give rise to a charge for services not a tax. However, for an economist that payment would have to be broken down and the profit element extracted since to an economist a tax is "any leakage from the circular flow of income; into the public sector, excepting loan transactions and direct payments for publicly produced goods and services up to the cost of producing those goods and services."[7] Such tests, however "meaningful and comprehensive," have had no part in the legal definition of a tax.

A subtler problem is the difference between a fine and a tax, particularly when government motives on such matters as cigarette smoking are to say the least, ambiguous. It could appear that there is no difference between a fixed rate of fine and a tax but the power of the court to vary the normal fine and to enjoin against continued breach[8] marks off the breach of the criminal law from the carrying on of a taxable activity. Fines or penalties imposed to regulate an activity are more complex; penalties imposed to encourage prompt compliance with filing or other requirements are really more in the nature of late filing charges or interest charges than fine.[9]

Objectives and functions

(a) The classical function of the tax system is the raising of the revenue to meet government expenditure. Nothing in this function dictates a particular form of tax. Alternatively the government might commandeer resources or print money or even borrow it, but taxation is either more efficient or more just than each of these.[10] The government expenditure, which requires to be met, is either the provision of services which the free market cannot provide such as defence, law and order and parks or the provision of services and education – often called public goods.[11] Whether in practice taxes are raised to meet expenditure or vice versa is a nice but worrying question.[12]

(b) In modern times great emphasis has come to be laid on the objective of redistribution of wealth. This has two quite distinct forms. The first is the doctrine that taxation should be based on ability to pay and is summarised by the cliché that the greatest burdens should be borne by the broadest

---

[7] Allan, *Theory of Taxation* p.24

[8] *A-G* v *Harris* (1961) 1 QB 74 (1960) 3 All ER 207 See Also *Fairfax* v *Federal Commissioner of Taxation*. (1965) 14 ATD 135 AT 143

[9] US Senate Report No. 92-437, Cong. 1st Sess. 74 (1971)

[10] R.C. Canada (1966) Vol. 2, pp. 2-7

[11] Allan, *op. cit.*, p.16

[12] See Diamond, Public Expenditure in Practice (1975) cited by Morgan, *Overtaxation by Inflation* (1977) p.59.

backs. The second form presupposes that the present distribution[13] is unjust and concludes that this should therefore be undone, an idea wrapped up in the dictum that the rich should be taxed until the pips squeak. This second principles sees confiscation as a legitimate objective of taxation. Perhaps a mixed economy, which accepts the incentive principles, may be taken as committing itself to the notion that some wealth is socially acceptable and in particular that productive wealth providing for example increased employment is positively desirable.

(c) The third objective is the management of the economy. The role of tax changes in altering the level of demand is now accepted although of course other mechanisms such as credit control and the raising of welfare payments are other useful devices in stabilising the economy. At present greater emphasis is placed on monetary measures.[14] However, the tax system is more than a matter of economics. It has been described as the most pervasive and privileged exercise of the police power. It determines the direction in which people may become wealthy by determining the directions in which they may not. It is therefore impossible to regard taxes as a means of obtaining revenue.[15]

The tax system may also be used for much more specific purposes, such as discouraging the use of alcohol or the purchase of cigarettes. The tax system thus becomes a legal maid of all work.

Criteria

Two hundred years ago, Adam Smith in *The Wealth of Nations* set out certain "canons of taxation," These have been the subject of some elaboration, but are still recognisable in the criteria used by the economists judging a tax system.[16] Conflict between these criteria is inevitable.

(a) *Equity* is traditionally divided into two sorts: horizontal equity, which means that those in equal circumstances should pay an equal amount of tax, and vertical equity which means that those in unequal circumstances should pay different amount of tax. The reason why equity is regarded as important is partly an inherent view that it is right and proper in the same way that equality before the law is right and proper, and partly the view that, if a system is believed to be fair and equal, taxpayers will be more

---

[13] The problem of determining the present distribution is difficult. See Royal Commission on Distribution of Income and Wealth. Atkinson, *Unequal Shares* (1972) and Polanyi and Wood, *How Much Inequality* (1974)

[14] For an instructive debate, see Friedman and Heller *Monetary* v *Fiscal Policy* (1969)

[15] Groves 1948, *Nat Jo.* Vol. 1 p.23

[16] Among other books see Prest and Barr *Public Finance;* Shoup, *Public Finance* and Musgrave *Public Finance in Theory and Practice.*

willing to co-operate with it. However the statement that equity is important does nothing to help us to determine what circumstances are equal and what unequal.[17] Equity may be satisfied by a proportional system just as much as by a progressive system of taxation and benefits.

(b) *Neutrality*:[18] A tax is neutral if it avoids distortions of the market. The Nigerian tax system has many rules, which break the principle of neutrality. Worse there are many technical rules which make significant tax differences according to which of two or more methods are adopted to achieve a given result.[19] The cffect is harmful since it encourages the expenditure of money on expert advice, expenditure which is in economic terms unproductive, and on schemes which may make a trade less efficient.

(c) *Certainty:* This means first that the scope of the tax should be clear. Penumbral areas cause resentment amongst taxpayers cast into the darkness and undermine the principle of equity, besides increasing the cost of the system. It means next the certainty that the tax can and will be enforced. A tax that is easily evaded causes resentment and often a decline in taxpayer morality. It means also that the government will be able to correctly predict how much tax is gathered in and so perhaps the effects of the tax.

(d) *Administrative efficiency:* Only those who regard the duty of the tax system as being to confiscate wealth in order to provide employment would be happy with a tax whose administration costs exceeded the tax yield. There is the further problem of compliance cost.[20] A good tax structure must take into account many factors: the effects on economic incentives; its fairness as between persons of similar taxable capacity; its effects upon distribution between rich and poor, whether it is compatible with desirable international economic relations and its simplicity, ease of understanding and absence of excessive administration cost.

Direct and indirect taxes

This distinction is important for Nigerian tax laws. According to Mill:[21]

> A direct tax is one which is demanded from the very person who, it is intended or desired, should pay it. Indirect taxes are those, which are demanded from one person in the expectation and intention that he shall

---

[17] Vertical Equity means graduated or disproportional taxation

[18] Groves (1948) *Nat Tax Jo.*, p. 18 and Bracewell Milnes (1976) *BTR* 110

[19] The reconstructing effect of section 18 CITA 1990

[20] See Abdulrazaq, M.T. (1993) *Nigerian Tax Offences and Penalties* (Batay Law publications), see also Sandford *Hidden Costs* (1973)

[21] Mill, *Principles of Political Economy*, Book V.chap.3

> indemnify himself at the expense of the other; such as the excise or customs. The producer or importer of a commodity is called upon to pay a tax on it not with the intention to levy a particular contribution upon him, but a tax through him the consumers of the commodity, from whom it is supposed that he will recover the amount by means of an advance in price.

This distinction has become less clear as the real incidence of taxation has been explored by economists. Thus some research suggests that the taxation of profits of companies results in the shifting of that tax on to customers or employers of the company; such a tax has however been classified as direct. This is because courts, such as the Privy Council on appeals from Canada, have paid attention to that part of Mill's formulation, which emphasized the intention and expectation that the tax would be shifted. There is thus a fundamental distinction between the economic recouping of a direct tax and the simple passing on (often in the form of a straight percentage of the price) which is the hallmark of an indirect tax; between the recovery of a direct tax by a more or less circuitous operation of economic forces and the passing on of a tax in recognizable form.[22] In applying this distinction the courts will treat a tax as direct notwithstanding that actual payment may be enforced against some intermediary so that income tax on employment income is not the less direct because the employer must deduct tax.

Applying these tests the Canadian courts, including the Privy Council, have held to be direct taxes not only such taxes as income tax, and capital duty[23] but also taxes on expenditure such as a levy on tobacco bought for personal consumption.[24] On the other hand, they have held to be indirect taxes not only such obvious items as customs and excise duties and sales tax but also stamp duty[25] a succession duty which could be collected from someone other than the beneficiary (e.g. a personal representative)[26] and gross revenue taxes.[27] Every tax must be judged on its sown. By rejecting – inevitably – the test of economic incidence, which would mean that almost every tax was at risk of being classified as indirect, the courts have been forced back on to a test of the general tendency of a tax to be passed on or not and this must lead to borderline cases.

The balance between direct and indirect taxation has long been a problem in Nigeria owing to the contrasting philosophies of different governments, which, believing that direct taxation was progressive and indirect taxation

---

[22] *Bank of Toronto* v *Lambe* (1887) 12 App Cas 575 Lord Greene in *A-G for British Columbia* v *Esquimault and Nanaimo Rly Co.* (1950) AC 87 at 113 See La Forest *Allocation of Taxing Power under the Canadian Constitution* (2nd edn. 1981) chap. 4, see also Abiola Sanni (2000) Division of Taxing Powers under the 1999 Constitution. *Modus International Law and Business Quarterly*, p. 109 volume 5 No. 3 September, 2000

[23] *Atlantic Smoke Shops Ltd.* v. *Cenlon* (1943) AC 550, (1943) 2 All ER 393

[24] *A-G for Quebec* v *Reed* (1884) 10 App. Cas 14

[25] *Cotton* v *R* (1914) AC 176, distinguishing *R* v *Lovitt* (1912) AC 212

[26] *R* v. *Caledonian Collieries Ltd.* (1928) AC 358

[27] La Forest, *op. cit.*, p. 74

regressive[28] acted accordingly. The room for change is now reduced by the very high demands placed upon the economy by government expenditure.

However, it should be noted that the divide between the two types of tax is not absolute. Indirect taxes may affect the cost of living and so be taken into account when fixing tax threshold levels.[29]

Indirect taxes are also of interest for the light they shed on social attitudes. It has been observed that it is generally a feature of the civilized world that the most unacceptable vices are punished by imprisonment or worse, the somewhat less serious by fines and the most venial by heavy taxes. It is possible to dismiss the idea that an Erewhon-like reversal of attitude might take place, so that for example sales of tobacco and alcohol will render the vendor liable to imprisonment, whilst excise will be imposed on soft drugs and the use of brothels – as well as income tax on the proceeds of both.[30]

Jurisdiction

Under section 272 of the Constitution of the Federal Republic of Nigeria, 1999, the High Court of a State has jurisdiction to hear and determine any civil proceedings in which the existence or extent of a legal right, power, duty, liability, privilege, interest, obligation or claim is an issue.[31] It may also hear and determine any criminal proceedings involving or relating to any penalty, forfeiture, punishment or other liability in respect of an offence committed by any person. However, the jurisdiction of a State High Court is subject to the provisions of Section 251 of the Constitution, which confers exclusive jurisdiction on the Federal Court in respect of some matters. Under section 251, the exclusive jurisdiction of the Federal High Court includes civil causes and matters:

a) Relating to the revenue of the Government of the Federation in which the said Government or any organ thereof or a person suing or being sued on behalf of the Federal Government is a party.
b) Connected with or pertaining to the taxation of companies and other bodies established or carrying on business in Nigeria and all other persons subject to Federal taxation.
c) Connected with or pertaining to customs and excise duties, including any claim by or against the Nigerian Customs Service or any member or

[28] E.g. Snowden cited in Mallet and George, *British Budgets* (1913-1921) p. 10: "These taxes violate every canon of taxation, because they tax a man not in proportion to his ability to pay nor according to those benefits he receives but according to his personal tastes".

[29] Pechman, IFS Lecture 1973 p.18

[30] Messere IFS Lecture Series No. 2(1974), p. 18

[31] See generally Ipaye, Ade, *Introduction to the Nigerian Tax System*, being a paper presented at the workshop on Tax Law and Administration organized by the Chartered Institute of Taxation of Nigeria and Rahmad Research and Consultancy Service, March 20-22, 2001, pp. 24, 25, 26

officer thereof, arising from the performance of any duty imposed under any regulation relating to customs and excise duties and export duties.

By virtue of Section 251 (3) of the Constitution, the Federal High Court also has jurisdiction and powers in respect of criminal causes and matters arising out of the foregoing.

It seems from these provisions that all matters pertaining to a Federal tax must go to the Federal High Court. These will necessarily include companies' income tax, petroleum profits tax, custom and excise duties, stamp duties payable by corporate bodies, capital gain tax payable by corporate bodies and education tax. However, because of the specialized nature of taxation, the income tax statutes provide that the cases should first go to the Federal Body of Tax Appeal Commissioners.

But what of personal income tax stamp duties payable by individuals and capital gain tax payable by individual? All these are charged by Federal law, but collected by State authorities. In our view, cases arising from these should go to State High Courts simply because the Federal Government or any of its organs is not a party to the case. Since States collect and expend these taxes, they cannot be said to do the collection on behalf of the Federal Government. Perhaps for this reason, the Personal Income Tax Act confers jurisdiction on State Bodies of Appeal Commissioners and State High Courts.

For the special case of value added taxation, the then Federal Government promulgated the Finance (Miscellaneous Taxation Provisions) (No.3) Decree (now Act) No.32 of 1996, by which a new Section 16(2) was introduced into the VAT Act. The section provides that a taxable person who is aggrieved by an assessment made on him may appeal to the Value Added Tax Tribunal. Furthermore, a new schedule 2 to the Act provides for the establishment and operation of five VAT Tribunals spread geographically throughout the country. The VAT Tribunal is given the same status as the Federal High Court; hence, appeals from the body go to the Court of Appeal.

Taxes collected by the Local Government authorities are often adjudicated upon in the Magistrate courts. For instance, issues of tenement rate go to an Appeal Tribunal and appeals from the Tribunal go to the Magistrates' courts.[32]

Avoidance, evasion, mitigation and planning

Politicians, tax officials and practitioners spend a lot of time and energy on the problem of tax avoidance. No one seems to have a very precise idea of what is meant by the term,[33] but it is to be distinguished from evasion, which is illegal. If two people marry in order to reduce tax burden they are practising tax avoidance; if they tell the Revenue that they are married when they are not, they

---

[32] See section 30-32, Tenement Rate Law of Lagos

[33] See IFS Tax Law Review Committee (TLRC), *Report on Avoidance*

are guilty of tax evasion, and may well be prosecuted. There is also an important distinction between a scheme under which no liability to tax arises, (tax avoidance) and one under which a charge arises but the tax cannot be collected.[34] The latter may be evasion and subject to penalty. Other terms used in discussion – and in case law – are tax mitigation and tax planning, which may be seen as subsets of tax avoidance or as independent categories, depending on the context in which one finds oneself; they are all, however to be distinguished from tax evasion.

Unfortunately, tax evasion itself has developed a number of "frayed edges". Thus, it is sometimes used to cover all cases of non-complaince[35] may be deliberate or accidental and may give rise to penalties under tax legislation, prosecution under criminal law, or both. Evasion may even result from taking a position on tax legislation, which is alter shown to be incorrect.[36] If these are all examples of evasion, its greatest cause may not be fraud or greed, but the complexity of the tax legislation; the category, instead of being one of undoubted opprobrium, can become a matter of judicial hindsight. It is such consideration which encourage those who believe in a low rate, broad-based tax system, with few opportunities for tax saving.

Tax mitigation[37] is distinguished from tax avoidance because judges when dealing with a provision turning on the presence of tax avoidance invented the term "mitigation" in order to mark off transactions, which would not be caught by the provision.[38] In this context therefore tax mitigation and tax avoidance are mutually exclusive. Today, tax avoidance arises where the taxpayer reduces a liability to tax without incurring the economic consequences that the National or State Assemblies intended to be suffered by any taxpayer qualifying for such reduction in that liability.[39] Tax mitigation arises where the taxpayer takes advantage of a fiscally attractive option afforded by the tax legislation, and genuinely suffers the economic consequences that parliament intended to be suffered by those taking advantage of the option. There are therefore two elements, economic consequences and legislative intent. The first element asserts that there should be some genuine economic consequences, while the second enables the court, on a case-by-case basis, to control, which consequences will qualify. Today, a couple marrying to reduce tax would be treated as examples of tax mitigation.

---

[34] See comments of Brightman J. in *Roome* v. *Edwards* (1979) STC 546, 561-5 (removed from bound volume – see (1979) BTR 262), See also the comments of Templeman I. J. in *IRC Stype Investment Ltd.* (1982) STC 625

[35] On causes of non-compliance, See Cooper (1994) 50 *Tax Law Review 35*

[36] *R* v *Allen* ((1999) STC 846

[37] See e.g. Lord Templeman in *Ensign Tankers (Leasing) Ltd* v. *Stokes (Inspector of Taxes)* (1992) AC.655 676-7 (1992) STC 226, 240-164, TC 617, 741-2 and Lord Goff at 684, 244-5 and 746-7 respectively

[38] E.g. Lord Templeman in *Commissioner of Inland Revenue* v *Challenge Corporation* (1987) AC 155, 167-8 (1986) STC 548, 554-5, PC (New Zealand)

[39] *IRC* v *Willoughby* (1997) STC 995

The problem with tax mitigation is that while it provides a coherent reason for saying, in a particular case, that the facts do not amount to avoidance, and so do not trigger the applicant of some rule, it does not provide a clear way of telling whether those particular facts fall one side of the line or the other – it can be a conclusion, not a test, and so restates the problem rather than solve it.[40]

Tax planning is what all sensible people do in order to reduce their tax liabilities. The boundary between tax avoidance and tax planning is shadowy at best, what matters is the boundary between successful and unsuccessful tax planning. Tax planning is bet understood by reference to the word "who", "what", "when" and "where".[41]

"Who"; tax planning may involve the careful selection of the particular taxpayer who will for example, receive the income or realize a loss; thus, it may be another member of the family with little other income or relief, or a subsidiary of a company. "What", with care, it may also be possible to influence the type of receipt, whether capital or income, or one type of income rather than another, e.g. employment income or business income.

"When": timing is also important, and paying attention to time may enable the taxpayer to postpone a liability to tax, for example by taking advantage of a deferral rule, or to avoid being caught by an artificial tax rule which forbids, for example, the carrying back of an unused capital loss.

"Where": location is important since placing income or assets outside the taxing jurisdiction may mean no liability to Nigerian tax, or no liability until income is remitted to Nigeria. The downside of this is that liability may be incurred under the foreign tax system. However, the foreign tax system may be different to the Nigerian system, and the exploitation of gaps between tax system is the forte of the international specialist.

Importance

The importance of tax avoidance is threefold. First, from the wider perspective it is not possible to assess the effectiveness of a tax system unless it can be seen by what degree of avoidance is practised and permitted by the system. Thus, to have a rule that trading profits of charities are not exempt from tax is one thing; to learn that this is routinely avoided by having a separate trading company which assigns its profits to its charitable owners makes the rule look less fierce. Secondly, while legislation to counter avoidance can be among the most complex in our tax code, it can also be among the simplest. Thirdly, from the lawyer's perspective, the case law on avoidance tell us much about the problems posed by legislation and statutory purpose.

---

[40] See Rosenberg (1988) 87 *Michigan L.R.*365-497

[41] See Tiley (2000) *Revenue Law* (Hart Publishing) pp: 85, 86, 87.

Sources

Statutes: The statute law for a particular tax is to be found in the statute, which introduced it as subsequently amended. Sometimes amendments are made to the text of the original Act; at other time a new provision is introduced to exist alongside the original Act. The result might be described as a patchwork where it not for the overtones of antique coziness that go with that words; is better described as a shambles. Sometimes the text relating to a particular tax is consolidated e.g. Companies Income Tax 1961, 1979 and 1990, but the perfection of consolidation is often marred within weeks.[42]

Codification has been suggested from time to time however no action was taken and it is unlikely that the tax law will be codified in the foreseeable future in a single text, except of course the various individual efforts at compilation.

Income tax is an annual tax and the charge is reimposed by the National Assembly in each year in the Finance Bill. The result is that Tax Acts are really in the nature of an Income Tax Clauses Act and apply whenever any Act imposes an income tax.[43] The Finance Bill also amends the rules for the other taxes.[44] The resulting combination of measures of great economic importance and matters of great technical subtlety discussed against the background of the hurly-burly of legislative procedure is, not surprisingly, capable of error.[45]

Interpretation of taxing statutes

As a result of tax laws being entirely statutory, tax disputes almost always raise the issue of statutory interpretation. As a rule, tax statutes are interpreted very strictly. There is no common law of taxation; hence no general principle of law can displace the true meaning and effect of a tax statute which has been validly passed. For tax liability to arise, therefore there must be a clear link between the charging provisions and the intended taxpayer. This link must be direct, not inferential.[46]

In line with these, judges generally agreed that the proper approach in the interpretation of tax legislation is to adopt the literal rule. The ordinary meaning of the provision in issue prevails. However, where the provision is found to be clearly ambiguous, i.e. where there are more than one ways of interpreting it, then the interpretation that most favours the taxpayer is adopted. This is because

---

[42] See Institute for Fiscal Studies Conference, 28th June 1974, p.18
[43] Per Atkin I.J. in *Martin* v. *Lowery* (1926) 11 TC 297 at 317
[44] The practice of having a single bill dealing with all taxes stems from Gladstone's battles with the House of Lords – See Magnus, Gladstone p.151
[45] On reform see Report of Raisman, Aboyade, etc., Fiscal Commission
[46] See S.A. *Authority* v. *Regional Tax Board* (1967) N.C.L.R.452; *Tennant* v. *Smith* (1892 A.C. at 154; See also Ipaye, Ade, ibid., pp.16, 17,18,19,20

tax is an imposition on the citizen. At common law, any statute by which the government seeks to expropriate its subjects must be construed strictly in favour of the subjects. As a result, the key issue in tax disputes is whether or not the words of a statute cover the alleged subject of taxation.

In *Cape Brandy* v. *IRC*, [47] Rowlatt J. presented a summary of the duties of a judge in tax adjudication thus:

> In a taxing Act, one has to look merely at what is clearly said. There is no room for any intendment. There is no equity about a tax. There is no presumption as to a tax. Nothing is to be read in, nothing is to be implied. One has to look fairly at the language used.[48]

This approach was approved and adopted in the Nigerian cases of *S.A. Authority* v. *Regional Tax Board*[49a] and *Aderawo Timber Company Ltd.* v. *F.B.I.R.*[49b] The nature of the provision under consideration did not matter. In *I.R.C.* v. *Ayrshire Employers Mutual Insurance Association Ltd.*[50] where a provision clearly intended to widen the tax net failed to achieve that purpose, Lord Simmonds declared:

> It is at least clear what is the gap that is intended to be filled and hardly less clear how it is intended to fill the gap. Yet I can come to no other conclusion than that the language of the section fails to achieve its apparent purpose and I must decline to insert words or phrase which might succeed where the draftsman failed.

However, the apparently settled judicial approach which gives no consideration to the intendment of a tax provision was slightly disturbed by Bello J.S.C. (as he then was) while delivering, the majority decision in *Mobil Oil Nigeria Ltd. v. Federal Board of Inland Revenue.*[51] According to him:

> In construing a statute, regard shall be given to the cause and necessity of the Act and then such construction shall be put upon it as would promote its purpose and arrest the mischief which it is intended to deter...Some companies have been manipulating their accounts with the intent to hide their true assessable profits and in that manner have been avoiding tax which they ought to have paid. The purpose of section 30 (of the Companies Income Tax Act) is to deter companies from engaging in such a fraudulent practice.

---

[47] (1921) 2K.B.403
[48] See also *Mangin* v. *IRC* (1971) A. C. 739
[49a] (1966) N.C.L.R. 452
[49b] (1996) N.C.L.R. 416 at 422 per Ikpeazu J.
[50] (1946) I. AII E.R. 637
[51] (1977) I.N.C.L.R.I

Perhaps, the proper inference to be drawn from this decision is that only anti-avoidance provisions (i.e., provisions are inserted in tax laws for the specific purposes of preventing tax evasion or avoidance) are to be construed liberally in order to give effect to the intention of the legislature. This would therefore be an exception to the general principle that there is no room for any intendment in the construction of a tax statute.

Justification for this approach could be found in the fact that anti-avoidance provisions are usually not plain and direct. Because of the purposes for which they were devised, such provisions are usually very widely drawn, and in the process, often so prolix as to be meaningless. If, in this circumstance, the strict interpretation approach is taken, many tax-evaders will still escape untouched and the legislature may be forced into even more complex and ambitious and avoidance provisions. Ultimately, the innocent taxpayer may become the easy prey of such provisions.[52]

Alternatively, the attitude of Bello J.S.C. (as he then was) could be seen as an indication that Nigerian judicial officers do not give any particular attention to the peculiarities of taxing statutes. This possibility was made clear in *Shell Petroleum Development Company (Limited)* v. *Federal Board of Inland Revenue*[53] where the same Supreme Court not only applied equity considerations but also gave administrative directives overriding effect in the interpretation of a tax statute. The trend was carried to an absurd level by the Court of Appeal in the case of *Phoenix Motors Limited* v. *NPFMB*[54] Against all known rules of tax statutory interpretation, the Court of Appeal declared that:

> If a statute is revenue based or revenue oriented, the provisions thereof must be construed liberally in favour of revenue or in favour of deriving revenue by government, unless there is a clear provision to the contrary. This is because it is in the interest of the generality of the public and to the common good and welfare of the citizenry for Government to be in revenue and affluence to cater for the people.

This is sufficient warning that there is no settled approach to interpretation of taxing statutes in Nigeria. The universal rule, which may of course be urged in Nigerian courts is that the beliefs and assumptions of those who interpret statutes cannot make the law. The onus is therefore on the legislature to ensure that tax is expressly imposed upon the subject. Where this has not been done, the response of the court should then depend on the factual situation before it. If the provisions in issue can reasonably be interpreted so as to mean what the legislature intended, then nit should be so interpreted. But where that is not possible or where, having regard to the intention of the legislature, ambiguity remains, then the taxpayer should have the benefit of the doubt.

---

[52] See the analysis of Lord Reid in *Greenberg* v. *IRC* 1972 A.C. 109 at 137

[53] (1996) 8 NWLR 256

[54] (1993) 1 NWLR (pt. 272) 718 at 731

A court would however be circumspect in declaring a taxing provision to be ambiguous[55] Taxpayers are not favoured just because the ingenious argument of counsel casts doubt upon the meaning of a provision. If the court is satisfied that of the two possible interpretations, one is clearly the right one, that right one must be adopted even when it is not favourable to the taxpayer. But if after a careful examination of all the causes, a judicial mind shall entertain any reasonable doubt as to what the legislature intended, then the taxpayer shall have the benefit of the doubt[56]. Real ambiguity in a taxing statute may be resolved in favour of government only by subsequent legislation; hence the taxpayer is entitled to stand upon a literal construction of the statutory provision, even if the result produced is anomalous.

By the same token, "once the intention to impose tax on the subject is sufficiently shown, it is vain to speculate on what would be the fairest and most equitable mode of levying the tax."[57]

Cases and revenue practice

Cases are authorities in the usual way according to the rule of precedent. However in assessing the value of a precedent in tax law, special complications arise from the fact that the appeal structure in Nigeria allows the courts to reverse a decision of the Commissioners only for error of law or because it cannot be supported on the evidence.[58]

The Revenue sometimes publishes reports of the decision of Tax Appeal although it is of little value as a guide for later cases. This cannot be said of decisions of the Federal or State High Courts. Although not law, statements of Revenue practice are of great importance in the practical administration of the system.[59] These statements are of different sorts. First there are extra-statutory concessions. These are few, tightly written and almost legislative in form.[60] Secondly there are the statements of practice, which are published on a regular basis; these are only slightly less formal than the concessions.[61] The Revenue position often prefers a broad legislative rule, which can then be interpreted "liberally" or not. The disadvantages of this are that a rule may be interpreted unevenly and there is the possibility, however, unlikely, of abuse.

---

[55] See *Wilcox* v. *Smith* 26 L. J. Ch. 596

[56] *Wilcox* v. *Smith, supra.*

[57] Per Lord Blackburn in *Coltness* v. *Black* (1881) 6 A. C. 315, quoted with approval in *S. A. Authority* v *Regional Tax Board* (1970) N.C.L.R. 276 See *also I.R.C.* v *Hinchy* 1960 A. C. 748SS

[58] Abdulrazaq M.T. (1996) An Analysis of Income Tax Appeal (Appeal Commissioners) Rules in *Nigerian Tax Notes* Vol.2. No.9 (Maples & Temples)

[59] For an example and practitioners' reaction, see (1975) BTR 87 and 196; See FIRS Tax Guide (2002)

[60] On legality, See Williams (1979) BTR 137 and *Vestey* v *IRC* (1980) AC 1148 (1980) STC 10

[61] On pros and cons see RC (Canada) 1966. Study No.22, pp.304-307; See FIRS Tax Guide (2002)

Thirdly there are advance rulings in individual cases.[62] There is no general scheme where tax payers can obtain advance rulings on the tax consequences of a particular transaction. However in practice, advice is often available. This practice seems both reasonable and desirable but could be expanded. The Revenue is not there to provide a free legal aid clinic, but it is in the Revenue's interests to be helpful. In certain circumstances the legislation will prescribe a clearance procedure, usually as part of broad anti-avoidance legislation.[63] In practice these clearances have been criticized as defective in that:

> they have to carry too much weight. They often require enormously difficult question of law to be decided, without right of appeal, at administrative level. Second, informal statutory terms they cover only a part of the ground. Extra-ordinary clearances are often given in practice, but the practice is unsatisfactory in that (a) it rests upon the exercise of an authorized discretion and (b) it often seems that the official in question, overworked but trying to be helpful when he can, is readier to listen to extra-statutory applications from the organizations and firms whom he knows and trusts than from others, which is understandable, but sometimes looks like one law for the rich and one for the poor.[64]

Administration

Responsibility for the administration of the taxes is entrusted to the Federal Board of Inland Revenue and the States' Board of Internal Revenue. The Boards appoint inspectors who carry out the work of assessment for income tax, CGT, Company Tax and VAT and Banks who collect these taxes.[65] The Board are under a duty to collect these taxes but is not guilty of an abuse of power in entering into special arrangements absolving taxpayers from liability to tax; further, a taxpayer has no sufficient interest to ask a court to investigate the tax affairs of another taxpayer.[66] In carrying out the duty laid on it ,the Board must act with administrative common sense.[67] However this discretion does not justify a court in construing a section so as to give the Board a discretion as to

---

[62] On pros and cons of advance ruling precedents See (1960) Can Bar Journal 6 at 14 and 91 at 115 – 116.

[63] E.g. section 18 CITA 1990

[64] Nolan, IFS Conference 28th June 1974, p.25, and see Potter (1975) BTR 175-177

[65] Part 1 CITA 1993 See also CITA 1990 section (2) (a) and PITA 1993 section 85a (2) a

[66] *IRC* v. *National Federation of Self Employed and Small Business Ltd.* (1981) STC 260 (Fleet Street amnesty not illegal) on amnesties See Pepper (1996) *BTR* 284. See also Abdulrazaq M. T (1992) *Nigerian Taxation and Fawehinmi* v. *Akilu*: Spreading the Dragnet of Tax Compliance. *Kwara Law Review* Vol. 1 No 1 pp86-101 (Journal of the Nigerian Bar Association, Ilorin Branch)

[67] Per Lord Wilberforce in *Vestey* v. *IRC* (1980) STC 10 at 19; the Board may remit tax in certain cases when the failure to collect was due to official error. Curiously the extent of this practice is governed by the taxpayer.

how to allocate a tax liability between different taxpayers, nor does it provide a legal basis for the practice of extra statutory concession[68] VAT and other indirect taxes are also administered by the Federal, State and Local Government tax authorities and Stamp Duties by the Commissioners for Stamp Duties.

Information received in the execution of duty may be disclosed to other bodies, including other government departments only with statutory authority. As there is no estoppel against the State, no legal reliance may be placed on statements by officers of the Board.[69] However compensation may be obtainable in tort.[70]

Administrative and transitional provisions

(A) Introduction

The Administrative and Transitional Provisions of the Personal income Tax Act of 1993 contained in Sections 85 – 85G provide the legislative framework for:

a) Joint Tax Board
b) Establishment of State Board of Internal Revenue
c) Functions of the State Board
d) Establishment of Technical Committee of the State Board
e) Establishment of Local government Revenue Committee
f) Functions of the Revenue Committee
g) Establishment and composition of Joint State Revenue Committee
h) Functions of the State Joint Revenue Committee

The above stated framework is discussed in a manner that highlights some of the important issues likely to arise in the exercise of the powers contained in the provisions and the legal implications for their workability as well as the effect on the Nigerian tax system.

Making the fiscal system work is said the two Musgraves, a large part of making democracy function.[71] The setting of the Nigerian tax system is important for a variety of reasons. Clearly, one has to know the basic rules governing the reporting of income, the calculation of tax and the enforcement of liability to tax. Secondly, one ought to be aware of Revenue powers to ensure that the basic structure works, including the imposition of interest or penalties under the tax legislation or the criminal law and the role of other agencies where tax fraud and other frauds overlap. However, it is also important to put this structure into a wider context. One part of that wider context is concerned with

---

[68] Per Lord Edmund Davies, ibid, at 35 see also Williams (1979) *BTR*

[68] PITA 1993 section 47, CITA 1990 Section 43

[69] *South-end on Sea Corporation* v. *Hodgson (Wickford) Ltd.* (1961) 2 All ER 46

[70] Wade, *Administrative Law* (4th ed) p. 327; See also Iluyomade & Eka *Cases & Materials on Administrative Law.* (Obafemi Awolowo University Press) 2nd ed.

[71] Musgrave and Musgrave, *Public Finance in Theory and Practice* (1st ed.), preface, Reprinted in 5th ed. (McGraw-Hill 1989), xvii.

the balance of power between taxpayers and the executive.[72] Tax is, after all, probably the branch of law through which most citizens come into contact with the state, especially if one includes, indirect contact through the PAYE system. Another part of that context is the need to be able to assess the efficacy of the rules in the same way as a criminologist looks at the efficacy of the criminal law. In the administration of the tax system one has to ask what the rules are for. Research in many areas of government regulation suggest that a flexible approach to enforcement may be much better than a top down, legalistic, going-by-the-book version.[73] However, this assumes that the regulator's purpose is to try to educate and to secure co-operation. Whether this is the right model for the tax system is precisely the question at issue. One needs to know when the demands of equity may have to reduce in the name of effective compliance. One has to know about the extent to which the professions are to be seen as enforcers of the system through codes of ethics imposed on qualified practitioners (and the extent to which a knowledge of the code forms part of the qualification process). In order to form some assessment of the system it is also desirable to know how efficient the services provided by tax professional are. However, the tax system should also be seen as a system, which has to work.

(B) Computing liability

The State Board of Internal Revenue and the Local Government Revenue Committee are under a duty to collect taxes but are not guilty of an abuse of power in entering into special arrangements absolving taxpayers from liability from liability to tax. One taxpayer has no sufficient interest to ask a court to investigate the tax affairs of another, [74] however, this must be distinguished from a situation in which the Revenue's approach to a question of interpretation of law is wrong.[75] In carrying out the duty laid on it the State Board or the Local Government Revenue Committee must act with administrative common sense.[76] However, this discretion does not justify a court in construing a section of an Act so as to give the State Board or the Local Government Committee discretion over how to allocate tax liability between different taxpayers, nor does it provide

---

[72] See e.g. Goldberg 1966 *BTR*

[73] For example, Bardach and Kangan, Going by the Book: *The Problem of Regulatory Unreasonableness* (Temple University Press, Philadelphia, 1982); Braithwaite. *To Punish or Persuade: The Enforcement of Coal Mining Laws* (SUNNY, Albany, 1985)

[74] *IRC V National Federation of Self-Employment and Small Business Ltd.* (1981) 2, All ER 93 (1981) STC 260 (Fleet Street amnesty not illegal); Abdulrazaq M.T. (1992) *Nigerian Taxation and Fawehinmi* v *Akilu*; "Spreading the Dragnet of Tax Compliance," *Kwara Law Review* Vol. 1. No. 2 pp 86-101.

[75] *R.* v *A.G. ex parte* (1986) 60 TC 1, (1987) 1 CMLR 72.

[76] *Vestey* v *IRC* (1980) STC 10, 19, 54, TC 503, 582, *per Lord Wilberforce*. The board remits tax in certain cases when the failure to collect was due to official error; the extent of this practice is governed by the circumstances of the taxpayer; ESC. A19.

a legal basis for the practice of extra-statutory concessions.[77] It is typical of the way the Nigerian tax system is run as a club whose members are the professions and the Federal or State Board's and Local Government Committee that there has been no pressure from club members to put concessions on a proper legal basis. However, judges remain critical[78] One day the court may have to decide whether it is theoretically possible to order the tax authorities to give taxpayer the benefit of a concession, i.e. to make an assessment, which is not in accordance with the law.

(1) Confidentiality/secrecy

Information received in the execution of duty may not be disclosed to other bodies, including other government department, without statutory authority. Release of information relating to the tax affairs of "an identifiable person" without such authority or consent may be a criminal offence[79] there is no statutory authority for releasing information to the police. The modern mantra of the anti-corruption crusade can undermine this confidentiality unless of course, the taxpayer agrees.

(2) Reliance on revenue statements

Conventional wisdom is that there is no estoppel against the State or Local Government; hence, no legal reliance may generally be placed on statements by tax officers so as to make the court determine a tax appeal in the way stated by those officers.[80] However, compensation be obtained through the Public Complaints Commission and may be obtainable in tort;[81] in addition, such statements may furnish the very basis for an application for judicial review of a revenue decision.[82]

(3) Discovery assessments

If an officer discovers that income or capital gains which should have been assessed have not been or that an assessments is or has become insufficient or that any relief is or has become excessive, that officer may make an assessment to recover the loss of tax. The notion of discovery assessment may only be made if either the taxpayer or agent has been guilty of fraud or negligence, or the

---

[77] *Vestey* v *IRC* (1980) STC 10, 35, 54 TC 503, 599 *per Lord Davies, citing Williams* (1979) BTR 137.

[78] See also Wade and Forsyth, *Administrative Law* (8th ed. OUP, 1994) 407.

[79] Section 47 (2) PITA 1993

[80] *Southend on Sea Corpn.* v *Hodgson (Wickford) Ltd.* 1962 1 QB 416, (1961) 2 All ER 46; See, *R.* v *IRC, ex parte J. Rothschild Hodings Plc* (1987) STC 163 TC 178 where an estoppel issue was raised in judicial review proceedings but failed on the facts.

[81] Wade and Forsyth, 339-334; See also comments of Lord Griffiths in *Matrix Securities Ltd* v *IRC* (1994) STC 272, 2S4. H, on possible compensation claim if the Revenue withdraws clearance after expense incurred in reliance on the clearance, see also Eden (1994) BTR 263, On wider issues, see the fascinating book by Farnsworth *Changing your mind. The Law of Registered Decisions.* (Yale 1999)

[82] Abdulrazaq, M.T. (1993) *Judicial Review in Nigerian Taxation* (Maples & Temples)

officer could not reasonably be expected to be aware, on the basis of the information then available to him, that additional tax was due.

The word "discover" covered a variety of circumstances; the word is apt to cover any case in which, for any reason, it newly appears that the taxpayer has been undercharged.[83] Therefore, an assessment may be made where the Revenue decides that a company should be treated as a dealing company rather than an investment company[84] where a new inspector takes a different view of the law from his predecessor,[85] or to correct an arithmetical error in the computation. Where taxpayer made a claim, which was erroneously agreed by an inspector, a later inspector is not entitled to make a "discovery assessment on finding the error.[86] The test is whether a reasonable man would conclude that the inspector had agreed the claim.

(4) Record keeping and penalties

If the tax payer is carrying on a trade, profession or business (including the letting of property) all necessary records must be kept. There are also rules as to the form in which records of a business must be kept.

(5) Subsequent events

Once an assessment has been made it cannot be changed although it may be open to Revenue to issue a second (additional) assessment rather than to seek an increase in the first on appeal.[87]

(C) Public law and other challenges to the tax authorities

Tax authorities are very powerful and so the law has created avenues for challenges to the tax authorities.

(1) Judicial review

This remedy is equally applicable to the decision of the Appeal Commissioners or to the original assessment; it is also applicable quite separately from the assessments process to any situation in which officers of the Revenue exercise a power committed to them by the State. An application may be made only if the court has granted leave. It requires an applicant to have sufficient interest or *locus standi.* The court will not allow an applicant to use judicial review where the point should be dealt with by appeal.[88] Conversely, allegations of unfairness

---

[83] *Cenlon Finance Co. Ltd* v *Ellwood* (1962) 1 All ER 854, 859, 40 TC. 176, 204, *per Viscount; Western Soudan Exporters* v *F.B.I.R.* INTC 239

[84] *Jones* v *Mason Investment (Luton) Ltd.* (1966) 43 TC 570 (1967) BTR 75 JGM.

[85] *Parkin* v *Cattell* (1971) 48 TC 462

[86] *Scorer* v *Olin Energy System Ltd.* (1985) STC 764; Section 54 PITA 1993.

[87] *Baylis Maternity Ltd* v *Hudgson* (1985) STC 764; Section 54 PITA 1993.

[88] See discussion by Dyson J. in *R.* v *IRC ex parte Bishop* (1999) STC 531; see generally *Saunders, Judicial Review in Tax Disputes* (Wiley, 1996) and Bartlett (1987) B.T.R. 10

in the conduct of the appeal are matters by the Appeal Commissioners[89] are matters for judicial review and not for appeal. When judicial review is sought applicants must ensure that they do not act too early or too late.[90] The grounds for judicial review are, of course, the same as in other areas of law, and were set out in 1985 in England by Lord Diplock[91] as comprising illegality, irrationality and procedural impropriety. Illegality covers errors of law; irrationality covers *Wednesbury* unreasonableness, i.e. a decision which is so outrageous in its defiance of logic or accepted moral standards that no sensible persons who applied their minds to the question could have arrived at it, procedural impropriety covers not only the failure to observe the rules of natural justice but also errors in the tribunal's own procedures. Today this formulation must also be interpreted to embrace the emerging doctrines of legitimate expectations and proportionality.

(2) Public law defence

The second remedy is to establish a public law defence to a Revenue enforcement action,[92] e.g. by arguing that the original assessment is *ultra vires* and therefore void. In *IRC* v *Aken,*[93] this line of argument was used – unsuccessfully – to argue that the profits or prostitution could not be taxable since, as a matter of law, the profits of an illegal activity cannot be subject to tax. The English Court of Appeal rejected this argument. Judges will no doubt keep this use of the *ultra vires* doctrine under very tight control to prevent it from becoming another avenue of appeal. Inspectors do not act *ultra vires* merely by making a mistake of law. Since *IRC* v *Aken* was decided the courts have developed the law on collateral challenge. It is open to citizens charged with a criminal offence to argue that the law under which they are charged is invalid[94] or that a *prima facie* case has not been made as was determined in the case of the *State v Abacha* by the Supreme Court.

(3) Damages

The third remedy is the altogether more ingenious suggestion that a cause of action lies against the State for damages, perhaps even exemplary damages, on

---

[89] *Mellor* v *Gurney* (1994) STC 1025.
[90] See *R.* v *IRC ex parte Ulster Bank* (1997) STC 832, *R* v *IRC ex parte Allen* (1987) BTR 10 (1997)
[91] *Council of Civil Service Union* v *Minister for Civil Service* (1985) AC 374, 410
[92] *Pawlowski* v *Dunnington* (1999) STC 550 (taxpayer allowed to argue legality of condition for Revenue action under PAYE regulations allowing action against employee for recovery of tax flowing deduction by employer) on differences between public law defence and judicial review. See ibid. 557 per Simon Brown L.J.
[93] *IRC* v *Aken* (1990) STC. 497, CA.
[94] *Boddington* v *British Transport Police* (1992) 2 AC 143: See Elliott 3 *Judicial Review* 144 Forsyth (1998) *Public Laws* 64 and Hare (1998) CIJ 429

the unlawful collection of or demand for tax.[95] This argument may gain credibility as a result of the argument is not necessarily a successful one.

(D) Tax compliance

Pity the poor tax collectors. In Russia in 1996, 26 collectors were killed and 74 injured in the course of their work, six were kidnapped and 41 had their homes burned down.[96] This gruesome tale is not unexpected in Nigeria once more seriousness is shown towards tax collection and reform in Nigeria.

(1) Court action

The Revenue or other tax authorities have a formidable battery of powers to collect tax.[97] It may sue in the magistrate's court or the High Court. The State's status as preferential creditor on insolvency remains for taxes for which the taxpayer acts as agent for Revenue, notably in respect of PAYER, withholding taxes and VAT. The revenue may also levy distraint on the goods and chattels (but not perishable food)[98] of the person liable and may obtain a warrant to enter premises during the daytime.

In severe cases, the Revenue may opt to press criminal charges in the criminal courts;[99] a criminal prosecution does not exclude penalties.[100] The revenue prefers the penalty procedure over criminal prosecution since prosecution is a drastic step which ought to be reserved for really serious cases, and because of the practical difficulties involved in preparing criminal cases.[101] The decision to prosecute in a particular case is amenable to judicial review.[102] If, however, a criminal prosecution succeeds, the imposition of a custodial sentence is very likely.[103] Whether private prosecution is consistent with the proper goals of the criminal law (as opposed to the convenience of tax administrators) is another matter.[104]

(2) Tax law and criminal law

There is something of a cultural gap between the precise technical world of the tax lawyer and the criminal lawyer, however, over-confidence about an

---

[95] Wide (1995) BTR 137. The argument may be weakened but not destroyed by the decision of the House of Lords in *O'Rourke* v *Camden B.C.* (1998) AC 188, on which see Camnwarth (1988)

[96] *The Economist*, 31 May, 1997, 19.

[97] It also has many powers to direct withholding tax at source, e.g. from visiting entertainers and sportsmen.

[98] *Morley* v *Pincombe* (1848) 2 Exch 101.

[99] For example, Section 86 PITA 1993; *R.* v *Hudson* [1956] 1 All ER 814, 36 TC 561; see also Keith report, Chaps. 9, 13, 22.

[100] Section 92 PITA 1993.

[101] Abdulrazaq M.T. (1993) *Nigerian Tax Offences and Penalties* (Batay)

[102] *R v IRC, ex parte Mead and Cook* [1992} STC 482, 65 TC 1.

[103] See Ahmad and Hingun [1995] BTR 581; Section 86 (1) PITA 1993.

[104] See Roording [1996] Crim LR 240; see McEwan [1981] Conveyancer 114.

avoidance scheme can become evasion and lead to a prison sentence,[105] for the taxpayer and adviser alike. The common law offence of cheating the public revenue still exists, being expressly preserved by the Criminal or Penal Code.[106] As A.T.H. Smith writes, "like many of the ill defined common law offences, cheating is one whose boundaries are indistinct, and the courts have not resisted the temptation recently to extend the law (or take an extensive view of its scope) when the issue has arisen."[107] Ormerod suggests that the *actus reus* of the offence has become so wide that it can best be stated in negative terms:

> There is no need for a dishonest act; an omission will suffice.[108] The act or omission must be intended to prejudice the Inland Revenue or the local tax authority. There is no requirement of operative deception, nor of a need to prove actual loss to the revenue or to any other. It is not necessary to prove that the conduct resulted in any gain to himself. The type of behaviour caught includes failing to account for VAT, withholding PAYE, failing to register for VAT and simply failing to disclose income.

Self-assessment has imposed new obligations on taxpayers to report and assess their liabilities accurately. The breath of the offence means that the only live issue at the trial will be dishonesty.[109]

Criminal lawyers dislike the width of the tax offence, particularly as expressed in *R.* v *Mavji* – the fact that the decision creates a liability for omission as opposed to acts and that it removes any requirement of deception[110] making something akin to fraud suffice). There are also wider objections to the role of criminal law and judicial activism, and unease over the central element of dishonesty.[111] The test used asks whether D's act was dishonest by the standards of reasonable and honest people and whether D realized that his act would be regarded as dishonest by such people. The former question is really one of law. This, of course, leads to another and more fundamental question, i.e. whether it is appropriate to have trial by jury at all on Nigeria.

(3) Criminal law and tax avoidance

Recent case-law from similar common law jurisdictions has examined the question of when tax avoidance becomes cheating the public revenue. First, it may be assumed that if the scheme is successful at the technical tax level, there

---

105 See Abdulrazaq, M.T. (1993) *op cit.*

106 For criticism (and reference to relevant literature) see Ormerod (1998), *Crim L.R.* 624 and A.T.H. Smith *Property Offences* (Sweet and Maxwell) 1994; paras.20, 106 et esq.

107 Smith, ibid, para. 20-106.

108 The appellant's submission (that there was no duty to disclose) would, if accepted, "provide nothing but a licence for cynical and deliberate tax evasion." *R.* v *Dimsey* (1999) STC 846, 859, per Laws LJ.

109 Ormerod, *op. cit.*

110 Smith, *op. cit.* para 20 - 1!1

111 Griew (1985) *Crim L.R.* 341; and other literature cited by Ormerod.

can be no criminal offence, the public revenue cannot be cheated if it has lost no tax.[112] This means that the transactions must be genuine (as opposed to shams). If the scheme succeeds as technical tax law, it does not matter that there was no initial full disclosure of all the facts provided the Revenue eventually aggress, or a court eventually holds, that no tax has been lost, a prosecution for attempting to cheat the public revenue should also fail.[113] the practical problem for the defence in such cases is to establish that the scheme works; the device of a trial within a trial. The theoretically correct solution would be to adjourn the criminal case until the tax answer has been reached by the tax tribunal.

Secondly, it may be assumed that in the converse situation where the scheme is a sham, there is potential criminal liability, especially if there has been suppression of relevant facts. This leaves the third (and middle) situation where the scheme is not a sham but still fails at the technical level so that a tax liability does arise but a tax payer fails to report. In *R.* v *Dimsey,*[114] the English Court of Appeal had no hesitation in upholding a conviction. It was held that an individual who had *de facto* control of a company and so arranged its affairs that the company made profits but did not declare them to the Revenue was cheating the Revenue. The position would be even stronger if the company was set up to operate in such a way. The case also shows that the words used in a judge's summing-up, like some cases stated, must be viewed in context; errors of tax law will not, of themselves invalidate the conviction. There is something wrong here; simply leaving such matters open seems perverse, the more so when one reads statements of judges who have no experience of tax law trying to explain some of the doctrines in terms one is meant to understand. At least this decision is an improvement on the earlier and most unsatisfactory[115] case of *R* v *Charlton*, even does nothing for those convicted in that case. Tax lawyers find this "robust" attitude inappropriate and wonder whether criminal law will find it possible to cope with the concept of innocent evasion.[116]

(E) Compliance

(1) Effectiveness of sanctions

Work has been carried out in United States to investigate the effects of sanctions under tax law on taxpayer behaviour. Although the conclusions reached are tentative they do not make encouraging reading for the Revenue. By looking at the extent of which taxpayers think they will be audited (perceived certainly)

---

[112] It is not, however necessary for the prosecution to prove a loss to the Revenue. See *R.* v *Hunt* (1994) STC 819, 827.

[113] Smith and Hogan, *Criminal Law* (9th ed.) Butterworths, 1999, 327-34

[114] (1999) STC 846.

[115] Thus, at no point did the judges in charge of the case address (or apparently, understand) the distinction between a sham transaction entered into for tax avoidance purposes; see generally Venables 7 *Offshore Taxastion Review* 1 and Brandon 8 *Offshore Taxation Review* 9.

[116] On problems of scope of evasion, etc. See Sawyer (1996) *BTR* 483.

and the severity of any sanction imposed (perceived severity). Long and Schwartz,[117] after looking at later returns by people who had been audited, concluded that audits appeared to be marginally effective in reducing the frequency of reporting errors but not their size, and that there were almost as many people who were initially compliant who became non-complaint, as taxpayers who had been non-compliant but who became complaint. The conclusion that the presence of audits did not decrease non-compliance naturally raises the question why this should be so. Answers tend to focus on the negative effects of the blanket enforcement of complex laws. These included the tendency to treat violators the same whether they acted inadvertently or intentionally; the lack of relative risk to the determined violator who would usually get away with paying tax and interest; and the lack of judicial review. Needless to say, other surveys suggest different results.[118] The Nigerian rules normally include penalties as well as interest, and also provide for appeals against penalties. However, while it is a matter for debate whether the Revenue is able to distinguish sufficiently between deliberate and inadvertent loss, there can be no doubting that the Nigerian tax rules are now about as complex as the United States rules were then. Another study suggests that audit may be better at deterring the overstatement of deductions as opposed to the under-reporting of income.[119] As a fascinating footnote one should record the (again US) survey on the effects of status in income tax audits. Using occupational status as a measure or status, Kinsey and Stalans conclude that tax payers of higher status tended to get more advantageous settlements than those of lower income status – but only a long as they represented themselves. Once tax practitioners were involved, status tended to get more advantageous settlements than those of lower income status – but only a long as they represented themselves. Once tax practitioners were involved, status advantages disappeared: "tax practitioners level the playing field by disrupting social influence and deference processes".[120] An altogether different line of work suggests ways in which one should behave when being audited, in order to get the best result. The provision of "soft lighting, alcohol videos and more" is not recommended since this suggests that the company has something to hide.[121]

(2) The professional's role: ethics

The role of the Nigerian Tax professional has emerged in a typically English, pragmatic way. Work is carried out not only by lawyers and accountants (in one

---

[117] Long and Scwartz presented to Annual Meeting of Law and Society Association Washington, DC June 1987 on work carried out in 1986.

[118] For example Witte and Woodbury (1985) 38 *National Tax Jo. 1.*

[119] Kinsey, *Theories and Models of Tax Cheating Criminal Justice Abstracts*, September 1996: 403-25

[120] Kinsey and Stalans, September 1996, looking at state as opposed to federal audits.

[121] See (1998) 46 Can Tax Jo. at 733 describing some of the advice given in a piece under review as "somewhat Machiavellian and borderline unethical

or other professional body of accountants) but also by the increasingly influential Chartered Institute of Taxation of Nigerian (CITN), which attained chartered status in 1992. There are also advisers who have no professional qualification as such, ranging from retired and highly skilled members of the Federal Inland or State Internal Revenue to complete freelancers with less impressive credentials.

Professional tax advisers face a range of problems concerning professional ethics. Clearly, they are under a duty to their clients, but they also owe a duty to observe the profession's standards. They must not make a tax return they know to be false (or they will face not only disciplinary procedures but also criminal prosecution). The CITN suggests that the client's position should be presented in a way, which is factually correct and is not intended to mislead an ordinarily competent inspector. If the Revenue makes an error in calculating tax, which favours the taxpayer, tax advisers are under a professional obligation to advise the client to inform the Revenue, and to refuse to act further for that client if the client does not follow that advice. However, there are many more difficult or grey areas where professionals may disagree on whether the Revenue should be informed of something, e.g. where the client takes a particular view which is different from the published Revenue view (here, the decision whether or not to inform must rest with the client). While there is no need to provide the Revenue with gratuitous information, relevant facts should never be concealed from the Revenue. This area of professional ethics is much studied in the United States and awaits proper study in Nigeria.[122] Some members of the profession may consider that the CITN attitude provide too much co-operation with the Revenue. It is unfortunate that these members are reluctant to engage in public debate.

(F) Tax administration and human rights

Although the African Convention on Human Rights says little directly on tax matters, the courts and similar conventions have begun to impose the rights indirectly.[123] The European Convention, for example, gives various procedural rights in civil cases, including a fair trial and appeal to an independent tribunal in criminal cases, more substantial rights such as a presumption of innocence, a right to be informed promptly of the nature and cause of the accusation, adequate and reasonable time and facilities to prepare the defence, a right to legal aid if insufficient means are available, and a right to examine prosecution witnesses. Although a tax dispute is not at present regarded as giving rise to a civil obligation. The Strasbourg Court of Human Rights has held that a civil claim, which originates in tax, e.g. an action in restitution for wrongly paid tax,

---

[122] See paper given at the ABA Conference (London) July 1985, including one on UK aspects by Avery Jones

[123] See Baker (2000) BTR 211

can be a civil right or obligation.[124] Similarly, although tax law is not the same as criminal law, the court has held that the concept of crime is autonomous, and so has held that an action for a tax penalty can be a "criminal charge".[125] Other issues which have been held to be capable of coming within the law include a 1000% tax penalty[126] an unjustifiably prolonged Revenue investigation[127] and a penalty imposed for fraud committed by someone else.[128] The classification of an automatic tax geared penalty in *Bendenoun* v *France*[129] as a criminal matter depended on the co-existence of several features; that the surcharge covered all citizens as taxpayers, that it was intended to deter, that it was substantial and that imprisonment could be imposed if it were not paid. How a penalty would be regarded if it lacked some of these feature is unclear.[130] The law guaranteeing respect for privacy and family life has also been invoked to counter Revenue searches without a warrant,[131] and, at Commission level only, a Revenue request for information about detailed personal expenditure.[132]

Finally, matters which may be looked at in future include: the scope of professional privileges, whether the Commissioners are an "independent" tribunal whether the Commissioners may continue to sit in private; whether points may be taken to the Commissioners by the Revenue when the taxpayers has no equivalent rights; the highly selective number of cases chosen for criminal prosecution; the right of the State to prosecute after a tax settlement has been reached; whether a taxpayer is given an effective right of appeal if the only remedy in a case is judicial review; the rule that any dispute tax must be paid before an appeal can be begun and the refusal of a court to allow a taxpayer accused of fraud to summon and cross-examine the informer. It is clear that there are many human rights issues, which can be raised; how far they will succeed is a very different matter.

Indirect taxes

The Oxford English Dictionary defines an indirect tax as one which is "not levied directly upon the person on whom it ultimately falls, but charged in some other way, especially upon the production or importation of articles of use or

---

[124] *National and Provincial Building Society* v *UK* (1997) STC 1466

[125] *Bendenoun* v *France* (1994) 18 EHRR 54 (Tax geared penalty); *A.P.M.P. and T.T.* v *Switzerland* (1997) 26 EHRR 541.

[126] *J.J.* v *Netherlands* (1998) Application 21351/93 28 EHRR 168.

[127] *Hazee* v *Netherlands* (1998) – much would depend on the degree of co-operation of the taxpayer.

[128] A.P.M.P and T.P. v Switzerland (1997) 26 EHRR 54.

[129] (1994) 18 EHRR 544.

[130] See Person-Osterman, *Cambridge Yearbook of European Legal Studies* (Hart, Oxford, 1999)

[131] *Funke* v *France* (1993) 16 EHRR 297 332, 357 (no warrant was needed under French law at that time)

[132] *Handy-Sprindler* v *Belgium* (192) 31 DR 23

consumption, the price of which is thereby augmented to the consumer, who thus pays the tax in the form of increased price." The economic analysis contained in this definition is shaky and in general such a distinction cannot be made.

Nevertheless, many people do; indeed, it has almost become part of the conventional political wisdom of Nigeria that the tax structure relies too much on direct taxation – especially income tax and too little on indirect taxes. In a period of inflation, a progressive income tax taxes an ever-increasing proportion of real incomes while the real yield of indirect taxes (which are in many cases levied as fixed monetary amounts) declines. This shift has not been intended, and it reinforces the case of indexation, which is the only way in which inflation can be prevented from accidentally bringing about changes which no one wants to bring about by design. So it is not surprising that the balance of direct and indirect taxation should now be a subject of attention. But some of the reasons which people have for believing that the present balance of direct and indirect taxation is wrong are bad ones. One is that it is thought that the disincentive effects of high rates of direct taxation can be reduced or avoided by a shift to indirect taxes. This argument is quite simply false. The hope that the disincentive effects of high marginal rates of taxation can be reduced by recasting direct taxes as indirect is therefore quite cynical. One cannot remove the disincentive effects of taxes by disguising them under a different name. What matters is the relationship between take – home pay and prices in the shops and this seems to be understood much better by the ordinary person than by many tax experts. There are, however, two possible grains of truth in these arguments. One is that people may be more resentful of the fact that over half of the product of their extra effort goes in tax if this fact is intimated to them on their pay-slip than if the same money is extracted by the shops in a slightly more roundabout way, and that this resentment itself leads them to do less work- that people are willing to deprive themselves if they can also see that they are simultaneously depriving the taxman. (Musgrave[133] describes this as the "spite effect") Some people may have this psychological make-up, but a social survey[134] found more people cited high prices than high taxes as an adverse influence on their incentive to work, and it is a weak argument for a particular tax structure that it would help to conceal the realities of the tax system from people who have pathological views about it.

The second point is that indirect taxes are generally less progressive than direct taxes – mainly, though not entirely, because there is a threshold of income, which is exempt from income tax while all expenditure, however small, is vulnerable to indirect taxation. This means the marginal rate of income tax is

---

[133] *The Theory of Public Finance* (McGraw – Hill, New York), See Kay and King (1978) *The British Tax System*, chap 8 (Oxford University Press)

[134] *Report of the Royal Commission on Taxation of Profits and Income, No 2*, Cmnd, 9105, H.M.S.O. London

generally substantially above the average rate; while for indirect taxes there is little difference between the two. These indirect taxes can yield the same revenue from lower marginal rates, and hence distinctive effects (which depend on these marginal rates) would be reduced if this were done. This argument is perfectly valid, but it rests on the reduction in progressivity, not on the shift in the structure of taxation, and this reduction could equally well – and more honestly – achieved by altering the rates of direct tax than by changes to different kinds of tax.

The second bad argument for preferring indirect to direct taxes suggests that the former are voluntary in a sense in which the latter are not: this notion is reflected in an older terminology which distinguishes 'escapable' and 'inescapable' taxes. It is true that any particular indirect tax can be avoided by any particular individual who chooses not to consume the taxed good. But it is also true, given that a certain amount of revenue is required, that taxes in general cannot be avoided by individuals in general. So an 'escapable' tax leaves the person who escapes it worse if – since he would have preferred, in happier circumstances, to have consumed the good which is taxed – and it makes everyone else worse off too, since it requires a higher rate of tax on those who continue to consume the good. Thus, the tax structure to which this argument would lead is the worst possible in terms of economic efficiency – it maximizes the welfare loss, which is additional to the basic and inescapable burden of the tax.

Principles of indirect taxation

What then would an efficient system of indirect taxes be like? A first principle is that there should be no taxes on intermediate goods, which are sold to other producers rather than to final customers. Taxes on things must of course ultimately be paid by people, so that levies on producers must finally be borne by taxpayers generally in one capacity or another, as consumers, workers, or owners of firms. Hence the imposition of taxes on producer goods does not reduce the tax burden in any way; in fact it will actually increase it by inducing producers to make different and (from a social viewpoint) less efficient choices of inputs. Essentially, the principal objectives for indirect taxes – raising revenue, achieving some distributional aims, or encouraging or discouraging particular consumption patterns – can all be more efficiently achieved by the imposition of taxes on final goods alone.[135] The burden of indirect taxation should therefore be confined to final goods; how should it be distributed among them? Economic efficiency requires that indirect taxes should be cast so as to minimize the distortion of consumer choice involved – that as far as possible, the revenue should be raised without diverting taxpayers into less preferred

[135] Diamond and Mirrlees, Optimal Taxation and Public Production, *American. Economic Review 41*; Kay & King, *op. cit.*, p. 132

patterns of consumption in their (collectively unsuccessful) attempts to avoid tax.

Personal taxation

Fringe benefits

High marginal rates of income taxation lead to income being sought and given in untaxed or lightly taxed forms. Thus, the employers of well-paid workers in the private sector will tend to offer, not a salary, but a 'total remuneration package' which will include a range of fringe benefits. Such benefits are generally provided on a more extensive scale in Nigeria than in most other countries: and as a proportion of salary they tend to rise sharply at the same points in the scale as do marginal rates of tax.

What are these fringe benefits? It is difficult to determine any sensible borderline between conditions of work and benefits. The employer who provides a congenial washroom for his employees is presumably simply offering a reasonable working environment, while the one who installs a coloured suite in the bathroom of their homes is providing a fringe benefit; but there is a spectrum of benefits in between, and taxation will lead to a tendency for all of them to be substituted for earned income.

Company taxation

"Why tax companies at all? A common reply is that corporate status conveys certain privileges, and companies should pay for these privileges. In particular, companies have limited liability status thus protecting their shareholders in the event of bankruptcy. At first sight this argument has some appeal, but on closer inspection it becomes less attractive. There is no reason to believe that the benefits of incorporation are proportional to profits (indeed the reverse might be the case) and one might as well argue for a license fee for companies. More fundamentally, although limited liability is very convenient form of contractual arrangement between shareholders and creditors, it is a voluntary agreement entered into by both sides. Before lending to the company the creditors know fully well that the shareholders' liability is limited and can adjust the terms on which they are willing to lend accordingly. There is no reason to tax one part than the other. The mere fact that some firms are incorporated is not a very strong argument for imposing a separate tax on them. Indeed, insistence on treating companies as entities distinct from the individuals who own them has provided a tax shelter for retained earnings. Another argument which has been used is that companies can afford to shoulder an extra burden, and that companies, as well as persons, should pay their fair share of taxes. This argument is completely mistaken. The effect of a tax is to reduce either leisure or consumption (whether this year or in the future via a reduction in savings) or both below the levels, which would have been chosen in the absence of the tax. Whether any given tax burden is distributed fairly can only be discussed by reference to the effects on the different individuals in society. Companies are owned by individuals and it is meaningless to talk about the "welfare" of Lever Brothers. The fact that a company has a legal personality of its own quite distinct from that of its managers, shareholders and employees cannot change the fact that a tax can only affect the well-being of those who work for or own the company, or consume its products.

The incidence of company taxes

Who then actually pays the corporation tax? We can therefore identify three main groups who may bear part of the burden of corporation tax. One is the people who supply entrepreneurship. A second is the people who supply capital to companies.

The third group of people who may share the burden of corporation tax are those who buy goods and services which are produced by companies. It should be clear from this that the incidence of corporation tax depends in part on the structure of the tax.

Petroleum profits taxation

The profits accruing to petroleum companies contain a supernormal component consisting of rent on the right to exploit the oil and gas fields. In order to recover some of these profits the Government has imposed a special tax system on petroleum activities. This rather complicated system has two objectives. First, to ensure a 'reasonable share' in the economic rent obtained by the exploitation of oil and gas. Second, to ensure that marginal fields do not escape. The difficulties encountered in designing a tax system to achieve these objectives derived from the need to fit the scheme into the existing company tax.

Capital taxation

It is clear that there are major weaknesses in the existing taxation of capital in Nigeria. There are two directions, not necessarily incompatible, in which efforts to reform the system could be made. The first would be to overhaul the methods of taxing capital gains and the second would be to adopt an annual tax on wealth. The motive for putting forward the idea of a tax on wealth largely derives from a feeling that the distribution of wealth is too unequal. It is clear that there is substantial inequity in the distribution of wealth, although it is difficult to know what standards of comparison we should when making value judgements about the distribution of wealth.

Local taxation

In general, we have been able to consider tax policy quite independently of public expenditure decisions, and that reflects the structure of decision-making in Nigeria. This is not possible in examining local government finance, since local authorities are autonomous units with a requirement to balance their budgets and to raise from rates or charges that part of expenditure which is not financed from Federal or State Government grants. The theory of Federal – local government financial relations distinguishes three main reasons for Federal Government support of local authorities. Federal grants are benefits of local expenditure, which arise outside the area of the authority, which undertakes the expenditure. Local Governments which are principally concerned for their constituents will not undertake enough of such activities, and those which do extend them will impose an unfair burden on local residents. These problems can be dealt with by specific Federal Government subsidies to certain activities.

A second function of grants is to redistribute revenue among local authorities. We might ask why it is necessary or desirable to redistribute among governments rather than directly to persons. The rationale is that without this, if a man lives in a poor area with a relatively local tax base or in one in which local authority services are particularly expensive, he will have to pay higher taxes to secure the same level of services than someone with the same income who is more favourably located. This is not only horizontally inequitable, but likely to lead to movements between local authority areas.

The third function of central grants is to alleviate 'fiscal imbalance'. If taxes are raised by that level of government which is able to levy them most effectively, while expenditure are determined at the level of government which is able to administer them most effectively, there is no reason to suppose that the resources and needs of any particular tier of government will match.

Procedure

It is useful to begin by settling out the implicit premises on which administrative arrangements for the Nigerian tax system are based. The central assumption is that the taxpayer is incompetent and dishonest. The procedure therefore seeks to ensure that as far as possible the correct amount of any tax liability is deducted from income before it is received, to ensure that the administrative burden on the taxpayer is reduced to a minimum and that whenever possible such obligations are imposed on employers and other payers of income and on the Revenue itself.

As a result it is not only unnecessary for the taxpayer to understand what his liabilities are and how they are computed, but it is difficult for him to understand this even if he wishes to do so. Additionally, the system avoids reliance on the supply of accurate information by the taxpayer, and seeks to check individual returns and secure independent verification of information supplied whenever possible. Thus, while other jurisdictions believe what the taxpayer says but penalize him rather heavily if he is found to be lying, in Nigeria prosecution for tax offences is very rare. The revenue law prefers to nudge the taxpayer until he brings his own declaration into line with what it already known.[136]

Finally, approaching an old problem from a completely new direction, while refusing to recognize conventional limitations can often lead to unexpected solutions.[137] We are constantly searching for solutions that lie beyond the obvious. With financial and intellectual reservoirs of great depth and breath to draw from in Nigeria, we need to combine insight, knowledge and original thinking to create new opportunities in tax administration. We can do it for ourselves and we need to do it as a matter of urgency.

---

[136] See generally Kay and King (1978) *The British Tax System* (Oxford University Press) chaps 8,9,11,14.

[137] The Vol 359 Number 8225, June 9th – 15th 2002 (U.K.) p.2

Chapter 2

Income tax

The charge of income tax

"Income tax, if I may be pardoned for saying so, is a tax on income...." This famous aphorism of Lord Macnaghten[1] has been frequently quoted, usually out of its proper context. If, however, one includes in the expression "income," for the purposes of the taxing statutes, those accretions to wealth which the statutes specially provide shall be so treated, whether or not such items would normally be regarded as "income," then the statement is broadly true. Income tax is a tax upon that which is properly regarded as "income" for the purposes of the appropriate taxing acts, that is to say "taxable income."[2]

There is no complete definition of income to be found anywhere in the Nigerian legislation but various rules are laid down for computing receipts liable to tax, and the decisions of the courts contribute to the law on the subject. Income tax is not a tax on capital and thus one of the major concerns of the Acts and of the tax cases is the distinguishing of capital from income. In *Aderawos Timber Trading Co. Ltd.* v *Federal Board of Inland Revenue*,[3] the appellant received 30,000 Nigerian pounds from a company called African Timber and Plywood (Nig.) Ltd. as a result of an agreement for concession to fell timber from the land on which the appellant had licence. The agreement included another amount to be paid per cubic foot of the area of concession.

The appellant had originally treated the 30,000 Nigerian pounds as rent and apportioned it over 5 years, and paid 7,000 Nigerian pounds tax on it for 3 years of assessment, 1962/63 to 1964/65, to the respondent. Subsequently, the appellant sought to treat the 30,000 Nigerian pounds as capital and demanded the refund of the 7,000 Nigerian pounds tax paid, from the respondent.

The appellant contended that the receipt was a windfall by way of sale of capital and not profit as it was to secure an agreement over a certain period. The respondent contended that since the company was in business of selling timber, all the receipt in that respect should be revenue receipt.

The Supreme Court held that:

a) The lump sum payment was derived from the trading activity of selling timber which constitutes a trading receipt and not capital.

---

[1] *London County Council* v *Att.-Gen.* [1901] A.C. 26 at 35.

[2] For a full discussion, see G.S.A. Wheatcroft, "What is taxable income?" [1957] *B.T.R.* 310.

[3] 1 NTC p.154; [1966] LLR 195.

b) Appeal dismissed.

The scope of the charge to tax is outlined in the P.I.T.A., s.3 and the C.I.T.A 1990 s.8. Tax is payable for each year of assessment upon all income or profits from a source inside or outside Nigeria accruing in, derived from, brought into, or received in, Nigeria.

P.I.T.A.,.s.3 provides as follows:

(1) Subject to the provision of this Act, tax shall be payable for each year of assessment on the aggregate amounts each of which is the income of every taxable person, for the year, from a source inside or outside Nigeria, including, without restricting the generality of the foregoing:

(a) gain or profit from any trade, business, profession or vocation for whatever period of time such trade, business, profession or vocation may have been carried on or exercised;

(b) any salary, wage, fee, allowance or gain or profit from employment including compensations, bonuses, premiums, benefits or other perquisites allowed, given or granted by any person to an employee other than:

(i) so much or any sums as my be admitted by the relevant tax authority to represent reimbursement to the employee or expenses incurred by him the performance of his duties, and from which it is not intended that the employee should make any profit or gain;

(ii) medical or dental expenses incurred by the employee;

(iii) the cost of any passage to and from Nigeria incurred by the employee;

(iv) any sum paid in respect of the maintenance or education of a child if any provision of this Act provides that any sum received by the employee during a year of assessment shall be deducted from the personal relief to be granted to him for the next following year;

(v) Deleted by 1996 No. 32;

(vi) so much of any amount of rent the employee is treated as being in receipt equal to the annual amount deemed to be incurred by the employer under section 4 of this Act;

(vii) so much of any amount of rent the employee is treated as having received under the provisions of section 5 of this Act;

(viii) so much of the amount of rent subsidy or rent allowance paid by the employer to or on account, for the employee not exceeding ₦100,000 per annum,

(ix) the amount not exceeding ₦15,000 per annum paid to an employee as transport allowance,

(x) meal subsidy or meal allowance, subject to a maximum of ₦5,000 per annum

(xi) utility allowance of ₦10,000 per annum,

(xii) entertainment allowance of ₦6,000 per annum,

(xiii) leave grant, subject to a maximum of 10 per cent of annual basic salary.

(c) gain or profit including any premiums arising from a right granted to any other person for the use or occupation of any property;

(d) dividend, interest or discount;

(e) any pension, charge or annuity;

(f) any profit, gain or other payment not falling within paragraphs (a) to (e) inclusive of this subsection.

(2) Deleted by 1999 no.30 for the purpose of paragraph (viii) of subsection (1)b of this section, the rate and the amount of rent or allowance in lieu of rent shall be:

(a) in the Lagos area and the Federal Capital Territory, Abuja, 28 per cent of annual basic salary, subject to a maximum of ₦10,000.00 per annum;

(b) in state capital cities, 28 per cent of annual basic salary, subject to a maximum of ₦6,000.00 per annum.

(c) in other places, 28 per cent of annual basic salary to a maximum of ₦4,000.00 per annum.

(3) For the purpose of this section:

(a) "allowance" includes any sum paid or payable in respect of expenses and any sum put by an employer at the disposal of an employee and paid away by the employer;

(b) "income" includes any amount deemed to be income under this Act;

(c) the gains or profits arising from a right granted to any other person for the use or occupation of property under any lease or assignment thereof, being rent paid or expenses to be paid in advance, shall be deemed to accrue to the recipient from day to day over the period for which such rent has been paid;

provided that where the period exceeds five years the whole of the rent so paid or expressed to be paid in advance shall be treated as accruing evenly from day to day over the five years commencing on the first day of that said period:

(d) "employment" includes any service rendered by any person in returns for any gains or profits;

(e) "dividend" means:-

(i) in relation to a company not being in process of being wound up or liquidation, any profits distributed whether such profits are of capital nature or not, including an amount equal to the nominal value of bonus shares, debentures or securities awarded to the shareholder, and

(ii) in relation to a company that is being wound up or liquidated, any profits distributed, whether in money or money's worth or otherwise, other than those of a capital nature earned before or during the winding up or liquidation.

C.I.T.A. 1990 section 8 also provides that:

(1) Subject to provision of this Act, the tax shall for each year of assessment, be payable at the rate specified in sub section (1) of section 29 of this Act upon the profits Accruing in, Derived from, Brought into or Received in Nigeria. The taxable profits under this section are those in respect of the following:

(a) any trade or business for whatever period of time such trade or business may have been carried on;

(b) rent or any premium arising from a right granted to any person for the use or occupation of any property; and where any payment on account of such a rent as is mentioned in this paragraph is made before the expiration of the period to which it relates and is included for the purposes of this paragraph in the profit of a company, then, so much of the payment as relates to any period beginning with the date on which the payment is made shall be treated for these purposes as accruing to the company proportionately from day to day over the last mentioned period or over the five years beginning with that date, whichever is the shorter;

(c) dividends, interest, discounts, royalties, charges or annuities;

(d) any source of annual profits or gain not falling within the proceeding categories;

(e) any amount deemed to be income under a provision of this Act or, with respect to any benefit arising from a pension or provident fund, of the Personal Income Tax Act;

(f) fees, dues and allowances (whatever paid) for services rendered;

(g) any amount of profits or gains arising from acquiring or disposing short-term money instruments like Federal Government Securities, Treasury Bills, Treasury and Saving Certificate, Debenture Certificates and Treasury Bonds;

(2) For the purposes of this section, interest shall be deemed to be derived from Nigeria if:

(h) there is a liability to payment of interest by a Nigerian company or a company in Nigeria regardless of where or in what form the payment is made; or

(i) the interest accrues to a foreign company or person from a Nigeria company or a company in Nigeria regardless of whichever way the interest may have accrued.

(2) In this section "dividend" means:

(a) in relation to a company not being in the process of being wound up or liquidated, any profits distributed whether such profit are a capital nature or not, including an amount equal to the nominal value of bonus shares, debentures or securities awarded to the shareholders; and

(b) in relation to a company that is being wound up or liquidated, any profit distributed whether in money or monies worth or otherwise, other than those of a capital

> nature earned before or during the winding-up or liquidation.

Example under Section 3(3)(c) P.I.T.A.

Abdulmumini lets his property Villa Taofiqat to Taslimat from January 1, 2003 at an annual rent of ₦10,000 for a term of twenty years, the first ten years rent to be paid in advance at the commencement of the term. Abdulmumini will be assessed to 20,000 in respect of the rent for each of the first five years of the lease, and will be deemed to have received nothing from this source for the next five years.

In effect all income is taxable if it either arises in Nigeria or arises abroad and is remitted or brought into Nigeria. However, foreign income of non-residents or temporary visitors to Nigeria is not exempted from tax. In spite of the case of *Karam* v *Commissioner of Income Tax*,[4] where the West African Court of Appeal was required to interpret the expression "accruing in, derived from, or received in, in respect of gains or profits from any trade..." Between 1944 and 1948, the firm shipped some goods to Nigeria and these were received and sold on behalf of the appellant who was in the Ghana and he was assessed to tax on the profits of the transaction. The question was whether the appellant was liable to pay income tax on the income of the goods. He appealed against his assessment on the ground that the profit in question was "an income accruing in, derived from and received" in Nigeria and not Ghana and, therefore, not assessable to tax in Ghana. The Court held by a majority of two to one that the true meaning of these words was "that the liability to pay income tax is limited in the geographical sense to transactions carried on in Ghana, and does *not* extend to transactions carried on outside it."[5]

Special provisions apply to the valuation of living accommodation. It is a common practice in Nigeria for employers to make available to their employers living accommodation at a nil or nominal rent. Section 5 P.I.T.A. provides that:

> (1) where any premises in Nigeria are made available to the occupier by reason of his or his wife's holding an office or employment and:
>
> (a) the occupier pays no rent for the premises; or
>
> (b) the rent which the occupier pays for the premises is less than the annual value of the premises, the employee shall be treated as being in receipt (in addition to any other emoluments) of emoluments at an annual rate equal to the annual value to the premises, as determined under subsection (2) of this section, reduced by the annual amount of rent which the occupier pays for the premises.

---

[4] 12 W.A.C.A. 331.

[5] Per Hooper J. at p. 337.

(2) Subsection (1) of this section shall apply to an occupier being a woman as it applies to an occupier being a man with the substitution of "her husband" for "his wife" and that subsection shall accordingly be so construed.

(3) In this section, "the annual value of the premises" means:
- (a) in relation to premises subject to any law governing assessment of local rates, the annul value of the premises as determined for purposes of local rates under that law;
- (b) in any other case, the annual value as determined by the relevant tax authority, and a reference in this section to annual value shall include a reference (whether applicable) to such proper proportion of the annual value:
  - (i) in relation to a period of occupation within a year, or
  - (ii) in relation to the part to the premises occupied, or
  - (iii) in relation to both a period of occupation within a year and
  - (iv) the part of the premises occupied, as may be determined by the relevant tax authority.

Taxation of dividends paid by Nigerian companies

Dividends under P.I.T.A. section 3 (3) (e) (i) and (ii) means:

- (i) in relation to a company not being in process of being wound up or liquidation, any profits distributed whether such profits are of capital nature or not, including an amount equal to the nominal value of bonus shares, debentures or securities awarded to the shareholder, and
- (ii) in relation to a company that is being wound up or liquidated, any profits distributed, whether in money or money's worth or otherwise, other than those of a capital nature earned before or during the winding up or liquidation.

Under P.I.T.A. section 12:

- (i) The income from a dividend from a dividend distributed by a Nigerian Company, shall be deemed to be derived from Nigeria, and
- (ii) shall be the gross amount of that dividend before the deduction of any tax which the company is required to deduct on payment therefore under the provisions of any law in force in Nigeria at the relevant time imposing taxation on the profits of companies.

Any amount of undistributed profit of a Nigerian company which is treated as distributed under the provisions of any law in force in Nigeria imposing tax on the profits of companies shall, for the purpose of this Act be deemed, to be income from a dividend accruing to any person who is a shareholder in the company in proportion to his share in the ordinary capital thereof at the relevant time, and the income for the dividend be taken for assessment in his hands shall be his due proportion thereof increase by such amount as my be specified by the relevant tax authority in respect of tax deemed to be deducted at source.

The income from a dividend distributed by a Nigerian company shall be deemed to arise on the day on which payment of that dividend becomes due.

Section 13 P.I.T.A. provides that the income from a dividend paid by a company other than a Nigerian company, or from any other source outside Nigeria, shall be the amount of that income brought into or received in Nigeria, provided that, if the income arose in a country to which section 39 of this Act applies, the amount of that income to be taken for assessment shall be the amount under subsection (5) of section 39 of this Act.

Also, section 15 P.I.T.A. states that where a dividend or interest is distributed or paid by a Nigerian company, the dividend or interest as the case may be, whenever necessary for the purpose of the First Schedule to the Act, shall be deemed to be derived from the territory in which the recipient of the dividend or interest, resides or, where the recipient id not resident in Nigeria, the person shall be a person to whom section 2 (1) (iv) applies.[6]

Income exempted

Section 19 P.I.T.A. states that:

> (1) There shall be exempt from the tax that income specified in the Third Schedule to this Act.
>
> (2) The minister may by notice include in the Third Schedule to this Act all or any person or class of persons chargeable to tax by virtue of this Act, so that person or class of persons from tax in pursuance of:
> (a) any treaty, convention or agreement between the Federal Government of Nigeria and any other country or any arrangement with or decision of an international organization of which the Federal Government of Nigeria is a member; or
> (b) any arrangement in that behalf subsisting between the government of the Federal and the Government of each State.
>
> (3) Nothing in this section or the Third Schedule to this Act shall be construed so as to:
> (a) exempt in the hands the recipients, any interest bonuses, salaries or wages paid wholly or in part out of income exempted thereby; or

[6] See W.R. Cotter (1964) *Taxation and Federalism in Nigeria*. British Tax Review, (B.T.R) p.107

authorize a state Government, a company or any person or agency or Government, a company or any person whether resident or not in Nigeria to provide tax exemption clauses in an agreement or arrangement without seeking approval first from the Minister of Finance and Economic Development and thereafter from the National Council of Ministers.

The P.I.T.A., 1993 does not define exempt income. In the case of *Northern Nigeria Investment Limited* v *F.B.I.R.*[7] Mr. Justice M.B. Belgore defined the expression "exempt income" as follows; "... exempt income is income primarily subject to tax but exempt under another provision of Law. The true position is not that exempt income is not subject to tax". In other words, exempt income is income subject to tax under a particular provision of the law, but only taken out of the taxing law by the relevant exempting provision. In *Australian Mutual Provident Society* v *IRC*[8] it was stated that the word "exempted from taxation" in s.86 of the Act did not cover income which was not within the reach of the New Zealand tax laws.

Administrative and transitional provisions

These are provided under Part X of the P.I.T.A. in section 85, these sections make provisions for the Joint Tax Board, the State Board of Inland Revenue, Technical Committee of the State Board and the Local Government Revenue Committee.

S.85 PITA (State Board of Internal Revenue)

1. There is hereby established for each State, a Board to be known as the State Board of Internal Revenue (in this Decree referred to as "the State Board") whose operational arm shall be known as the State Internal Revenue Service (in this Decree referred to as "the State Service").
   (1) The State Board shall comprise:
      (a) the executive head of the State Service as Chairman, who shall be a person experienced in taxation and be appointed by the Governor from within the State Service;
      (b) the Directors and Heads of Departments within the State Service;
      (c) a Director from the State Ministry of Finance;
      (d) the legal Adviser to the State Service;
      (e) three other persons nominated by the Commissioner for Finance in the on their personal merit; and
      (f) the Secretary of the State Service who shall be an ex-officio member.

[7] Suit No. FRC/L/2A/75 p.57; See Ayua, *Nigerian Tax Law* pp 72, 73 (Spectrum)
[8] (1962) A.C. 135.

2. Any five members of the State Board, of whom one shall be the Chairman or a Director, shall constitute a quorum.
3. The secretary of the State Service shall be appointed by the Board from within the State Service.
4. Notwithstanding that the Legal Adviser to the State Service is a member of the State Board, he may appear for and represent the State Board or State Service in his professional capacity in any proceedings in which the State Board or State Service is a party, and the Legal Adviser shall not in such circumstances give evidence on behalf of the State or State Service.
5. The secretary shall summon a meeting of the State Board whenever the business requiring its attention warrants, or on the request of a member.
6. A majority decision of the members on any matter obtained by the Secretary in written correspondence shall be treated ion all respects as though it were a decision of the Board in an actual meeting unless any member has requested the submission of the matter to such meeting.

Section 85(B) provides as follows:

(1) The State Board shall be responsible for:
   (a) ensuring the effectiveness and optimum collection of all taxes and penalties due to the government under the relevant laws;
   (b) doing all such things as may be deemed necessary and expedient for the assessment and collection of the tax and shall account for all amounts so collected in a manner to be prescribed by the commissioner;
   (c) making recommendations, where appropriated, to the Joint Tax Board on tax policy, tax reform, tax registration, tax treaties and exemption as may be required, from time to time;
   (d) generally controlling the management of the State Service on matter of policy, subject to the provisions of the law setting up the State Service; and;
   (e) appointing, promoting transferring and imposing discipline on employee of the State Service.

(2) The State Board shall be autonomous in the day to day running of the technical, professional and administrative affairs of the State Service.

(3) Subject to subsection (4) of this section, the section, the State Board may, by notice in the Gazette or in writing, authorize any person to:
   (a) perform or exercise on behalf of the State Bòard, any function, duty or power conferred on the State Board; and
   (b) receive any notice or other document to be given or delivered to or in consequence of this Act or any subsidiary legislation made under it.

(4) Notwithstanding the provisions of subsection (3) of this section, the State Board shall not delegate any power conferred on it under sections 2, 6, 7, 17, 45, 46, 49, 52, 53, 54, 56, 77, 85, 91, 94, 95 and 96 of this Act to any person.

Technical committee of the state board

Under section 85(C):

(1) there shall be a Technical Committee of the State Board (in this Decree referred to as "the Technical Committee") which comprise:
   (a) the Chairman of the State Board as chairman;
   (b) the Directors within the State Service;
   (c) the Legal Adviser to the State Service;
   (d) the Secretary of the State Service.

(2) The Technical Committee shall:
   (a) have powers to co-opt additional staff from within the State Service in the discharge of its duties;
   (b) consider all matters that require professional and technical expertise and make recommendations to the State Board;
   (c) advice the State Board on all its powers and duties specifically mentioned in section 85B of this Act;
   (d) attend to such other matters as may, from time to time, be referred to it by Board.

Local government revenue committee

Section 85(E) states that:

(1) There shall be established a Revenue Committee that shall be responsible for the assessment and collection of all taxes, fines and rates under its jurisdiction and shall account for all amounts so collected in a manner to be prescribed by the Chairman of the Local Government.

(2) The Revenue Committee shall be autonomous of the Local Government Treasury and shall responsible for the day to day administration of the Department which forms its operational arm.

Methods of collection

There are two methods of collection and these are direct assessment and deduction at source. The former consists of an assessment made by the Relevant Tax Authority of the total income for a year of a taxpayer and thus also of the tax payable for that year. The latter method, of which P.A.Y.E. is the principal example, is more sophisticated. Here the revenue authorities require the payer, in the case of P.A.Y.E. the employer, to deduct an appropriate amount from each weekly or monthly instalment of salary paid to an employee, in anticipation of the employee's tax liability for the whole year. This liability usually, month by month, or as the case may be is ascertained from tax tables supplied to an employer on request. The tables are complete and take into account such complications as employees who have not worked a full year and are therefore liable to less tax for that year. Similarly, the tax liability of an employee whose personal reliefs alter during the tax year is adjusted by alteration of his code number.

Employers are required to make regular returns to the tax authorities in their areas. These returns are usually monthly and should show the number of employees during the month, the total tax deducted and total deductions paid into a Government Treasury.

The main advantage of the P.A.Y.E. system is that it reduces tax evasion since an employer is less likely to evade his employee's tax than the employees themselves would be if they had themselves to account for their income. The system also enables much of administrative work and expense shifted onto the shoulders of employers who are required to act as collectors for the Revenue.[9]

Payment of tax

In the case of direct assessment tax is normally payable in two equal instalments, the first within two months of the date of service of the notice of assessment and the second not later than the fourteenth day of December in the relevant tax year. The date of payment of the second instalment varies from territory to territory. Where tax is not paid by the due date, a penalty of 10 per cent of the tax is imposed and the employer may also be liable to criminal sanctions.[10]

Where the P.A.Y.E. system applies, tax is paid in instalments deducted by the employer from salary payments. If at the end of a tax year it is found that an under or over payment of tax has been made, this is easily put right by a simple adjustment which will be reflected in a diminished or increased "pay packet" on the next "pay day" and an adjustment in the code number.[11]

Returns

Under section 41 P.I.T.A.:

(1) For each year of assessment, a taxable person shall without notice or demand therefore, file a return of income in the prescribed form and containing the prescribed information with the tax authority of the State in which the taxable

[9] See section 80 P.I.T.A.; See also Willoughby & Harvey (1969) *op. cit.*, pp. 10, 11.
[10] See section 81 P.I.T.A.
[11] See Section 67,75, P.I.T.A; See *R.T.A.* v *African Press Ltd.* INTC 160

person is deemed to be a resident together with a true and correct statement in writing containing:

(a) the amount of income from every source of the year preceding the year of assessment computed in accordance with the provisions of this Decree and rules or regulations made there under; and

(b) such particulars as by the return may be required for the purpose of this Decree and rules or regulations made thereunder with respect to any such income, allowance, relief, deduction or otherwise as my be material for that purpose.

(2) The form or return shall contain a declaration which shall be by or on behalf of the taxable person that the return contains a true correct statement of the income computed in accordance with the provisions of this Decree and rules or regulations made thereunder or that particulars given in the return are true and complete.

(3) A taxable person shall file with the relevant tax authority the returns as stipulated in this section within 90 days from the commencement of every year of assessment.

(4) A written return, statement or an information affecting the liability to tax of an individual for a year of assessment made or given by a person to a tax of an individual for a year of assessment made or given by a person to a tax authority may be treated as having been given to another tax authority in the territory of which that individual is deemed to be resident for that year and, if an error or omission in the return, statement or an information constitutes an offence under the income tax law of that other tax authority, proceedings may be taken by that other tax authority in respect of that offence as though the return, statement or information had been made or given to that other tax authority in the first instance.

Also under section 44 P.I.T.A., a taxable person required by this Act to file a return of income shall in the return calculate the amount of tax payable and under section 45, the relevant authority may give notice in writing to a person when and as often as it thinks necessary requiring him to deliver within a reasonable time limited by such notice fuller or further returns respecting any matter as to which a return is required or prescribed by this Decree.

When a taxpayer fails to make a return, an assessment will be made on the total income, which the taxing authority to the best of its judgement, considers was received by the taxpayer during the year. Such an assessment will tend inevitably to be arbitrary but that is the fault of the taxpayer. Similar action is taken where a return is not accepted as correct.[12]

Additional assessments may be made in respect of unassessed profits provided that the Revenue Act within six year of assessment in question. Although where the failure to assess occurred as a result of the fraud, wilful

---

[12] See section 53 P.I.T.A; See *Sundu* v *Commissioner of Income Tax* (1955) 14W.A.C.A. 656; See also, *F.B.I.R.* v *Omotesho* INTC 257; *F.I.B.R.* v *Azigbo Bros Ltd* I NTC 88

default or neglect of the taxpayer, an additional assessment may be made at any time.[13]

Penalties

In addition to the penalty for late payment of tax already mentioned, the C.I.T.A. and P.I.T.A. provide certain other penal sanctions for offences relating to income tax.[14] The penalties include:

(a) Failure to comply with the requirements of a notice served on the taxpayer;
(b) Supplying incorrect information in relation to any matter or thing affecting the liability to tax of the taxpayer or any other person or of a partnership;
(c) Failure to make a correct return when requested;
(d) The making of any false statements, returns, or the preparation of false accounts with a view to the evasion of tax liability;
(e) The failure or refusal to pay tax.

The punishments for these offences vary and are rather detailed. There are wide powers given to the tax authorities with leave of the court to compound offences.

Objections and appeals

Under section 60 P.I.T.A., a taxable person being aggrieved by an assessment to income tax made upon him, having failed to agree with relevant tax authority in the manner provided in subsection (3) of section 57 of this Act, may appeal against the assessment on giving notice as provided in section 61 of this Act within thirty days after the date of service of notice of the refusal of the relevant tax authority to amend the assessment as desired.

Where no valid objection or appeal has been lodged under section 65 P.I.T.A. and within the time limited by section 57 or 60 of this Act or where due notice has not been given of a further appeal against a decision of the Appeal Commissioners or Judge, as the case may be an assessment as made, or agreed to under the provisions of subsection (3) of section 57 of this Act determined

---

[13] See section 54 P.I.T.A; See *C.O.R.* v *Attah INTC* 190; *John Khawam Ltd* v *F.B.I.R.* (3) 1 NTC 407.

[14] See C.I.T.A. 1990 section 71-78; P.I.T.A. Section 86-93; See also Abdulrazaq M.T. (1993) *Nigerian Tax Offences and Penalties* (Batay Law Publications)

under the proviso to that subsection or on appeal, as the case may be, shall be final and conclusive for all purpose of the Act as regards the amounts of the assessable, total income and the tax charged thereby.

Appeals from company assessments are made to the Appeal Commissioners and thence appeal lies to the Federal High Court on a point of Law. Companies are expressly entitled to legal representation before Appeal Commissioners. Where there is failure to object or appeal against an assessment or the decision of an appeal committee within the stipulated periods the assessment becomes absolutely binding upon the taxpayer.[15]

[15] See section 54, 57, and 58 C.I.T.A. 1990; see Olowofoyeku, A.A. (1989) 'The Nigerian Tax Appeal System – a Peculiar Mess?' *Gravitas Review of Business and Property Law*, Vol 2, No 8, p. 30; See also *R.* v *General Commissioners for St Marylebone*, ex.p. Hay (1983) STC, 346, 359 ; see also *Mobil Oil Nigeria Ltd* v *F.B.I.R.* 1 NTC 424

Chapter 3

Reliefs and rates

These reliefs are allowed to individuals and are set off against the total income of a taxpayer in order to ascertain his taxable income, that is, the amount of income on which tax is to be charged. It should be noted that:

a) Personal reliefs are available only to an individual and therefore cannot be claimed by a company;
b) There is, unlike losses, no carry forward, that is to say where the income for any year of assessment is insufficient to exhaust all a taxpayer's personal reliefs the amount unused of such reliefs may not be carried forward and used to reduce tax liability for the following year; and
c) The reliefs are generally only granted to persons resident in Nigeria.

Under section 33(3) P.I.T.A., the reliefs given are as follows:

(a) a deduction of the amount of any alimony not exceeding three thousand naira paid to a former spouse under an order of a court of competent jurisdiction in the case of an individual whose marriage had been dissolved;

(b) a deduction of two thousand five hundred naira in respect of each unmarried child who was maintained by the individual during the year preceding the year of assessment and who, on the first day of that preceding year, had either not attained sixteen years of age, or was receiving full time instruction in a recognized educational establishment, or was under articles or indentures in a trade or profession:

(i) no deduction under this paragraph shall be allowed to any individual in respect of more than four children and for the purpose of applying this restriction, a husband and his wife or wives not separated from him by deed or an order of any court shall be treated as one and the same individual,

(ii) no additional deduction shall be allowed in respect of the costs incurred in connection with the education of any child in respect of whom he is entitled to a deduction under this paragraph,

(iii) where the cost of maintaining a child is shared between two or more persons, the relevant tax authority may apportion the sum of five hundred naira as may seem to it to be equitable between those persons, and the deduction to be allowed under this paragraph to any individual in respect of that of that child shall be his apportioned share of that sum,

(iv) a widow who remarries shall be allowed a deduction of five hundred naira for every child (up to a maximum of four children) in respect of the children born by her to her deceased husband;

(c) a deduction of the costs incurred by the individual during the year preceding the year of assessment in maintaining or assisting to maintain a close relative of the individual or of the individual's spouse who was either incapacitated by old age or infirmity from maintaining himself or is the widowed or is the widowed mother (whether so incapacitated or not) of the individual's spouse:
Provided that:
(i) no deductions shall be allowed in respect of any relative whose income of the year of assessment exceed one thousand naira,
(ii) the aggregate of all deductions to be allowed to two or more individuals for any year in respect of any one relative subject to a maximum of two relatives, shall not exceed two thousand naira and, if the total of the cost incurred by them in respect of the same relative exceed that sum, then the amount of the deductions to be allowed to any such individual shall be that same proportion of that sum and the cost so incurred;
(iii) the aggregate of all deductions to be made under this paragraph in ascertaining the chargeable income of any one individual for any year, shall not exceed four thousand naira;

(d) a deduction of the annual amount of any premium paid by the individual during the preceding year of assessment to an insurance company in respect of insurance on his life or the life of his spouse, or for a contract for a deferred annuity on his own life or the life of his spouse;

(e) deduction of additional three thousand naira or 20 *per cent* of the earned income, whichever is higher, in the case of a disabled person who uses special equipment or the services of an attendant in the course of a paid employment.

General

All claims to personal reliefs must be made on the proper form, normally the income tax return form, and the tax authority may require supporting documentary evidence of claims made, such as receipts for school fees paid.

Under section 35 P.I.T.A.:

(1) The relevant tax authority may require a claimant to a deduction under section 33 of this Act to produce such documentary evidence as may be available in support of any claim and in the absence of that evidence or if that evidence is, in the opinion of the relevant tax authority inadequate, the relevant tax authority may refuse to allow the deduction or allow such part only of the amount claimed as the relevant tax authority may decide.

(2) Notwithstanding any provisions of this Act:
(a) where a person has failed to produced documentary evidence in support of a claim to a deduction under section 33 of this Act, no objection to an assessment or, if the person is an employee, to any rate which tax is required to be deducted from his remuneration under the provisions of this Decree shall be valid on the grounds that deduction, or the full amount thereof, has not been allowed or taken into account by the relevant tax authority; and

(b) where an individual claims a deduction under this Decree for a year of assessment, or produces evidence in support of a claim previously made and not admitted in full by the relevant tax authority within two years the end of such year, such repayment or set-off of tax, or reduction in any assessment shall be made so as to give effect to any amount or additional amount of the deduction which the relevant tax authority is satisfied should properly be allowed.

Rate of tax

Subject to the provisions of the P.I.T.A. under section 37, the income tax that may be payable on the chargeable income of an individual ascertained in accordance with the provisions of this Act shall in respect of each year of assessment, be assessed at the rate or rates specified in the Sixth Schedule of this Act so however that where after all deductions allowable under this Act, the individual has no chargeable income or where the tax payable on the chargeable income of that individual is less than 0.5 *per centum* of the total income of that individual, the individual shall be charged to tax at the rate of 0.5 *per centum* of his income.

Income tax

Under the sixth Schedule of P.I.T.A. the income tax timetable is as follows:

Income to be taxed	*Rate of tax*	*Per centum*
For every Naira of the First N20, 000	5k per N1 or	5%
For every Naira of the next N20, 000	10k per N1 or	10%
For every Naira of the next N40, 000	15k per N1 or	15%
For every Naira of the next N40, 000	20k per N1 or	20%
For every Naira of the next N120, 000	25k per N1 or	25%

Minimum taxable income

Under section 43 P.I.T.A. notwithstanding that a tax authority requires a taxable person to file a return containing the amount of his income for each year of assessment, no return of income shall be filed by a person whose only source of income in any year of assessment is employment in which he earns thirty thousand naira or less from that source.

Chapter 4

Trade, business, profession or vocation

The meaning of trade

For the purposes of the charge to tax in respect of the profits of a trade,[1] the term "trade" is defined to include "every trade, manufacture, adventure concern in nature of trade."[2] As this circular, and somewhat unhelpful, definition of the expression "trade", the courts have had to establish for themselves what in essence amounts to trading; thus, in any particular case, in order to ascertain whether or not an individual has traded or has engaged in an adventure in the nature of trade, reference must be made to the considerable body of case law on this subject, and the principles emerging therefrom.

It has been judicially stated that the word "trade" must be given its ordinary dictionary sense, namely "a pecuniary risk, a venture, a speculation, a commercial enterprise,"[3] and that the other words in the statutory definition cited above must be considered as enlarging that sense. In *I.R.C.* v *Livingston* Lord President Clyde stated:[4]

> I think the test which must be used to determine whether a venture such as we are now considering is or is not, 'in the nature of trade' is whether the operations involved in it are of the same kind, and carried on in the same way, as those which are characteristic of ordinary trading in the line of business in which the venture was made.

In the context of what constitutes a trade Lord Wilberforce stated in *Ransom* v *Higgs* that: [5]

> Trade involves, normally, the exchange of goods, or of services, for reward, not of all services, since some qualify as a profession, or employment or

[1] See *General Tax Guide for Tax Administrators and Practitioners (FIRS)* (June 2002) p.17.
[2] Ibid.; See generally *Whiteman & Wheatcroft Income Tax* ; (Sweet & Maxwell) pp 246-276, 2nd ed.
[3] Per Scott L.J. in *Smith Barry* v *Cordy* (1946) 28 T.C. 250, at p. 258. In *Liverpool London and Globe Insurance Co.* v *Bennett* [1912] 2 K.B. 41, at p. 55; 6 T.C. 327, at p. 371 it was stated that the words "in the nature of trade" only qualify "concern" and not "adventure." This point was not referred to when the decision was affirmed in the House of Lords ([1913] A.C. 610) and judges frequently use the phrase "adventure in the nature of trade".
[4] 1927 S.C. 251 at p. 256; 11 T.C. 538 at p. 542
[5] [1974] 1 W.L.R. 1594 at p. 1611

> vocation, but there must be something which the trade offers to provide by way of business. Trade moreover, presupposes a customer (to this too, there may be exceptions, but such is the norm), or, as it may be expressed, trade must be bilateral – you must trade with someone. The mutuality cases are based in part at least upon this principle.

Another important consideration relating to what constitutes a trade was mentioned by Lord Wilberforce in the same case:[6]

> Trade is infinitely varied; so we often find applied to it the cliché that its categories are not closed. Of course they are not; but this does not mean that the concept of trade is without limits so that any activity which yields an advantage, however indirect, can be brought within the net of tax.

The latter point referred to by Lord Wilberforce is illustrated by a series of dividend-stripping cases which have been held not to constitute trading, because "they were no more than a planned raid on the Revenue."[7]

The meaning of profession or vocation

(i) Profession

The most helpful judicial exposition of its meaning is to be found in the judgment of Scrutton L.J. in *I.R.C.* v *Maxse*,[8] where he stated that:[9]

> It seems to me as at present advised that a 'profession' in the present use of language involves the idea of an occupation requiring either purely intellectual skill, or of any manual skill controlled, as in painting and sculpture or surgery, by the intellectual skill of the operator, as distinguished from an occupation which is substantially the production or sale or arrangements for the production or sale of commodities. The line of demarcation may vary from time to time. The word 'profession' used to be confined to the three learned professions, the Church, Medicine and Law. It has now, I think, a wider meaning.

Membership of a professional organization is an indication that an individual is carrying on a profession,[10] but it is by no means conclusive.

---

[6] [1974] 1 W.L.R. 1594 at 1610

[7] [1974] 1 W.L.R. 1594 at p. 1611. Lord Wilberforce stated that the principle in dividend-stripping cases "must be carefully watched for illegitimate extension": See ibid., at p. 1611

[8] [1919] 1 K.B. 647; 12 T.C. 41

[9] Ibid., at p. 656 (K.B.) and at p. 61 (T.C.)

[10] See *Currie* v *I.R.C.* (1921) 12 T. C. 245

It is a question of fact whether or not whether an individual is carrying on a profession, so that the determination of the Appeal Commissioners will not be upset unless they have misdirected themselves in law.[11]

The decided cases do little more than provide illustrations of what the courts have or have not regarded as professions. The following have been regarded as carrying on a profession: a journalist,[12] an actress,[13] an architect,[14] an optician,[15] and headmaster of a school.[16] On the other hand, the following have been regarded as not engaging in professional activities: a stockbroker,[17] an insurance broker,[18] a firm of chartered secretaries (on somewhat special facts),[19] a photographer,[20] a film producer (again on special facts)[21] a dance band leader,[22] and an individual who made his living by successfully backing horses.[23]

(ii) Vocation

The word "vocation," in the words of Denman J. in *Partridge* v *Mallandaine*,[24] "is analogous to 'calling,' a word of wide significance, meaning the way in which a man passes his life." In that case, it was held that a bookmaker who accepts bets is carrying on an organized vocation.

Similarly, in *Graham* v *Arnott*,[25] it was held that an individual who habitually supplied racing forecasts to newspapers for reward was chargeable to tax. On the other hand, it will be noted that in *Graham* v *Green*,[26] an individual was held not to be so chargeable in respect of gains derived from betting. Again, in *Down* v *Compston*,[27] the winnings of a golf professional on bets on his own matches were held not to be the earnings of a vocation.

---

[11] Ibid.

[12] *I.R.C.* v *Maxse* [1919] 1 K.B. 647; 12 T.C. 41

[13] *Davies* v *Braithwaite* [1931] 2 K.B. 628; 18 T.C. 198

[14] *Durant* v *I.R.C.* (1921) 12 T.C. 245, at p. 255; no decision to this effect, but Rowlatt J. expressed this view in his judgment

[15] *Carr* v *I.R.C.* [1944] 2 All ER 163. Cf. *Webster v I.R.C.* [1942] 2 All ER 517

[16] *I.R.C.* v *North and Ingram* [1918] 2 K.B. 705

[17] *Christopher Barker & Sons* v *I.R.C.* [1919] 2 K.B. 222

[18] *Durant* v *I.R.C.* (1921) 12 T.C. 245

[19] *Burt & Co.* v *I.R.C.* [1919] 2 K.B. 650

[20] *Cecil* v *I.R.C.* (1919) 36 T.L.R. 164

[21] *Asher* v *London Film Productions Ltd.* [1944] K.B. 133

[22] *Loss* v *I.R.C.* [1945] 2 All ER 683

[23] *Graham* v *Green* [1925] 2 K.B. 37; 9 T.C. 309. An accountant and income tax repayment agent has been held not to be carrying on a profession: *Currie* v *I.R.C.* (1921) 12 T.C. 245, but in view of the statement made by the members of the Court of Appeal in giving judgment this case must be regarded as somewhat doubtful.

[24] (1886) 18 Q..B.D. 276, at p. 278; 2 T.C. 179, at p. 180

[25] (1941) 24 T.C. 157

[26] [1925] 2 K.B. 37; 9 T.C. 309

[27] (1937) 21 T.C. 60

A dramatist,[28] a land agent[29] and a jockey[30] have all been regarded as carrying on a vocation, whilst, on the other hand, a film producer[31] was not so treated.

Profits of trades, businesses, professions or vocations

Section 3(1)(a) of the P.I.T.A. charges to the tax the gains or profits arising from any trade, business, profession or vocation, for whatever period of time such trade, business, profession or vocation may have been carried on or exercised.

There is no formal definition of what constitutes trading in the Nigerian tax legislation and therefore in a doubtful case the matter must ultimately be decided by the courts. Lord Jessel M.R. in *Erichsen* v. *Last* (1881) 8 Q.B.D. 414 stated at p.416:

> There is no principle of law which lays down what carrying on a trade is. There are a multitude of things which together make up the carrying on of a trade, but I know of no one distinguishing 'incident for it is a compound fact made up of a variety of things.

In *Arbico Limited* v. *Federal Board of Inland Revenue*,[32] the appellant was a building contractor and the objects of its memorandum included the power to deal in property. The appellant acquired four building plots and built residential accommodation on one of them. The building was sold to the Federal Government of Nigeria at a profit which was appropriated to the appellant's working capital. The sale was the first sale of property by the appellant.

The respondent assessed the appellant to tax on the profit made on the property contending that the profit was in respect of trade or business of the appellant. The respondent further later contended that since the appellant's memorandum of association includes the power to deal in property, there was a presumption that the sale was in furtherance of its trading objectives.

The appellant contended that the transaction was not a trade but a realization of capital and that the sale, being an isolated transaction was not trading within the meaning of the Act. The appellant also contended that the word 'Trade' had been given extended definition beyond its ordinary meaning in the Companies Income Tax Act, 1961.

---

[28] *Billam* v *Griffith* (1941) 23 T.C. 757; this conclusion was reached although the taxpayer was engaged in another occupation, and given the fact that the had written several plays in his spare time, only one had been accepted.

[29] *Humphrey* v *Peare* (1913) 6 T.C. 201

[30] *Wing* v *O'Connell* [1927] I.R. 84

[31] *Aher* v *London Film Productions Ltd.* [1944] K.B. 133

[32] (1968) 1 All N.L.R. 263; See also *Rev. Shodipo* v *F.B.I.R.* 1 NTC 273

The Supreme Court of Nigeria held that:

(1) The sale was a transaction by way of trade notwithstanding that it was an isolated transaction.

(2) Isolated transactions could constitute trade if the intention of the company was to deal in that line of business within its memorandum of association.

(3) The word 'trade' could be defined extensively to include isolated transactions.

The appeal was dismissed.

In *Erichsen* v *Last* Brett LJ said, "where a person habitually does and contract to do a thing capable of producing profit and for the purpose of producing profit, he carries on a trade or business."[33] Lord Reid said in *Ransom v Higgs* that the word "is commonly used to denote operations of a commercial character by which the trader provides to customers for regard some kind of goods or services," and in the same case Lord Wilberforce said, "Trade normally involves the exchange of goods or services for reward...there must be something which the trade offers to provide by way of business. Trade moreover presupposes a customer".[34] Other judges have suggested what amounts to a commercial deal,[35] while others again have asked what the operation is if it is not trade, to which the answer that it is investment will be sufficient if that can be established.

The question whether there is a trade, as defined, is one of fact. This means that it is for the Body of Tax Appeal Commissioners not only to determine the primary facts, such as what transactions were carried out, when, by whom and with what purpose, but also to conclude that the transaction was or was not a trade as defined.[36] Although this conclusion is an inference it is usually treated as one of fact. Where the findings are inconsistent it is for the court to judge.[37]

It should be remembered that it is not always to the advantage of the Revenue to argue that a particular transaction is an adventure in the nature of trade, since losses resulting from an adventure will be eligible for loss relief.[38]

---

[33] (1881) 8 QBR 915, 46 TC 463; See Tiley (1981) *Revenue Law* p.169 - 189

[34] [1974] 3 All ER 949 at 955, per Lord Reid, and per Lord Wilberforce, at 964.

[35] Lord Radcliffe in *Edwards* v *Bairstow and Harrison* [1955] 3 All ER 48 at 58, 36 TC 207 at 230.

[36] *Leeming* v *Jones* [1930] 1 KB 279, 15 TC 333, CA affid, sub nom; *Jones* v *Leeming* [1930] AC 415, 15 TC 333, *Hillerns and Fowler* v *Murray* (1932) 17 TC 77.

[37] *Simmons* v *IRC* [1980] STC 350, [1980] 2 All ER 798.

[38] *Scott* v *Hoddinott* (1916) 7 TC 85 but *Lewis Emanuel & Son Ltd* v *White* (1965) 42 TC 369. Compare the Australian Income Tax Act, s. 52 which states that a loss can be claimed in respect of property acquired for profit-making only if the tax payer notifies the Commissioner of Taxation not later than the date on which he furnishes his first return after acquiring the property, that it was acquired for the purpose of profit making by sale. Tax on a profit in such circumstances is charged by Australian Income Tax Act s. 26.

Liability – who is trading?

The trade must be carried on by the person whom it charges; the tax is levied on the traders and not on the transactions each with a different partner, it is possible to conclude that in view of the frequency of the transaction he was carrying on a trade but that his partners were not.[39]

Where no profit accrues to the person by whom the trade is carried out no charge can be made on that person. In *Ransome* v *Higgs,*[40] land was owned by a company owned by H and his wife. H agreed to a scheme by which the company developed the land and paid the profits to a discretionary trust. It was held that the trade of developing the land was not carried on by H. as Lord Reid put it, *"He did not deal with anybody. He did not buy or sell anything. He did not provide anyone with goods or service for reward. He had no profits or gain."*[41] There was no evidence that the trade carried on by the company was in fact carried on by H. H had not compelled but merely persuaded the company to conduct a trading operation and so could not be said to be the trader.

In deciding who is trading the court looks to the facts. In *Smart* v *Lowndes,*[42] a half share in land owned by the taxpayer's wife was held to be the taxpayer's trading stock. Where a trading operation is carried out by a company there is authority for the view that the gain realized on the sale of shares in the company can be trading receipt: *Associated London Properties Ltd* v *Henriksen.*[43] Although the English Court of Appeal was clear that the decision turned on its facts, it is not completely clear what these facts were. If the facts had been that the new company was simply the agent of its owners so that in fact the trade was carried on by them and not by the company, the case could be treated as just a useful illustration of a general principle; however the case appears to involve a fine disregard of the separate legal personality of the company.

Definitions of trade

(1) Illegal trading

The question whether the profits of an illegal trade are taxable has produced conflicting dicta in most jurisdictions but the answer clearly ought to be, and on

---

[39] *Pickford* v *Quirke* (1927) 13 TC 251; *Marshalls Executors* v *Joly* [1936] 1 All ER 851, 20 TC 256.

[40] [1974] STC 539, [1974] 3 All ER 949, see Twitley, [1974] BTR 335.

[41] At 955.

[42] [1978] STC 607 narrowing still further *Williams* v *Davies* [1945] 1 All ER 304, 26 TC 371.

[43] [1944] 26 TC 46.

balance of authority now is, yes.[44] It was decided in *Partridge* v *Mallandine*[45] that a bookmaker's profits were taxable notwithstanding that wagering contracts were unlawful, and in *Lindsay, Woodard and Hiscox* v *IRC*[46] that profits of illegal contract were taxable. These cases merely decide however that the profits of a contracts which the law will not enforce are nonetheless taxable. No such explanation can be advanced for the decision of the Privy Council in *Minister of Finance* v *Smith*[47] that the profits of illegal brewing during the prohibition era were taxable. Today the true principle is that the taxpayer cannot set up the unlawful character of his act against the Revenue.[48]

There have been some suggestions that the profits of burglary would not be taxable, because crime is not a trade.[49] It is however submitted that these should not be followed.[50] Any other conclusion may lead to distinctions between acts illegal *per se* and acts which are merely incidental to the carrying on of a trade. There may be difficulty in calculation of profits as there is a civil obligation to restore the goods to their owner and it should be remembered that a consistently unprofitable trade may not be a trade at all.[51]

(2) Adventures in the nature of trade

The question whether there is a trade or an adventure in the nature is one of fact but the question cannot be ignored for that reason. What follows is an attempt to synthesise the many cases and to indicate not only what factors the courts take into account but also the frail nature of those factors.

The United Kingdom Royal Commission in its final Report in 1954 listed six "badges of trade" as follows: (i) the subject-matter of the realization, (ii) the length and period of ownership (iii) the frequency or number of similar transactions by the same person, (iv) supplementary work on or in connection with the property realized, (v) the circumstances that were responsible for the realization and finally (vi) motive. These badges are principally important in determining what is an adventure in the nature of trade.

---

[44] But see Day [1971] BTR 104.

[45] (1886) 18 QBD 276, 2 TC 179.

[46] (1933) 18 TC 43.

[47] [1927] AC 193.

[48] *Southern* v *AB* [1933] 1 KB 713, 18 TC 59; *Mann* v *Nash* [1932] 1 KB 752, 16 TC 523; *contra* *Hayes* v *Duggan* [1929] IR 406.

[49] E.g. per Lord Sand in *Lindsay* v *IRC* (1932) 18 TC 43 at 56.

[50] Fines are not deductible expenses: *IRC* v *Alexander von Glehn* [1920] 2 KB 553, 12 TC 232; cf. however *Day and Ross Ltd* v *R*.[1976] CTC 707; holding that fines for excess axle loads on lorries resulted from the day-to-day operations of the business and so were deductible. See discussion by Brooks in 1977 Can Tax Jo 16. See also Tiley (1981), *op. cit.*

[51] See Tiley (1981), *op. cit.*

An example

In *Wisdom* v *Chamberlain,*[52] the taxpayer had assets worth between £150,000 and £200,000. Fearing that sterling might be devalued his accountant concluded that silver bullion would be a suitable hedge and tried to buy £200,000's worth. However the brokers would only sell £100,000 worth, a transaction, which was financed on a loan from the brokers of £90,000 at 3% above bank rate. Five months later the accountant managed to get £200,000 worth of bullion from the brokers on the basis that the original purchase would be repurchased by the brokers, at a loss to the taxpayer of £3,000. The new deal was financed by loans of £160,000 from a bank and £40,000 from the brokers, both for a maximum period of one year and at high rates of interest. The brokers were under an obligation to buy back for £210,000 within a certain period. Between October 1962 and January 1963 the bullion was disposed of at a profit of £48,000 after deducting interest payment of £7,000.

The commissioners held that this was a transaction in the nature of trade and the English Court of Appeal held that they were amply justified in reaching that conclusion. For Harman LJ this was "*a transaction entered into on a short term basis for the purpose of making a profit out to the purchase and sale of a commodity and if that is not an adventure in the nature of trade I do not really know what it is*".[53] Salmon LJ observed that if the taxpayer had realized his other assets and used the proceeds to finance the purchase of the silver the case might have been quite different. The facts of the case however presented a trading adventure – "*and a very sensible and successful one. I for my part cannot see that it is any the less a trading adventure because you describe it as something to offset the loss incurred by a fall in the value of sterling or as a hedge or insurance against devaluation.*"[54]

Badges of trade (purpose of profit)

An intention to make a profit is not a necessary ingredient of a trade. Operations of the same kind as, and carried out in the same way, as those which characterize ordinary trading are not the less trading operations because they make a loss or there is no intention to make a profit.[55] However a scheme which inevitably involves a loss may not be a trading transaction.[56]

[52] [1969] 1 All ER 332, 45 TC 103.
[53] At 336, 106.
[54] At 339, 108.
[55] See Lord Reid in *J.P. Harrison (Watford) Ltd v Griffiths* (1960) 40 TC 281; affid sub nom. *Griffiths v J.P. Harrison (Watford) Ltd* [1962] 1 All ER 909, 40 TC 292, and cases there cited. See also *Building and Civil Engineering Holidays Scheme Management Ltd v Clark* (profit but not trading (1960) 39 TC 12. A related issue is whether a particular transaction carried out by one who clearly is trading forms part of the trade even though a loss must result.
[56] *FA and AB Ltd v Lupton* [1971] 3 All ER 948, 47 TC 613.

One must distinguish a trade from a merely charitable endeavour. In the *Religious Tract and Book Society of Scotland* v *Forbes*,[57] the question was whether colportage, that is the sending out of colporteurs whose job was to sell Bibles and to act as cottage missionaries, was a trade. The Court of Exchequer (Scotland) ruled that the activity, which could not possibly be carried on at a profit, could not be a trade, with the result that the losses on colportage could not be set off against what were undoubtedly trading profits from the society's book shops. It would therefore appear that while the impossibility of profit will prevent the activity from being a trade, the absence of a profit motive will not.

If there is an intention to make a profit but then to apply it in some worthy way, there is a trading activity. The tax system is concerned with the acquisition and not with the distribution of profit.[58]

Motive for acquisition

The motive attending the acquisition of an asset is a factor which, when there is doubt, is to be thrown into the balance.[59] An acquisition under a relative's last will and testament is clearly different from a purchase with a view to speedy re-sale.[60] If the taxpayer embarks on an adventure which has the characteristics of trade his purpose or object cannot prevail over it. But if his acts are equivocal his purpose or object may be very material.[61]

The acquisition of an asset with the intention of making a profit on the resale does not inevitably signify an adventure in the nature of trade since whether a person is hoping to carry out a deal or hoping to make a good investment some capital appreciation is anticipated.[62] The time at which resale is foreseen is of greater importance.

However, if the taxpayer argues that it was not his intention to make a profit through resale the onus is on him to produce some plausible explanation for his purchase, such as that he intended to enjoy the income before reselling.[63] Further, the taxpayer's assertion that he intended to buy an asset for investment purposes, whether as an investment fund for old age or as a hedge against devaluation[64] will not be allowed to stand against other facts. The Revenue thus

---

[57] (1896) 3 TC 415.

[58] *Mersey Docks and Harbour Board v Lucas* (1883) 8 App Cas 891, 2 TC 25.

[59] As in *Lucy and Sunderland Ltd v Holt* [1961] 3 All ER 1062, 40 TC 132 and *West v Phillips* (1958) 38 TC 203, [1958] BTR 76 (Bates).

[60] But distinguish *Pilkington v Randall* (1965) 42 TC 662 where one beneficiary bought the interest of another.

[61] Per Lord Reid in *Iswera v Ceylon Taxation Commr* [1965] 1 WLR 663 at 668.

[62] *IRC v Reinhold* (1953) 34 TC 389.

[63] *Reynold's Executors v Bennett* (1943) 25 TC 401.

[64] *Wisdom v Chamberlain, supra.*

get the best of the best of both worlds; the taxpayer's state of mind can make up for equivocal acts while unequivocal acts cannot be distorted by intent.[65]

If there is no prospect of immediate profit through resale this may suggest that the acquisition is not an adventure in the nature of trade.[66] However, whatever the taxpayer's original intention may have been that may change.[67]

A separate question concerns companies which, as legal persons, have their capacity limited by their objects. The court, in deciding whether there is an adventure or not, may look at the objects of the company,[68] but a statement therein limiting the company's powers to investment is not conclusive against liability to income tax.[69] On the other hand, if a company is set up which has power to purchase land and to turn it to account, such operations are likely to be regarded as trading operations[70] and it has been suggested that the mere setting up of a company points to a trading intention because of the implied continuity of the company.[71]

The individual

Where a single transaction is involved and is of a nature close to, but separate from, what is undoubtedly a trade carried on by him, it is likely that the courts will conclude that the transaction is an adventure in the nature of a trade.[72] In *T. Beynon Ltd* v *Ogg*[73] where the company acted as agents for the purchase of wagons and brought some on their own account, the profits on the resale of those wagon were held taxable, as they were in *Cape Brandy Syndicate* v *IRC*[74] where South African brandy was acquired for blending and resale in this country by three persons who happened to be members of certain firms engaged in the wine trade. In these cases the taxpayer was held assessable on the profits of the adventure in the nature of trade, but the profits formed part not of his general trading activities, but rather a distinct taxable source.

The second way in which the individual may become important is if he possesses some special skill. There is some authority that if a person has a skill

---

[65] E.g. *Mitchell Bros v Tomlinson* (1957) 37 TC 224.

[66] Ibid.

[67] Ibid.

[68] *Cooksey and Bibbey v Rednall* (1949) 30 TC 514 at 521.

[69] *Earmes v Stepnell Properties Ltd* [1967] 1 WLR 593, 43 TC 678; affd [1967] 1 All ER 785, 43 TC 693, CA, *Emro Investments Ltd v Aller* (1954) 35 TC 305.

[70] *IRC v Reinhold* (1953) 34 TC 389 and see *IRC v Korean Syndicate Ltd* [1921] 3 KB 538, 12 TC 181 and *Ruhamuh Property Co Ltd v FCT* (1928) 41 CLR 1648; see also *Lewis Emanuel & Son Ltd v White* (1965) 42 TC 369.

[71] Per Lord Carmont in *IRC v Reinhold* (1953) 34 TC 521.

[72] Per Lord Normand in *Cayzer and Irvine & Co. v IRC* (1942) 24 TC 491 at 496.

[73] (1918) 7 TC 125.

[74] [1921] 2 KB 403, 12 TC 368.

and makes money by it, the profit is more likely to be taxable[76] but today the absence of a skill appears to be natural.[77]

(1) The subject matter

The courts take the view that some commodities are more likely to be acquired as investments than as the subject of a deal. There are two main groups of examples. Objects recommended for investment in the light of these cases include wine, gold coins and reversionary interests. Antiques and works of art are likewise recommended provided they are retained for some time and not sold by commercial methods.

First, if the object yields income, whether in form of rent or dividends, that object is more likely to be an investment than is one, which yields no income.[78] Where the court can see some fruit, the source of the fruit is likely to be a tree. A subtle case is *Snell* v *Rosser Thomas & Co Ltd,*[79] where the taxpayer – a developer – bought a house and 5¾ acres of land. The house produced rent from tenants but the land produced no income and was therefore stock in trade.

In determining whether or not there is income the court looks not simply at the flow of money to the taxpayer but also at any outflow. So in *Wisdom* v *Chamberlain*[80] the interest payments were of importance while in *Cooke* v *Haddock*[81] rent of £167 a year had to be set against the £320 a year interest.

Property which produces income may none-the-less be trading stock so that the proceeds of sale must enter a profit and loss account. The question depends on the individual circumstances of the case. Thus, stocks and shares bought by a bank in order to make good use of funds in hand and subsequently disposed of in order to finance repayments to depositors are treated as trading stock of the banking business.[82] Equally, a company which in addition to building ships ran a passenger service and bought and sold four ships for that service in rapid succession was held taxable on the profits from the resales of the passenger ships.[83]

Secondly, if the object does not yield income but can be enjoyed in kind so that there is pleasure or even pride in its possession,[84] as where a person buys a

---

[76] Per Scott LJ in *Smith Barry v Cordy* (1946) 28 TC 250 at 260 but doubts as to the correctness of this decision were raised in *Ransom v Higgs* [1974] STC 539, [1974] 3 All ER 949.

[77] Per Goff J in *Johnston v Heath* [1970] 3 All ER 915 at 921.

[78] *Salt v Chamberlain* [1979] STC 750.

[79] [1968] 1 All ER 600, 44 TC 343 and consider the factory in *W.M. Robb Ltd v Page* (1971) 47 TC 465.

[80] [1969] 1 All ER 332, 45 TC 103.

[81] [1960] 39 TC 64.

[82] *Punjab Co-operative Bank Ltd v Amritssar IT Comr Lahore* [1940] 4 All ER 87, [1940] AC 1055; a similar rule applies to insurance companies. *General Reinsurance Co Ltd v Tomlinson* [1970] 2 All ER 436, 48,TC 81.

[83] *J. Bolson & Son Ltd v Farrelly* (1953) 34 TC 161.

[84] See Lord Normand in *Fraser v IRC* (1942) 24 TC 498; *quaere* how a trust can enjoy such an object – in which case one should consider the liability of pension funds which purchase pictures.

picture for purposes of aesthetic enjoyment, any profit on resale will escape income tax. Conversely, the purchase of a commodity which gives no such pleasure and which cannot be turned to account except by a process of realization, may well give rise to a taxable profit. Examples of this turn not only on the nature of commodity, such as the railway wagons in *Gloucester Railway Carriage and Wagon Co Ltd* v *IRC*[85] but also on the quantity as in *Rutledge* v *IRC*[86] where there were one million rolls of lavatory paper.

Land is another asset which can easily yield taxable profits.[87] If one owns a house and lives in it, the house is unlikely to be trading stock. However, occupation is not conclusive and courts are reluctant to disturb a finding by the Commissioners that there was an adventure in the manner of trade. In *Page* v *Pogson,*[88] the taxpayer had built a house for himself and his wife and then sold it six month after completing it. He then built another house and Upjohn, J. felt himself unable to reverse that finding although doubting whether he would have reached that decision himself.

(2) Processing – supplementary work

The alteration of the asset by the taxpayer may suggest that there is an adventure in the nature of trade. So if a purchaser were to carry through a manufacturing process which changed the character of the article, as where pig-iron is converted into steel, there is likely to be a trade, but merely to put the asset into a condition suitable for a favourable sale, such as cleaning a picture or giving a boat a general overhaul, would not suggest a trade. In the case from which these illustrations are taken *IRC* v *Livingstone,*[89] the taxpayer, a ship repairer, together with a blacksmith and a fish salesman's employee, purchased a cargo vessel which they converted into a steam drifter and then sold without themselves using it for fishing. The alterations took nearly four months and were carried out by two of the three for wages. The Court of Session held that the profit was taxable.

The mere enhancement of value, as by obtaining planning permission,[90a] is not sufficient nor will be the normal use of the asset. So whereas the planting of rubber trees did not indicate a trade in *Tebrau (Johore) Rubber Syndicate Ltd* v *Farmer,*[90b] the blending of brandy in the *Cape Brandy Syndicate* case did.[91]

---

[85] [1925] AC 469, 12 TC 720. See Ziegel [1961] *BTR* 155 at 164.

[86] (1929) 14 TC 490 and see also *Martin v Lowry* (44 million yards of aeroplane linen), [1927] AC 312, 11 TC 297.

[87] See Crump [1961] BTR 95; Pearce, [1962] *BTR* 144 and TA 1970, s. 488.

[88] (1954) 35 TC 545; cf. *Sharpless v Rees* (1940) 23 TC 361 and *Shadford v Fairweather* (1966) 43 TC 291.

[89] 1927 SC 251, 11 TC 538.

[90a] *Taylor v Good* [1974] STC 148, [1974] 1 All ER 1137 noted [1974] BTR 184 (Nock).

[90b] (1910) 5 TC 658.

[91] [1921] 2 KB 403, 18 TC 358.

Jenkinson v *Freedland*[92] must be regarded as a most unusual case. There the taxpayer bought two stills, which were coated with a resinous substance and succeeded in removing them by a process of his own devising. It was held that there was no trade on the particular facts but this turns largely on the eventual sale of the stills by the taxpayer to his own company.

(3) Realization – reasons

"*Some explanation, such as a sudden emergency or opportunity calling for ready money, negatives the idea that any plan of dealing prompted the original purchase.*"[93] There are few reported cases in which the point has been successfully made. In *Mitchell Bross* v *Tomlinso,n*[94] a decision to sell houses originally bought for letting was motivated by changes in rent control legislation which made letting uneconomic and the rising costs of repairs and the need to realize partnership assets on the death of a partner, but the court held that the only reasonable conclusion was that the trade had commenced before the death of the partner, but the court held the only reasonable conclusion was that the trade had commenced before the death of the partner and even before some of the houses had been bought, let alone sold. In *Stott* v *Hoddinott,*[95] an architect was obliged as a term of a contract to take up shares in the company granting him the contract. He subsequently sold those shares in order to provide funds to take up shares under later contracts with other companies. It was held that this was a capital transaction so that he was not entitled to relief in respect of the loss which he sustained.

(a) Realization – machinery

The presence of an organization through which the disposal of the asset is carried out is one of the hallmarks of a trade, not least because the expenses of such an organization will be deductible in computing the net profit on the deal.[96] Equally, another factor in deciding whether or not a trade has been discontinued is whether the trade organization has ceased to exist in an identifiable form.[97] However, the presence or absence of an organization is anything but conclusive in deciding whether or not there has been an adventure in the nature of trade. As Lord Wilberforce said in *Ransom* v *Higgs*, "organization as such is not a principle of taxation, or many estimable ladies throughout this country would be imperiled."[98]

---

[92] (1961) 39 TC 636.
[93] RC 1955, Cmd. 9474, § 115.
[94] (1957) 37 TC 224. See also *Page v Pogson*.
[95] (1916) 7 TC 85.
[96] Lord Radcliffe in *Edwards v Bairstow and Harrison* [1955] 3 All ER 48 at 58, 36 TC 207 at 230.
[97] *Andrew v Taylor* (1965) 42 TC 557.
[98] [1974] 3 All ER 949, 966.

Thus in *West* v *Phillips*,[99] where the taxpayer built certain houses for letting and subsequently set up an estate agency business run by a separate company for the purposes of selling the houses that action was regarded as simply a convenient method of realizing investment property consisting of a large number of component parts. On the other hand, in *Hudson* v *Wrigthson*[100] where the appellant was a retired druggist who had bought some houses and later sold them but had never had an office or staff, the Commissioners concluded that there was a trade and their decision was not reversed.

(b) Realization – the number of steps

The number of steps taken to dispose of the asset is a fragile indicator of a trade.[101] The purchase of goods in bulk and their resale in smaller quantities is the essence of a wholesale – retail-trading operation. So in *Cape Brandy Syndicate* v *IRC*[102] one of the factors in favour of a trade was that the brandy was disposed of in some 100 transactions spread over 18 months. On the other hand the fact that a large number of disposals of land occurred did not make them trading transactions in *Hudson Bay Co* v *Stevens.*[103]

Conversely a single disposal can nonetheless amount to an adventure in the nature of trade.[104]

(4) Frequency of transactions

The frequency of transactions is only one factor; an investor is still an investor even though he changes his investments. In J. *Bolson & Son Ltd* v *Farrelly* where the taxpayer company ran a passenger service but bought a large number of boats in a short time for the service and resold them after modification, Harman J agreed that the Commissioners' finding that there was trade was inevitable. He said, "*A deal done once is probably not an activity in the nature of trade, though it may be. Done three or four times it usually is. Each case must depend on its own facts.*"[105]

However, while it is clear that repeated transactions may support the adventure in the nature of trade and that an isolated transaction many nonetheless be an adventure in the nature of trade, there is also authority that where a transaction is repeated the court may use that fact to place the label of trade on to the original transaction. In *Leach* v *Pogson,*[106] the taxpayer had set

[99] (1958) 38 TC 203 at 213; see also *Rand v Aberni Land Co* (1920) 7 TC 397.
[100] (1934) 26 TC 55. Cf. *Bradshaw v Blunden* (1956) 36 TC 397.
[101] Per Lord Russel in *IRC v Reinhold* (1953) 34 TC 389 at 395.
[102] [1921] 2 KB 403 at 417, 12 TC 368, at 376. For another example *Martin v Lowry* (1926) 11 TC 297 at 320.
[103] (1909) 5 TC 424.
[104] E.g. *T. Beynon & Co Ltd v Ogg* (1918) 7 TC 125.
[105] (1953) 34 TC 161 at 167. See also *Foulds v Clayton* (1953) 34 TC 382 at 388. *Likewise Pickford v Quirke* (1927) 13 TC 251.
[106] (1962) 40 TC 585.

up a driving school in early 1954; the business was incorporated. In December 1955 he transferred it to a newly formed company in return for cash and shares. He subsequently started other schools which he likewise transferred to companies. It was agreed that he was liable to income tax on the profits from the subsequent transactions but the taxpayer argued that he was not liable in respect of the profit on the first. It was held that he was so liable and that the subsequent transactions could be used to support that conclusion. It is probably of great importance that in that case, while he had no intention of embarking upon the business of establishing and selling motoring schools when the first one was set up, he did have that intention before he sold it. The case would thus appear to be correctly decided although perhaps more appropriately dealt with as a case of a change in the character of the transaction.

(5) Duration of ownership

A fast buck is the essence of a deal. A long period between the acquisition of an asset and its disposal may corroborate an intention to hold it as an investment.[107] Conversely, a quick sale invites a scrutiny of the evidence to see whether the acquisition was with that intent.[108] One element of an investment is that the acquirer intends to hold it at any rate for some time, with a view to obtaining either some benefit in the way of income in the meantime or obtaining some profit, but not an immediate profit by resale.[109] In *Earmes* v *Stepnell Properties Ltd*[110] the Commissioners' finding that there was no trade was reversed by the courts. Land subject to zoning for school use in the county development plan was held by a firm of civil engineers and building contractors. The firm had agreed in principle to sell it to the council, but then sold it at its agricultural value (£2,100) to the taxpayer company which was intended to be an investment company. About that time the basis for valuation in compulsory purchase cases was altered from existing use to market value. After much delay in obtaining a ruling from the Minister as to alternative development, a matter crucial to valuation, the land was sold to the county council for £50,000. As Harman LJ put it:[111]

> This sort of property is not of any use to a building company nor can it be described as a form of investment of any sort for as it was, and without purchase by the county council it was a mere piece of agricultural land yielding about 2% on its price... This...was land earmarked for sale, at a profit.

---

[107] Per Donovan J in *Harvey v Caulcott* (1952) 33 TC 159 at 164.
[108] Per Cross J in *Turner v Last* (1965) 42 TC 517 at 522-13.
[109] Per Buckley J in *Eames v Stepnell Properties Ltd* (1966) 43 TC 678 at 692.
[110] [1967] 1 All ER 785, 43 TC 693.
[111] AT 794; 701.

However, while an asset acquired on a short-term basis[112] will be the subject of an adventure, it does not follow that this will always be so. Thus in *IRC v Reinhold,*[113] the taxpayer admitted that he acquired the property with the intention of reselling it and that he instructed his agents to sell whenever a suitable opportunity arose. The land was sold after three years. This isolated transaction escaped income tax. Much more doubtful however is the decision of Danckwerts J in *McLellan, Rawson & Co Ltd* v *Newall*[114] in which the Commissioners' decision that there was a taxable profit was reversed, even while he was still negotiating for their purchase.

(6) Timing

It is a question of fact not only whether there is an adventure in the nature of trade but also when it begins – and ends. Where an asset is acquired and subsequently disposed of, it is open to the court to conclude from the evidence that the whole transaction was an adventure in the nature of trade. It is however open to the courts to conclude that an asset was acquired with the intention of retaining it as an investment but that trading subsequently commenced so that the profit accruing on resale will be taxable.[115] What is clear is that at any one time the asset must either be trading stock or a capital asset; it cannot be both.[116]

In computing the profit where the trade is begun subsequently to the asset being acquired, the asset must be brought into the account at its market value at that time.[117]

(7) Sales by personal representatives and liquidators

A personal representative may be empowered to carry on the deceased's business by the terms of the will, however his acts may amount to carrying on a trade whether or not there is such a power.[118] If he is held to be trading this liability to tax is his and not *qua* executor.[119] As personal representative his job is to realize the assets of the estate and distribute them among the beneficiaries. There is therefore a presumption that if all he did was to realize the asset in a way advantageous to the estate then he was not carrying on a trade.[220]

Whether the acts amount to carrying on a trade is a matter of degree and must depend on the nature of the trade, as two cases concerning farming show

---

[112] E.g. *Wisdom v Chamberlain; supra,*

[113] (1953) 34 TC 389.

[114] (1955) 36 TC 117.

[115] *Taylor v Good* [1973] STC 383, [1973] 2 All ER 785.

[116] *Simmons v IRC* [1980] STC 350, [1980] 2 All ER 798.

[117] Ibid. This is the converse of *Sharkey v Wernher*. See also CGTA 1979, s. 122, cases in which this rule should have been applied include *Leach v Pogson* and *Mitchell Bros v Tomlinson.*

[118] *Weisberg's Executors v IRC* (1933) 17 TC 696.

[119] *Cohan's Executors v IRC* (1924) 12 TC 602. Note Romer LJ in *Hillerns and Fowler v Murray* (1932) 17 TC 77 at 92.

[220] Per Sargant LJ in *Cohan's Executors v IRC* (1924) 12 TC 602 at 620; approved by Greene MR in *Newbarns Syndicate v Hay* (1939) 22 TC 461 at 472.

In *Pattullo's Trustees* v *IRC,*[221] the taxpayers were the representatives of a tenant farmer who also carried on the trades of cattle breeder and feeder. The farm and the cattle dealing business were bequeathed specifically so that the only asset to be realized was the feeding business. The deceased died in November at which season the cattle would already be on the land of other farms feeding from it and manuring it. The trustees felt they had to complete these contracts for economic reasons. They also bought more cattle in order to consume the remaining feedstuffs on these farns. The cattle were all sold by the following June. The Commissioners held that the trustees were carrying on the business of cattle feeding and were not simply preparing the assets for sale, even though this was their motive. The Court of Session held that there was evidence to support the Commissioners.

However, in *IRC* v *Donaldson's Trustees,*[222] the Commissioners held there was no trading and their conclusion was supported by the Court of Session. In this case the deceased was a farmer whose sole interest was a pedigree herd of Aberdeen Angus cattle. He died in March 1955 and the trustees were advised to sell the heifer calves in September 1955 and the bull calves in February 1956. This they did to keep the cattle alive and well in the meantime. The manager was told that they were to be sold and the farm was rearranged for preparing them for sale instead of grazing and breeding. It was held that the occupation of the farm was simply for the termination of husbandry and there was no trade.

It is thus a question of fact and degree whether the acts amount to the realization of the asset or to trade.[223] However, if the acts are equally consistent both with the carrying on of a trade and with mere realization, the act will be mere realization since to hold otherwise would deprive the executors of their right *vis-à-vis* the Revenue to realize their testator's assets in the ordinary way.[224] In *Donaldson's Trustee* the personal representatives were able to show a positive change from the normal pattern of farming. In *Pattullo's Trustees,* the Revenue could show, by the purchase of extra cattle, a continuation or development of the trade.

Where the deceased was carrying on a trade in partnership with others, his executors may insist that on his death the assets should be realized so that they may administer the estate. Where such assets are realized the court may hold that as far as the estate is concerned the process is one of mere realization as in *Marshall's Executors, Hood's Executors and Rogers* v *Joly*;[225] it was proved that the executors did not consent to the continuation of the trade but insisted upon their share of the assets. In the absence of such a finding the court will uphold a finding by the Commissioners that there was a continuation of the

---

221 (1955) 36 TC87.
222 (1963) 41 TC161.
223 *Wood v Black* (1952) 33 TC 172.
224 Per Greene MR in *Newbarns Syndicate v Hay* (1939) 22 TC 461, at 476.
225 [1936] 1 All ER 851, 20 TC 256.

trade. In *Newbarns Syndicate* v *Hay*[226] not only did the process of realization take ten years but the executor attended all partnership meetings as a voting participation, something he was not entitled to do as the mere executor of a deceased member; there was thus an implied agreement to continue the trade.

(8) Liquidation

Like the personal representative, the liquidator's duty is to realize the assets.[227] Here too the courts ask the question: what reason is there to suppose that the winding up was done for any purpose other than the normal carrying out of the duties of a liquidator?[228] There is a presumption that a mere disposal is not a trading operation. In *Wilson Box (Foreign Rights) Ltd* v *Brice*[229] the company was formed to turn patent rights to account. However no trade of dealing in patents was commenced. During liquidation certain patent rights were sold. The Special Commissioners held that there was a trading operation but the Court of Appeal held that there was no evidence to support this. On the other hand the payment to the liquidator of sums in respect of trading contracts made before the date of liquidation will be trading receipts.[230]

(9) Retirement

To dispose trading stock after announcing one's retirement may well be trading, since the moment when trade ceases is a question of fact. Declarations by the trader are not of themselves decisive. In *J. and R.O'Kane Ltd* v *IRC*,[231] the taxpayers had carried on the business of wine and spirit merchants. They announced their intention to retire in early 1916 but did not complete the disposal of their stock until late 1917, an operation which was carried out mostly in 1917 and which took the form of many small sales. The only purchases made for the business after the announcement of their retirement were under continuing contracts with distillers. The Special Commissioners held that the trade did not end in early 1916 and that the proceeds of the disposal sales were therefore taxable as the profits of the trade. The House of Lords held that there was abundant evidence for the Commissioners' findings.

---

[226] (1939) 22 TC 461.

[227] Per Atkin LJ in *IRC v Burrell* [1924] 2 KB at 73, 9 TC 27 at 42. In these cases it is irrelevant that the assets were the trading stock of the company or represented undivided profit. The same principles apply to trustees holding on an assignment for the benefit of creditors (*Armitage v Moore* [1900] 2 QB 303, 4 TC 199, supplying steam power is trading not realizing) and to a receiver for debenture holders (*IRC v Thompson* [1936] 2 All ER 651, 20 TC 422).

[228] *Wilson Box (Foreign Rights) Ltd v Brice* [1936] 3 All ER 728, 20 TC 736, esp. per Lawrence J at 742, and per Slesser LJ at 747; and per Ungoed Thomas J, in *John Mills Production Ltd v Mathias* (1967) 44 TC 441 at 456.

[229] [1936] 3 All ER 728, 20 TC 736.

[230] *IRC v Oban Distillery Co. Ltd* (1932) 18 TC 33.

[231] (1922) 12 TC 303.

On the other hand, in *IRC* v *Nelson,*[232] there was only a twelve day gap between the decision to retire and the disposal of the stock, and the whole stock was sold together with the rest of the business, the casks, the trade name and office furniture and fittings in one sale to one customer. The Commissioners held that the disposal was not by way of trade and the Court of Session held that there was evidence to support the conclusion.

Problems also arise on the completion of executory contracts entered into before retirement. In *Hillerns and Fowler* v *Murray,*[233] the trade was run by partnership which was dissolved by lapse of time under the terms of the partnership deed. At that time the partners held trading stock and they acquired other stock after that time under contracts entered into before the dissolution. The trading stock was used to fulfil orders placed by customers before the dissolution. But no new contracts whether for purchase or sale were entered into after dissolution. The commissioners held that there was evidence of trading after the dissolution; the Court of Appeal held that there was evidence to support their conclusion. The mere declaration by the partners that offices would remain open only for the carrying out of existing contracts could not give them immunity from the Income Tax Acts. The argument was put that this was simply the best way of realizing the assets of the partnership. Romer LJ after pointing out that the realization of the assets to best advantage might involve trading, went on "in most cases, in the winding-up of a partnership, it is necessary for the proper getting in of the assets and winding-up of the affairs of it, to carry on the business for a short time, or to carry on the business to a limited extent".[234] So the presumption that is said to exist that a sale by an executor is a realization of an asset and not a trading activity, does not apply to mere dissolution.

Where however it is clear that trading has ceased, subsequently disposals will escape income tax. Thus in *Beams* v *Weardale Steel Coal and Coke Co Ltd,*[235] the company's iron works had shut down by 1915. In 1933, they sold off some slag heaps and the Commissioners held this was not a part of their trade. It was not suggested that this was a new trade. The Revenue's appeal was dismissed.

Where a trader sells his trade to another, he ceases to trade. Whether his successor, in selling former trading stock commences to trade or simply realizes assets is a matter of fact.[236] If the successor is a company which is under some obligation to hand over the whole or part of the profits of the trade of the predecessor, it may be that new owner is simply the agent of the old, so that the former owner does not cease to trade.[237] An alternative conclusion on the facts may be that the old trade has ceased but the former owner has commenced a

---

232 1939 SC 689, 22 TC 716.
233 (1932) 17 TC 77.
234 At 92, and see Lord Hanworth, at 87.
235 (1937) 21 TC 204
236 *Lucy and Sunderland Ltd v Holt* [1961] 3 All ER 1062 at 1066, 40 TC 132 at 139.
237 *Baker v Cook* [1937] 3 All ER 509, 21 TC 337.

new trade through the agency of the new owner.[238] The choice between the two solutions is not merely academic since apart from the commencement and cessation provisions there are such questions as unused loss relief and capital allowances which will be lost under the second solution.[239]

(10) Mutual business

It is necessary to distinguish a profit from a trade from an excess of contribution over expenditure. If I allow myself ₦100 a week for housekeeping but spend only ₦90, no one would contend that the ₦10 saved was taxable profit. The immunity of the ₦10 from tax rests on two principles, either of which is sufficient; the one is that no man can trade with himself and the other is that the sum does not represent a profit.

This immunity has been applied to groups of people who combine for a purpose and contribute towards expenses, as in the case of a golf club whose members pay a club subscription. Here too, any excess of income from subscriptions over expenses is free from tax.[240] Each member is entitled to be a share of the surplus and it is irrelevant that there is only a limited liability to contribute to any deficiency.[241] Whether there is an identity[242] of contributors to fund and the recipients from the fun, it is impossible that the contributors should derive profits from contributions made by themselves to a fund which could only be expended or returned to themselves.[243] Even if the club had a bar at which drinks were served at prices which yielded a profit there is no liability to tax since the bar is merely a part of the club, and is open only to members who thus make certain additional contributions to the fund. A different situation arises if the bar is open to the public,[244] since there is now no identity of contributors to the fund with recipients from it; profits from the bar would be taxable even if the rest of the club ran at a loss. Liability would also arise if the facts showed that the bar was a distinct trading venture separate from the rest of the club.

---

[238] *Southern v Watson* [1940] 3 All ER 439, 23 TC 566; see also *Parker v Batty* (1941) 23 TC 739.

[239] Ibid

[240] *Carlisle and Silloth Golf Club v Smith* [1913] 3 KB 75, 6 TC 48 and 198; dist, *Carnoustie Golf Course Committee v IRC* 1929 SC 419, 14 TC 498.

[241] *Faulconbridge v National Employers Mutual General Insurance Association Ltd* (1952) 33 TC 103.

[242] But not equality, per Lord Macmillan in *Municipal Mutual Insurance Ltd v Hills* (1932) 33 TC 430 at 448; as long as the relationship is reasonable.

[243] See per Lord Normand in *English and Scottish Joint Co-operative Wholesale Society Ltd v Assm Agricultural ITC* [1948] 2 All ER 395 at 400; [1948] AC 405 at 419. *IRC v Eccentrics Club Ltd* [1924] 1 KB 390, 12 TC 683 and Finlay J in *National Association of Local Government Officers v Watkins* (1934) 18 TC 499 at 506.

[244] *Grove v Young Men's Christian Association* (1903) 4 TC 613

The mutuality principle has been used to exempt a local authority[245] from liability to tax on its rates but today its scope is limited to mutual insurance companies,[246] and members' clubs.[247]

The principle of mutuality applies even though the contributions are made to a separate legal entity, such as a company, so long as the company exists simply for the convenience of its members of a mutual insurance company. Income from investments is taxable in the usual way. Any excess of premium income over liabilities will also be the income of the company. However, so long as such income is returnable to the members either in the form of bonuses or by way of reduction of premiums, that income is exempt from tax since although the company is trading this sum is not a profit to its members. Should a member surrender his policy, he will lose his entitlement to future bonuses even though he has contributed to them. Likewise if a person becomes a member of the company by taking out a policy he may become entitled to a portion of the surplus contributed by someone else. Such possibilities do not prevent there being mutually, since the excess of contributions must go back to the policy holders as a class even if not precisely in the proportions in which they have contributed to them.

It is however essential that such companies should be mutual companies, that is, one where only the policy holders are the members of the company. If the company has shareholders who do not hold life policies but who are entitled to the profits of this business the company is not a mutual company.[248]

The mutuality doctrine is not without its limits. First, as just indicated, it applies only to the mutual dealings between the contributors. Mutual insurance companies are taxable on the ordinary income accruing from transactions with non-members. Thus in *New York Life Assurance Co.* v *Styles*[249] where the House of Lords held that the company was not taxable on its profits from premium income from members' participating policies, it was agreed that the company was taxable on its profits from policies for fixed sums without profits and from its general annuity business with strangers, since they were not members of the company, just as it was taxable on its investment income. Exemption is afforded not to the profits from members but to the non-profit of mutual dealings.

Secondly, the doctrine applies only if there is genuine mutuality. In *Fletcher* v *IRC*[250] a members' club owned a bathing beach in Jamaica. They permitted guests at certain hotels to use the beach on payment of an entrance fee. The club was clearly taxable on the profits of these fees since they were

---

[245] See Lord Thankerton in *IRC v Forth Conservancy Board* [1931] AC 540 at 554, 16 TC 103 at 123; contrast *IRC v Stonehaven Recreation Ground Trustees* 1930 SC 206, 15 TC 419.

[246] *British Broadcasting Corpn v Johns* [1964] All ER 926, 15 TC 419.

[247] E.g. Ilorin City Club or Lagos Island Club.

[248] *Last v London Assurance Co.* (1885) 10 App Cas 438, 2 TC 100.

[249] (1889) 14 App Cas 382, 2 TC 460; see also *Municipal Mutual Insurance Ltd v Hills* (1932) 16 TC 430, HL.

[250] [1971] 3 All ER 1185; [1972] AC 414.

carrying on a trade with non-members. They then altered their arrangements, abolishing the payment of a fee by the hotel guests and making the hotel voting members of the club.[251] However, each hotel member, like each individual, held only one share. The hotels were, like the individual members, to pay a sum by way of subscription, and in addition a sum which was based on the number of its guests using the beach. The gross receipts were £1,750. The Revenue sought to tax the club on the profit element in the relevant proportion of the hotel membership subscription. Lord Wilberforce said that if mutuality was to have any meaning, although a uniform fee was not essential, "*there must be a reasonable relationship, contemplated or in result, between what a member contributed and what, with due allowance for interim benefits of enjoyment he may expect or be entitled to draw from the fund; between his liabilities and his rights.*"[252] The great use of the beach made by hotel guests was not sufficient allowance and so the mutuality principle did not apply.

Thirdly, as *Municipal Mutual Insurance* v *Hills*[253] showed, not all business between a company and its members is mutual business. A business cannot escape tax on its profits for a year simply because at the end of the year, it discovers that all its business has been with its members but its principal function is as a mere entity for the convenience of its members.[254] The mutuality principle is satisfied because nothing belongs to the corporation which is several from what belongs to the aggregation of individuals.[255] When a company has share capital with a chance of dividends and, to one side of that, dealings with people who happen to be the owners of the share capital affording benefits to those people one by one individually, there is no reason to ignore the incorporation. In *English and Scottish Joint Co-operative Wholesale Society Ltd* v *Assam Agricultural ITC*,[256] a company was set up to own and manage a tea estate with the bulk of its produce going to its two shareholders who advanced money by way of loan to be set off against the price due for the tea supplied by the company to its shareholders and so was taxable. This conclusion could not have been avoided by restricting the company's business to sales to its members.[257] A different result might have been reached if the business had not been incorporated and a different practical result would have been earned.[258]

---

[251] An earlier scheme had made the hotels members but without voting rights and it had been held that this scheme failed because the hotels were not truly members (see at 1188).

[252] At 1191.

[253] *Supra.*

[254] Per Lord Normand in *English and Scottish Joint Co-operative Wholesale Society Ltd v Assam Agricultural ITC* [1948] 2 All ER 395 at 399; [1948] Ac 405 at 417.

[255] Per Rowlatt J in *Liverpool Corpn Trade Association Ltd v Monks* (1926) 10 TC 442 at 453 See also *Lord Watson in New York Life Insurance Co v Styles* (1889) 14 App Cas 381 at 393, 2 TC 460 at 471.

[256] [1948] 2 All ER 395, [1948] AC 405.

[257] At 417, 399.

[258] At 421, 401 (perhaps by treating the application of profit as a discount reducing the Price); see *Pope v Beaumont* [1941] 3 All ER 9, 24 TC 78.

Another test is to decide whether any gains or profits accruing are concerned with fixed or circulating capital. If concerned with the former, the gains or profits are not taxable, if the latter, then they are. (see *John Smith and Son* v. *Moore* (1991) 12 T.C. 266 at p. 282; *J. & R. O'Kane & Co.* v. *I.RC.* (1992) 12 T.C. 303). This distinction is accepted commercially and normally observed in a properly prepared balance sheet.

The scope of this charge to tax, it will be appreciated, is a wide one for if profit making activity is not caught for tax as a trade it may yet be chargeable as a business, profession or vocation. It was held by Finlay J. in *St. Aubyn's Estate Ltd. v. Strick* (1932) 17 T.C. 412 at pages 418 – 419, that the word "business" is wider in its scope than "trade" and therefore it is arguable that the charge to tax under the P.I.T.A. is very wide.

Basis of assessment

Normally income received other than from an employment or pension is charged to tax on a preceding year basis: *P.I.T.A. 1993, s.22 (1)*. Profits of trades, businesses and professions are usually computed for tax purposes from the profit as ascertained at the end of the accounting year ending in the preceding year of assessment.[259]

For example if a business makes up its accounts to December 31 each year, in the tax year 2004, it will be assessed on the profits as computed for the accounting year ended December 31, 2003.

There are exceptions to the preceding year basis of assessment. When they apply, tax, broadly speaking is assessed on the profits of the current rather than the preceding year. If profits are falling assessment on a current year basis is more advantageous to the taxpayer, whereas if profits are increasing the preceding year basis is more advantageous.

Example:

Year ending November 30	**Year of Assessment**
2002 – N40, 000	2002/3 – Profits of a/c year ending 30/11/01
2003 – N100, 000	2003/4 – N40, 000
2004 – N250, 000	2004/5 – N100, 000
2005 – N200, 000	2005/6 - N150, 000
	2006/7 – N200, 000

[259] S. 23(2) P.I.T.A.

Clearly, the preceding year basis is advantageous to the taxpayer as he earns N100, 000 in 2003 but during that tax year pays tax on only N40, 000 and so on. Where profits are falling the preceding year basis becomes dis-advantageous.

The exceptions to preceding year basis of assessment

(A) Basis of assessment for new business

Under section 24 P.I.T.A., the assessable income of an individual from a trade, business, profession or vocation carried on by him in Nigeria for the year of assessment in which he commenced to carry on the trade, business, profession or vocation in Nigeria and for the two following years of assessment (which years are in this subsection respectively referred to as "the first year", "the second year" and the "third year") shall be ascertained in accordance with the following provision:

(a) for the first year the assessable income shall be the amount of the income of that year;

(b) for the second year the assessable income shall unless such notice as hereinafter mentioned is given be the amount of the income of the income of one year from the date of the commencement in Nigeria of the trade, business, profession or vocations;

(c) for the third year the assessable income shall, unless such notice as is hereinafter mentioned be given, be computed in accordance with the provisions of section 23(1) of this Act;

(d) the individual carrying on the trade, business, profession or vocation shall be entitled, on giving notice in writing to the relevant tax authority within two years after the end of the second year, to require that the assessable income both for the second year and the third year (but not for one or other only of those years) shall be the income of the respective years of assessment:

Provided that he may, by notice in writing given to the relevant tax authority within twelve months after the end of the third year, revoke the notice, and in such case the assessable income both for the second year and the third year shall be computed as if the first notice had been given;

(e) where such a notice as aforesaid has been given or revoked, such additional assessment, or, on a claim being made for the purpose in writing, such reductions of assessments or repayments of tax shall be a made as may be necessary to give effect to paragraph (d) of this subsection.

But the taxpayer can, under section 24(d) of the P.I.T.A. 1993 elect to have the second and third years of assessment (both or neither) taxed on the actual profits of these years (i.e. from January to December each year) instead as above. The notice electing to be taxed on "actual" must be served on each relevant tax authority within two years of the end of the second year of assessment.

By choosing the moment to commence a business and then making a slow start it is possible to use these provisions to legitimate advantage.

Example:

Trading commences October 1, 2002. First year's trading profits computed to September 31, 2003 are N120, 000 – i.e. the profits of the first accounting year.

Thus the first year's assessment is the proportion of the year's profits for the period October 1 to December 31, 2002.

= $^3/_{12}$ x 12,0000 = 30,000 – basis of assessment for tax year2001/2.
Second year's assessment is the profits of the first twelve months trading – i.e. trading – i.e. October 1, 2002 – September 31, 2003
= N120, 000 – basis of assessment for tax year 2003/4.

Third year's assessment is on a preceding year basis – i.e. the profits as computed for the accounts year ending in the preceding year of assessment. The preceding year of assessment was the tax year 2003/4 and the accounting year ending in that year was again the first year of trading – October 1, 2002 – September 1, 2003

=N120, 000 – basis of assessment for tax year 2002/4.

Third year's assessment is on a preceding ye3ar basis – i.e. the profits as computed for the accounts year ending in the preceding year of assessment. The preceding year of assessment was the tax year 2003/4 and the accounting year ending in that year was again the first year of trading – October 1, 2002 – September 31, 2003.

=N120, 000 – basis of assessment for tax year 2005/6.

It can therefore be seen that a slow start can affect a new business tax assessment for at least three years. If initial expenses can be made as high as possible low assessments are likely for three years and thus if after deducting legitimate expenses a small loss has been made this will mean three consecutive nil assessments. It follows therefore that the following formation of a trading company it may be advantageous to pay high salaries, director's fees and so on during the first year of trading so as to keep the net profit down.

To illustrate the working of the option to assess on actual for the second and third years more facts must be added:

Profits for the accounting year October 1, 2002 – September 31, 2003 – N60, 000.

Profits for the accounting year October 1, 2003 - September 31, 2004 – N 80, 000.

(a) If no option is exercised the assessments will be as follows:

First year N30000	Tax Year	2002/93
Second year N120000 „ „		2003/4
Third year N120000 „ „		2004/5
Fourth year N60000 „ „		2005/6

(b) Where the option is exercised the assessment will be as follows:

First year N30000 Tax Year 2002/3

Second year $^9/_6$ x 120000 = 90000
$^3/_{12}$ x 60000 = 15000 N10,5000 tax year 2003/4

Third year $^9/_{12}$ x 60000 = 45000
$^3/_{12}$ x 80000 = 20000 N6, 5000 tax year 2004/5

Fourth year N60000 tax year 2005/6

Fifth year N80000 tax year 2006/7

It will be seen that on these figures there is a considerable tax advantage in exercising the option for the second and third years of assessment since in (a) above, tax will be payable for these years on N240, 000 whereas in (b) tax is payable on only N17, 000 a saving of tax on N70, 000.

It should be noted that although this option works in favour of a taxpayer there is another option in favour of the tax authorities which arises on the discontinuance of a business.

(B) Basis of assessment for a discontinued business

Under section 25 P.I.T.A. 1993, where an individual permanently ceases to carry on a trade, business, profession or vocation, in Nigeria, his assessable income therefrom shall be:

(a) as regards the year of assessment in which the cessation occurs, the amount of the income of that year:

(b) as regards the year of assessment preceding that in which the cessation occurs, the amount of the income as computed in accordance with the provisions of section 24 of this decree, or the amount of the income of such year, whichever is the greater, and he shall not be deemed to derived assessable income from such trade, business, profession or vocation for the year of assessment following that in which the cessation occurs.

Example:

Accounts made up to September 31 and business discontinued on September 31, 2006.

In the last year of assessment (2006/7) taxed on actual profits earned between October 1, 2006 and September 31, 2007 which requires an apportionment to be made as in the example above. For the penultimate year of assessment (tax year 2005/6) basis will be the profits earned in the accounting year ended on September 31, 2004 unless the profits made during the period October 1, 2005 to September 31, 2006 are greater when the tax authority will opt to assess tax on the latter amount.

It will be seen therefore that it is unwise to cease trading when profits are increasing since the profits made are likely to be higher when computed on an actual basis for the penultimate year of assessment than when computed on the preceding year basis. On the other hand, where profits are falling no advantage will accrue to the tax authorities. Furthermore, if the business is to be continued, it may be worthwhile forming a company to carry on the business. Where this is done the business of the unincorporated trader will be treated as discontinued and the business, which will have the benefit of the commencement provisions as already, explained. It will not be possible to continue with artificial cessations of the business and the formation of new companies or partnerships from time to time with a view to taking advantage of the commencement provisions many times over owing to s.17 P.I.T.A. and s.18 C.I.T.A. Also in the case of a partnership, on a change of its membership the business is treated as continuing for tax purposes.

When does trade commence?

It is important to determine when a trade commenced, because expenditure is only deductible if incurred after that time.[260] If an expense is incurred in the twelve months before trading the amount is treated as a loss incurred in the year of commencement. Preparing to commence a trade is not the same as commencing a trade. In *Birmingham and District Cattle By-Products Co Ltd* v *IRC*[261] the appellant company was incorporated on 20th June 1913; its directors then arranged for the installation of plant and machinery and entered into

---

[260] *City of London Contract Corpn v Styles* (1887) 2 TC 239; See Tiley (1981) *Revenue Law* p. 192-197

[261] (1919) 12 TC 92 (an excess profits duty case).

agreements for the purchase of its raw materials and the sale of its products; the raw materials were received on 6th October. The company's trade began on 6th October when they began to take the raw materials and to turn out their product. However in *Cannop Coal Co Ltd* v *IRC*[262] where the trade was to be the mining of coal by sinking pits in the Forest of Dean the company had since 1909 extracted a certain amount of coal from a drift nearby for use in its machines and, finding it had extracted more than it needed, sold the excess to the public, the company was held to have commenced trading when it sold the excess coal to the public and not when in 1912 coal began to emerge from the pits. That the coal company was engaged in a trade in those three years seems beyond argument and it was too fine a point to say that the trade was different from the mining of coal from the pits. Thus, the mere formation of an intention to commence trading is not the moment of commencement, nor is the incurring of capital expenditure for the purpose of preparing to trade.

A difficult question concerns the use of small-scale pilot projects involving resale to the public to decide precisely what product to make. It was important in *Cannop Coal Co Ltd* v *IRC* that the sales were substantial[263] and it may therefore be that pilot projects are not trading.

Commencement – new trade or development of existing one

There is no rule of law that a person, whether or not a company, cannot carry on more than one business and it is immaterial that there is one consolidated balance sheet. The question is one of fact and degree. As Rowlatt J put it in a case where the two activities had both been bought from another company, *"the real question is, was there any inter-connection, any interlacing, any interdependence, any unity at all embracing those two businesses"*.[264] So if a trader commences a new trade alongside his established one, the two trades are treated separately,[265] even for purposes of loss relief, capital allowances and stock relief; the sources are distinct. It is a question of fact whether a particular development is an expansion of an existing trade or the commencement of a new one; it may happen that the amalgamation of two trades is to be treated as the cessation of both and the commencement of one new trade.[266]

A modern example is *Seaman* v *Tucketts Ltd.*[267] In 1956 control of the company was acquired by a new group. The company carried on the trade of manufacture and sale of confectionery; this included the purchase the purchase

---

[262] (1918) 12 TC 31 (another excess profits duty case). In both instances the Revenue won.
[263] In one year 68% of the coal was resold and in another 84%.
[264] *Scales v George Thompson & Co Ltd* (1927) 13 TC 83 at 89.
[265]. *Fullwood Foundry Ltd v Ltd v IRC* (1924) 9 TC 101.
[266] (1963) 41 TC 422.
[267] See Rowlatt J in *Kirk and Randall Ltd v Dunn* (1924) 8 TC 663 at 670.

and resale of such goods from other manufacturers, which ended early in 1958. in September 1958 the two retail shops were closed and in November 1958 manufacture ceased. By April 1959, the existing stocks and the factory had been sold. The company which had previously bought sugar and cellophane for its own business now bought these for resale to the new parent company at cost plus 19%. Two years later it began to supply confectionary again. Reversing the Commissioners, Pennycuick J held that the only true and reasonable conclusion was that, at the end of 1958 when the manufacturers had ceased, a new trade of sugar merchants, including the buying and selling of cellophone payer, had been commenced and the case was remitted to the Commissioners to determine whether the confectionery trade had been discontinued or had been merely quiescent.

The question is one of fact and degree. *Seaman* v *Tucketts* Ltd shows that not only may there be a termination of one trade and the commencement of another but there may also be a contraction of one trade and the commencement of another, even though that other deals with a commodity employed in the original trade. There is also authority that a substantial change in management policy can lead to discontinuance and a new commencement.[268] However a legal practitioner does not, on becoming a Senior Advocate of Nigeria (SAN), start a new profession.[269]

Succession[270]

Problems of commencement also arise where a trade which has been carried on by one person is transferred to another; such a transfer is called a succession and must be distinguished from the mere purchase of the assets used in the trade.

If the new trade is not absorbed into the old but is a distinct entity then not only will the commencement provisions apply but there will be no merging once those provisions are spent.

Where a succession to a trade occurs, neither losses nor unused capital allowances incurred by the first trader can be used by the successor.[271a]

One other point concerns the former trader. Generally, expenditure incurred shortly before discontinuance may not be for the purposes of the continuing trade and so is not deductible.[271b] However expenditure made with a view to the trade after transfer may be incurred for the purposes of the trade and

---

[268] See Rowlatt J in *Kirk and Randall Ltd v Dunn*. ibid.
[269] *Seldon v Croon-Johnson* [1932] 1 KB 759, 16 TC 740.
[270] See [1959] *BTR* 193 (Graham).
[271a] E.g. *Rolls-Royce Motors Ltd v Bamford* [1976] STC 162.
[271b] *Godden v Wilson's Stores (Holdings) Ltd* (1962) 40 TC 100, CA.

not for the purposes of the present trader and so deductible by the first trader despite the succession.[272]

Rule 1. A succession to a trade must be distinguished from the purchase of the assets of a trade. Thus where a company which had a tramp shipping business bought a ship second hand from another trader there was no succession to that person's trade, but only the purchase of a ship.[273] These are however questions of fact and it was important in that case that the purchaser acquired no list of customers along with the ship, that the ship had no special route along which and only along which she used to ply trade and that no goodwill came with the ship.

Since the origin of the concept of succession lay in application of the rule that profits be measured by the average of three previous business years, there had to be a "*very close identity*" between the business in the former proprietorship and the business in the new proprietorship.[274] A very close identity is however not the same as a complete identity. Thus a successor to a business with say fifty shop may choose to shut up some of them, make alterations in the goods that he sells, change his supplier or may cut out a particular class of customer or a particular area.[275] The question whether such changes prevent there being a succession to the business is one of fact.

There may be a succession even though there is no purchase of the entire assets. In one case a circular was distributed to the former trader's customers that the new owners had acquired the "*trading connection*" of the former traders. The Commissioners held that there was no succession; the courts felt unable to reverse that conclusion.[276] Conversely in another case where a circular to the public described the new firm as successors, but they took over no books, no lists of customers by the customers and none of the staff except a few workpeople, they were held to be successors by the Commissioners and the courts again declined to intervene.[277]

Rule 2. There can be no succession to a part of a trade. However as Rowlatt J said, "*I do not think that it means that if what is succeeded to is not the same extent of trade or even does not include a particular lone of customers, it necessarily follows that there cannot be a successor to a trade.*[278]

[272] *Per Lord Clyde in IRC v Patrick Thomson Ltd* (1956) 37 TC 145 at 157; noted [1958] BTR 89 (Baker).

[273] *Watson Bros v Lothian* (1902) 4 TC 441. Compare *Bell v National Provincial Bank of England* [1904] 1 KB 149, 5 TC 1.

[274] Per Rowlatt J in *Reynolds, Sons & Co Ltd v Ogston* (1930) 15 TC 501 at 524, approved by Lord Hanworth MR at 527.

[275] Per Sir Wilfrid Greene MR in *Laycock v Freeman, Hardy and Willis* (1938) 22 TC 288 at 297.

[276] *James Shipstone & Son Ltd v Morris* (1929) 14 TC 413 at 421; and see *Stockham v Wallasey UDC* (1906) 95 LT 834.

[277] *Thomson and Balfour v Le Page* (1923) 8 TC 541 at 548.

[278] *James Shipstone & Son Ltd v Morris* (1929) 14 TC 413 at 421; and see *Stockham v Wallasey UDC* (1906) 95 LT 834.

Rule 3. There is no succession through the accidental acquisition by a trader who continues in business, of custom left by another who goes out of business. For there to be a succession there must be a transfer by one trader to another of the right to that benefit which arises from connection and reputation.[279] Thus if a trader goes out of business and his former rival captures his customers there is no succession; however if there were a transfer of the business and its goodwill to the rival, there would be.

Rule 4. There is no succession if the trade has ceased before being acquired by its new owner, nor if the new owner closes it down immediately he acquires it. Thus if a business has gone bankrupt and remained in the hands of the trustee in bankruptcy for twelve months before the assets were sold, it is likely that such a sale would be treated as a sale of assets rather than of the business.[280] Indeed there is authority that where a business has been making heavy losses and practically has to sell to avoid shutting down, it is likely that there is no succession.[281] However, where a business suffered extensive fire damage and ceased to trade with the Public but kept together its employees and various pieces of equipment, a delay of seventeen months between the fire and the acquisition of the business by a new owner did not prevent there being a succession.[282]

The question for the Commissioners is "*whether it is true and fair to say that the business in respect of which the successor is said to be making profits is the business to which he succeeded*". In *Laycock* v *Freeman, Hardy and Willis,*[283] the respondent company bought shoes from wholesalers and resold them to the public. Some 20% to 30% of its supplies came from two subsidiary companies which it controlled. In 1935 the subsidiary companies went into voluntary liquidation and the liquidator assigned all the assets and goodwill to the respondent company which also took over all the staff. The respondent company took all the products of the factories previously owned by the subsidiary companies and sold them in their shops. It was held that there was no succession. The business of the subsidiary companies was that of wholesale manufacturing concerns; that business had ceased; manufacturing was still carried on but the business of wholesale manufacturing was not.

To be distinguished from *Laycock* v *Freeman, Hardy and Willis* is *Briton Ferry Steel Co Ltd* v *Barry*[284] where the appellant company produced steel bars which were then supplied to six wholly owned subsidiaries. In 1934, the six subsidiary companies were wound-up and the conversion of the bars into blackplate and tinplate was carried on by the appellant company using the plant

---

[279] *Thompson and Balfour v Le Page* (1923) 8 TC 541 at 548.
[280] Per Green LJ in *Reynolds, Sons & Co Ltd v Ogston* (1930) 15 TC 524 at 413.
[281] Per Rowlatt J in *Wilson and Barlow v Chibbett* (1929) 14 TC 407 at 413.
[282] *Wild v Madam Tussauds* (1926) Ltd (1932) 17 TC 127.
[283] Per Sir Wilfrid Greene MR in *Laycock V Freeman, Hardy and Willis Ltd* [1938] 4 All ER 609 at 614, 22 TC 288 at 298.
[284] [1939] 4 All ER 541, 23 TC 414, applied *IRC v Spirax Manufacturing Co Ltd* [1938] 4 at 431-2.

and workforce of the former companies. The Commissioners held that there was a succession to the trades carried on by the subsidiaries. The fact that the company through its shares already controlled them was irrelevant, as was the fact that another subsidiary company controlled their sales.[285] The Court of Appeal refused to interfere with that decision. *Laycock* v *Freeman, Hardy and Willis* was distinguished. In that case the business of the subsidiaries, that of making profits by wholesale sales, had ceased, and one of retail manufacturing begun. In the present case the business of the subsidiary companies, that of making profits by conversion of steel bars into blackplate and tinplate and resale still existed, but was being carried on by someone else,[286] and the retail side was handled by a separate legal entity. The fact that someone had previously supplied the steel bars was irrelevant.

These cases produce one odd result. If there is a manufacturing concern with five distinct stages in it, each stages in it, each stage carried out by a separate company, it would appear that if one company takes over its neighbour, there will be a succession if the acquiring company is at an earlier stage in the process but not if it is at a later stage.

A further problem concerns the calculation of the profit of the trade acquired. In *Laycock* v *Freeman, Hardy and Willis* the Court of Appeal held that it was "*wholly illegitimate*" to invent a notional sale from the wholesale stage of the enterprise to the retail stage at a price which would yield a stage a notional "*wholesale profit*".[287] But in *Briton Ferry Steel Co Ltd* v *Barry* the same Court, having again rejected a notional sale, directed that the transfer of the steel bars from the one artificial side of the trade to the other should be treated as carried out at the actual cost of production. This ensures that the profit from the whole operation would be attributable to the newly acquired sector of the trade.[288] One cannot help feeling that the court was being a little ingenuous.

Discontinuance

There is a discontinuance if the trader ceases to carry on his trade; this will also occur if he ceases to trade in the way in which he had previously traded.[289] It is a question of fact whether the particular change is the ceasing of one trade and the commencement of another or is simply a normal development of his previous trade.

A trade does not cease if it is merely in abeyance. Thus a mere interruption in production does not cause discontinuance[290] nor does a disposal of assets[291]

[285] Per Macnagheten J [1938] 4 All ER 429 at 434-5, 23 TC 414 at 431-2.
[286] Per Sir Wilfrid Greene MR at 479, 547 and 431
[287] Per Sir Wilfrid Greene MR [1938] 4 All ER 609 at 616, 22 TC 288 at 300.
[288] Per Sir Wilfrid Greene MR [1939] 4 All ER 541 at 550, 23 TC 414 at 434.
[289] For a deemed discontinuance to assist a person who reduces his business.
[290] *Merchiston Co Ltd v Turner* [1910] 2 KB 923, 5 TC 520.
[291] *Aviation and Shipping Co Ltd v Murray* [1961] 2 All ER 805, 39 TC 595; note [1969] BTR 264

nor even the appointment of a liquidator.[292] Business is not confined to being busy and long periods of inactivity may occur.[293] It is however a question of fact whether a particular trade has lapsed into a period of quiescence or has ceased. A trade may be treated as permanently discontinued notwithstanding that the former trade later commences a new trade which in all respects identical with the previous ceased trade.

In *Kirk and Randall Ltd* v *Dunn,*[294] the new owners of a trading company obtained no new contracts and tried to sell the premises; they then had their works and plant requisitioned during the First World War. However the managing director tried to obtain contracts overseas. Rowlatt J, reversing the Commissioners, held that the company was still trading as there was evidence of business activity resulting in expenditure and loss.

However in *J.G. Ingram & Son Ltd* v *Callaghan*[295] where the period was much shorter the Court of Appeal upheld the Commissioners' finding that there was not just unprofitability but inactivity and so a discontinuance. In this case, the company had by May 1961 ceased to produce rubber goods, had sold off its stock and dismissed its staff. The plan being to switch to plastics. From September 1961 to June 1962 products were manufactured by another subsidiary of the owner and sold over the company's name. In this way the goodwill was kept alive but the operations of the company were confined to little more than bookkeeping and perhaps debt collecting; the trade was not kept alive between those dates.

Computation for tax purposes of the profits of trade

A) Accountancy principles

One of the greatest problems in the ascertainment of the full amount of the profits or gains of the trade is the role of accountancy practice. It is clear that the aim of the accountant is in some senses the same as that of the revenue – both are seeking to measure the income of a precise – and so an artificial – period.[296] It is also clear that the mere fact that an accountant or his employer wishes to charge a particular expense to capital or revenue will not be sufficient to

(Silberrad)

[292] *Wadsworth, Morton v Jenkinson* [1966] 3 All ER 702; noted [1967] BTR 80 (JGM)

[293] *The South Behar Rly Co Ltd v IRC* [1925] AC 476, 12 TC 657; cf. Morning Post Ltd v Graham (1940) 23 TC 414.

[294] (1924) 8 TC 663.

[295] [1969] 1 All ER 433, 45 TC 151, CA. The same conclusion was reached in *Tryka Ltd v Newall* (1963) 41 TC 146, Ch. D, noted [1964] BTR 286, and *Goff v Osborne & Co (Sheffield) Ltd* (1953) 34 TC 441.

[296] See Walton J in *Willingale v International Commercial Bank Ltd* [1976] STC 188 at 194-5; See Tiley (1981) *op cit* p. 201 - 203

determine its status at law.[297] While the ordinary principles of commercial accounting must, as far as is practicable, be observed, income tax law must not be violated.[298]

There are two distinct approaches to the relationship between questions of law and principles of accountancy. One asserts that the court should first look to see what accountancy says and then see whether any rule of law contradicts it;[299] the other that the court should first determine the question as a matter of law and then see whether accountancy gives a different answer and then determine which should prevail.[300] It will be appreciated that the former gives much greater weight to accountancy practice than the latter.

Tax law and accountancy practice conflict in a number of ways. First, it is an elementary accountancy principle that capital expenditure on a depreciating asset must be written off over the lifetime of the asset. However the tax law allows the deduction of capital expenditure only that expenditure falls within Capital Allowances system. Again prudent accountancy practice writes off abortive expenditure as a revenue expense but for law abortive capital expenditure is not deductible.[301] Again certain items of expenditure will be deducted by the accountants in ascertaining the income for the year but disallowed by some express provision such as business entertainment expenses.[302] However, the courts have not confined their decisions on points of accountancy to those situations where an express statutory provision is in point. The courts have also ruled on such questions as the correct method of assessing work in progress,[303] and the correct method of valuing stock in trade,[304] matters where there is no express provision and in the latter case the courts have ruled that there is such a thing as the correct method even though accountancy knows of many methods. By treating these issues as questions of law the courts have enabled themselves to keep complete control. The reasons for this divergence between tax law dates back to 1799 and so to a time well before the first Companies Act, to a time when the business unit was relatively small and when ownership and management were not completely distinct concepts.

---

297 *Associated Portland Cement Manufacturers Ltd v Kerr* [1946] 1 All ER 68, 27 TC 103. See also *Heather v P.E. Consulting Group* [1973] 1 ER 8, 48 TC 320.

298 Viscount Salmonds in *Ostime v Duple Motor Bodies Ltd* [1961] 2 All ER 167 at 169, 39 TC 537 at 566.

299 E.g. Salmon J in *Odeon Associated Theatres Ltd v Jones* [1972] 1 All ER 681 at 689, 48 TC 279 at 283A and Lord Haldane in *Sun Insurance Office Ltd v Clark* [1912] AC 443 at 455, 6 TC 59 at 78; Lord Clyde in *Lothian Chemical Co Ltd* v *Rogers* (1926) 11 TC 508 at 520; also Tucker Report Cmd. 8189 § 135.

300 Brightman J in *E.C.C. Quarries Ltd v Watkins* [1975] 3 All ER 843 at 855. See [1975] BTR 309 (Coombes) and, more generally, [1959] BTR 323 (Crump) and [1972] BTR 308 (Burgess).

301 See Abdulrazaq M.T. (1985) Law of Business Taxation and Accounting Principles. *Nigerian Accountant* April/June Vol XVII No.2 p.3-5,7,9 (ICAN)

302 Ibid.

303 *Ostime v Duple Motor Bodies Ltd.*

304 E.g. the prohibition of LIFO.

The courts' reluctance to abandon these matters to the accountancy profession has been supported on three grounds. (1) Such a course would have a potentially cramping influence on the development of accountancy practice; (2) the courts might not be the best forum to determine what accountancy practice is;[305] there would be no greater certainty than there is at present.[306] These reasons are however not particularly convincing.[307] They may easily be met by insisting first that questions of accountancy practice are questions of fact not of law, thus avoiding the deadening hand of the doctrine of precedent, and secondly by perhaps requiring not proof that all accountants would adopt a particular method but proof that a method had substantial accounting support. The third point seems doubtful. First, while it must be conceded that there are different methods of income measurement,[308] all methods tend to produce similar results overall when applied consistently from year to year and perhaps the one thing upon which there is uniform accountancy opinion is that there must be consistency from year to year.[309]

A recent decision in which the courts departed from accounting practice is *Willingale* v *International Commercial Bank Ltd.*[310] The taxpayer bank held a number of bills of exchange issued by borrowers all over the world and maturing over periods from one to ten years. The issue was whether the bank should bring the proceeds of such bills into the account only when the bills matured (or were disposed of) or whether following the practice applied to the clearing banks, it should bring in a part of the expected profit each year. The House upholding all the lower tribunals held that although the bank had made up its accounts on the practice stated it was entitled to insist that for tax purposes the other basis should be taken, as this would be in conformity with a fundamental principle that profits should not be taxed until ascertained. The division was by a bare majority and has been heavily criticized. One of the more restrained comments is that the decision makes no kind of commercial or logical sense and is out of line with previous decisions, a half dozen at least of which emanate from their Lordships' House.[311]

---

305 Royal Commission (Canada) vol. 4, pp. 218-220 and 581-584.

306 It is certainly much easier to conclude that a certain rule of tax accounting is contrary to generally recognized accounting principles than it is to define such principle: (1948) *Nat Tax Jo* 341 (Seghers)

307 See generally Harries, "Measuring Business Income", 19th Canadian Tax Foundation Conference 1967, at pp. 93-98.

308 Thus in *Southern Railway of Peru Ltd v Owen*. The House of Lords felt that the accountancy figures were not sufficiently relaiable. See [1956] *BTR* 172 (Edey) and [1957] BTR 351 (Philips).

309 But the Revenue may change the basis from year to year, e.g. cash to earnings basis, and have challenged accounts on bases which they have previously accepted, e.g. *B.S.C. Footwear Ltd v Ridgeway* [1970] 1 All ER 932, 47 TC 511 (30 years) and *Ostime v Duple Motrs Bodies Ltd* [1961] 2 All ER 167, 39 TC 537 (28 years)

310 [1978] STC 75, [1978] 1 All ER 754 and note Vinelott J in *Pattison v Marine Midland Ltd* [1981] Simons's Tax Intelligence 218.

311 Blom Cooper [1978] *BTR* 229. See also [1977] *BTR* 236 and [1978] BTR 69 (J.F.A.-J).

B) Assessment of profits of a trade

The Act does not define "profits" and so it should be given its ordinary meaning. The *Oxford English Dictionary* defines it as "the pecuniary gain in any transaction; the amount by which value acquired exceeds value expended; the excess of returns over the outlay in capital."

Various judicial pronouncements have been made as to the meaning of "profits." For example, in *Mersey Docks and Harbour Board* v *Lucas*, [312] the Board was required to pay its surplus income into a fund after making expenses and interest charges. The question was whether such surplus was profit assessable to tax. It was held by the House of Lords that:

> the word 'profits' as here used means the incomings of the concern after deducting the expenses of earning and obtaining them before you come to the application of them...It is exactly the same thing as if there had been a declaration that after paying the current expenses and all other out goings...the clear surplus of the profits and gains of the undertaking should be applied in a certain manner...[313]

In *Russell* v *Town & Country Bank*,[314] Lord Herchell defined "profits" as:

> the surplus by which the receipts from the trade exceed the expenditure necessary for the purpose of earning those receipts...

and he went on to say that:

> ...unless and until you have ascertained that there is such a balance, nothing exists to which the name profit can properly be applied.[315]

Similar views have been expressed on several occasions.[316]

In dealing with the provisions of the English Income and Corporation Tax Act 1970 charging tax "on the full amount of the profits or gains" accruing from a trade, profession or vocation, Whiteman and Wheatcroft observed that:

> For this purpose there is no distinction between 'profits' and 'gains' and both words bear the same meaning, that is, the net profits of the trade or profession computed for the relevant period on normal commercial principles in accordance with established legal concepts, and subject to any specific qualifications imposed by the Income and Corporation Tax Act.[317]

---

[312] (1883) 8 App. Cas. 891; 2 T.C. 25.
[313] Per Lord Selbourne L.C.
[314] (1888) 13 App. Cas. 418.
[315] Ibid. at P. 424.
[316] E.g. see *The Anaconda Case* [1956] A.C. 85 at p. 102; *Greshman Life Assurance Society v Styles* [1982] A.C. 309 at p. 322; *Sun Insurance v Clark* [1912] A.C. 443 at p. 460.
[317] Whiteman and Wheatcroft, *British Tax Encyclopaedia, Income Tax and Surtax*, para. 6-26, p.

They also concluded that:

> In general...if accounts are prepared in a normal commercial manner and in accordance with current accountancy practice the profits shown by these accounts will be taken as the taxable profit, subject to any specific statutory provisions and to the overriding power to the court to disregard accountancy practice where that practice appears to be based on a mistaken view of the law.[318]

For assessment of profits there are three elements to be considered:

(a) Receipts
(b) Payments
(c) Adjustments

(a) Receipts

All receipts must be brought into account in computing the gross profit figure, with the following exceptions:

(i) *No-trading Receipts*: But these may be taxable under PITA 1993 s.3(1)(f) as "any profit gain or other payment not falling within paragraph (a) to (e) inclusive of this subsection."

(ii) *Capital Receipts*: These are not easy to define and the problem of what is and what is not a capital receipt has given rise to a host of cases.

In *Mallet* v *Staveley Coal & Iron Co. Ltd.*,[319] Lord Hanworth M.R. distinguished fixed and circulating capital:

> I think one has to keep clear in one's mind that in dealing with any business there are two kinds of capital, one the fixed capital, which is laid out in the fixed plant, whereby the opportunity of making profits or gains is secured, and the other the circulating capital, which is turned over and over in the course of the business which is carried on.

It is not always easy, however, to determine whether an asset belongs to one category or the other, and little or no assistance can be obtained by examining the nature of the asset itself. This difficulty is referred to by Romer L.J. in *Golden Horse Shoe (New) Ltd.* v *Thurgood*:[320]

254; see also Whiteman and Wheatcroft, *Income Tax* (2nd ed.), para. 6-26.

[318] Ibid.

[319] [1928] 2 K. B. 405 at p. 413; 13 T.C. 772 at p. 780 (C.A.); See also *Arbico v F.B.I.R.* INTC 146; *C.I.T. v Nigerian Properties Co Ltd*, 1 NTC 15; See further Pinson *op cit* p. 33-39

[320] [1934] 1 K.B. 584 at p. 563; 18 T.C. 280 at p. 300 (C.A.).

> Land may in certain circumstances be circulating capital. A chattel or chose in action may be fixed capital. The determining factor must be the nature of the trade in which the asset is employed. The land upon which a manufacturer carries on his business is part of his fixed capital. The land with which a dealer in real estate carries on his business is part of his circulating capital. The machinery with which a manufacturer makes the articles that he sells is part of his fixed capital. The machinery that a dealer in machinery buys and sells is part of his circulating capital, as is the coal that a coal merchant buys and sells in the course of his trade.

Again, the character of an asset may change in the course of business; thus land originally acquired as an investment may later become part of the owner's circulating capital or stock-in-trade. Indeed, the value of the distinction between fixed and circulating capital as a criterion for determining the nature of a receipt may be questioned; but it is thought that the distinction has some value if it is recognized that the character or the asset is but one of a number of factors which are material. Where a receipt comes from the sale of ordinary trading stock or from the rendering of services, it will be brought into the computation of the annual profits or gains for tax purposes. A sum realized on the sale of a fixed asset may be a trading receipt. If, for example, the asset is sold on terms which secure to the vendor a right to future commission on sales by the purchaser the commission thus received is a trading receipt of the vendor.[321] The question in such cases is whether there is a sale of an asset providing for the payment of capital sums by instalments on a sale coupled with a collateral bargain for the sharing of commission.[322]

A sum received by a trader for undertaking *not* to carry on some trading activity may not be a receipt of the trade. Thus in *Higgs* v *Olivier*,[323] following the production of the film *Henry V* and to assist in its promotion, Sir Laurence Olivier entered into a covenant under which he received £15,000 in consideration of an undertaking by him to appear in no other film for any company other than the covenantee company for a period of 18th months.

It was held that the sum was not taxable. It did not come to the recipient as income of his vocation; it came to him for refraining from carrying on one facet of his vocation, namely "that part of it which showed him as an actor on the celluloid stage." It should be observed that there was a finding of the special Commissioners in that case that the covenant formed no part of the agreement under which the appellant make the film. Where, however, a trader agrees to some restriction on his trading activities as part of an arrangement to obtain supplies of raw material, the sums receivable by him are trading receipts.

---

[321] *Orchard Wine and Spirit Co. v Loynes* (1952) 33 T.C. 97.

[322] *Lamport & Holt Line Ltd. v Langwell* (1958) 38 T.C. 193 (C.A.)

[323] [1952] Ch. 311; 33 T.C. 136. *Cf.* payments made to employees for restrictive covenants: *Beak v Robson* [1943] A.C. 352; 25 T.C. 33.

Thus in *Thompson* v *Magnesium Electron Ltd.*,[324] the respondent company entered into two agreements with I.C.I.:

a) an agreement for the purchase of chlorine at a stated price per ton; and
b) an agreement not to manufacture chlorine or caustic soda (its by-product), in consideration of a payment of £x for each ton of caustic soda which the respondent company would have produced if it had manufactured its won chlorine, for which latter purpose it was to be treated as having produced an agreed number of tons for each ton of chlorine purchased from I.C.I.

It was held that the two agreements should be read together as an arrangement for the supply of chlorine and that the sums received under agreement (a) were taxable.

In *I.R.C.* v *Biggar*,[325] a grant paid under the EEC Dairy Herd Conversion Scheme to a farmer who agreed to switch from dairy farming to raising cattle for beef was held to be a receipt of the trade of farming.

In this case the General Commissioners held that the grant was a capital receipt, in reliance on the decision in *Higgs* v *Olivier* (above); but Lord Emslie (allowing the Revenue's appeal) explained the difference between the cases as follows:

> In *Higgs*, Sir Laurence Olivier would, but for the restrictive covenant, have carried on acting in and producing and directing films as well as carrying on his vocation on the legitimate stage on radio and elsewhere. The restriction which he accepted severely limited his ability to exploit his art and exposed him to inevitable loss. In the Bigger, case there is no question of there being a restriction of this kind which is capable of being equiparated with sterilization of part of a taxpayer's capital assets. The scheme was a conversion scheme in terms of which on the one hand the taxpayer agreed to stop producing milk and milk products and, on the other hand, to begin producing meat instead. They agreed, in short, to continue to farm to their full capacity. Only the product changed.

There are many cases where the problem of distinguishing an income from a capital receipt presents great difficulty and, as Lord Macmillan said in one such case, "the task of assigning it to income or capital is one of much refinement." Some of these cases must now be considered.

(1) The compensation cases

The problems now to be considered arises where a trader is deprived of some profitable asset and receives compensation by way of damages or otherwise for the loss suffered or anticipated. It should be kept in mind that the cases

[324] (1944) 26 T.C. 1 (C.A.).
[325] (1982) S.T.C. 677 (C.S.).

discussed below preceded the introduction of the tax on capital gains and that compensation payments are often taxable as capital gains.

Compensation for sterilization of assets. The leading case is *Glenboig Union Fireclay Co. Ltd.* v *I.R.C.*,[326] where the facts were as follows:

> The appellants manufactured fireclay goods and sold raw fireclay. They were lessees of fireclay fields in the neighbourhood of the Caledonian Railway and a dispute arose with the railway company as to their right to work the fireclay under railway. An action by the railway company to restrain the appellants was eventually unsuccessful, but during its pendency the appellants were restrained from working the fields (but incurred expense in keeping them open). When the House of Lords decided against the railway company, that company exercised its statutory powers to required part of the fireclay to be left unworked on payment of compensation. Held, that the amount received for compensation was a capital receipt, not subject to tax.

Lord Wrenbury stated the principle as follow:

> Was that compensation profit? The answer may be supplied, I think, by the answer to the following question: is a sum profit which is paid to an owner of property on the terms that he shall not use his property so as to make a profit? The answer must be in the negative. The whole point is that he is not to make a profit and is paid for abstaining from seeking to make a profit ...... it was the price paid for sterilizing the asset form which otherwise profit might have been obtained.

It must not be supposed, however, that *all* payments for sterilization of assets are capital receipts. In the *Glenboig* case, the asset of which the appellants were deprived was a capital asset (i.e. fixed capital); moreover, sterilization was complete. If the appellants had been dealers in fireclay beds (which would then be circulating capital or stock-in-trade), or if the asset had been only partially sterilized or sterilized in the last year of its effective life, the payment might be regarded as of an income nature. The real test, it seems, is whether the thing in respect of which the taxpayer has recovered compensation is the depreciation of one of the capital assets of his trading enterprise or a mere restriction of his trading opportunities.

The *Glenboig* case should be contrasted with *Burmah Steam Ship Co. Ltd.* v *I.R.C.*[327] where the facts were as follows:

> Repairers of a vessel exceeded the time stipulated by contract for the completion of an overhaul damages were paid in compromise of a claim for loss of profit. The payment was held to be a trading receipt.

---

[326] (1921) 12 T.C. 427 (H.L.).

[327] (1931) 16 T.C. 67 (Ct. of Sess.)

The character of a payment for sterilization of assets is not determined by the manner in which the compensation payment is calculated. In the *Glenboig* case, for example, the compensation was estimated on the basis of the profits lost to the appellants; yet the payment was held to be a capital receipt.

> There is no relation, *said Lord Buckmaster,* "between the measure that is used for the purpose of calculating a particular result and the quality of the figure that is arrived at by means of the application of that test."

Compensation for cancellation of business contracts. In *Van den Berghs Ltd.* v *Clark,*[328] an English company manufacturing margarine and other butter substitutes had a Dutch company as its principal trade rival. In 1908 and 1013 certain "pooling agreements" were entered into between the companies under which each company retained its separate identity but agreed to conduct business on certain agreed lines to the mutual advantage of both companies. After some years these agreements became unworkable and it was agreed that they should be rescinded and that the Dutch company should pay the English company £450,000 "as damages." It was held that this was a capital receipt. The following passage in Lord Macmillan's judgement[329] is frequently cited:

> The three agreements which the appellants consented to cancel were not ordinary commercial contracts made in the course of carrying on their trade; they were not contracts for the disposal of their products, or for the engagement of agents or other employees necessary for the conduct of their business; nor were they merely agreements as to how their trading profits when earned should be distributed as between the contracting parties. On the contrary the cancelled agreements related to the whole structure of the appellant's profit-making apparatus. They regulated the appellant's activities, defined what they might and what they might not do, and affected the whole conduct of their business. I have difficulty in seeing how money laid out to secure, or money received for the cancellation of so fundamental an organization of a trader's activities can be regarded as an income disbursement or an income receipt ... It is not the largeness of the sum that is important but the nature of the asset that was surrendered.

This passage is the foundation of the distinction, often made, between payments for the cancellation of ordinary trading contracts and payments for the cancellation of contracts affecting the structure of the taxpayer's profit-making apparatus (which are not).

---

[328] [1935] 431; 19 T.C. 390. See also *Barr, Crombie & Co. Ltd v I.R.C.* (1935) 26 T.C. 406; *I.R.C. v Fleming & Co. (Machinery)* (1951) 33 T.C. 57; *Wiseburgh v Domville* (1956) 36 T.C. 527 (C.A.); *Keir & Cawder Ltd. v I.R.C.* (1958) 38 T.C. 23; *Sabine v Lookers Ltd.* (1958) 38 T.C. 120 (C.A.); *Creed v H. & M. Levinson Ltd.* (1981) 54 T.C. 477; (1981) STC 486.

[329] [1953] A.C. 431 at pp. 442-443; 19 T.C. 390 at pp. 431-432.

In contrast to the decision in the *Van den Berghs* case is *Kelsall Parsons & Co.* v *I.R.C.*[330] The appellants were manufacturers' agents; that is, they had contracts with a number of manufacturers whose products they sold on a commission basis. They had sold Ellison products for some time under agency contracts which had occasionally been varied, and the agreement in force in 1934 was due to expire on September 30, 1935. In May 1934, however, Ellisons requested that the agency agreement should be terminated and, in due course, £1, 500 was paid as compensation for the premature determination. This amount was held to be taxable receipt.

The *Kelsall Parsons* case can be distinguished from the *Van den Berghs* case in the following respects:

a) In the *Kelsall Parson* case, the taxpayer was a manufacturers' agent, so the acquisition and loss of an agency was a normal incident of the business.

> The agency agreements, *said Lord Normand,* so far from being a fixed framework, are rather to be regarded as temporary and variable elements of the.... Profit-making enterprise.

b) In the *Kelsall Parsons* case, the abandoned agreement had only one year to run (a [331]factor to which importance was attached) and the compensation was "really a surrogatum for one year's profits." In the *Van den Berghs* case, however, the cancelled agreements had 13 years to run.

There are numerous reported cases in which the courts have been called on to decide whether a payment is taxable as income, within the *Kelsall Parsons* principle, or escapes tax as income under the *Van den Berghs* principle.

(2) Unclaimed balances and released debts

In *Morley* v *Tattersall,*[332] a firm of bloodstock auctioneers received sums from sales for which they were liable to account to the vendors, their clients. These sums were not trade receipts; they were the clients' money. Substantial sums were never collected by the clients and remained in the firm's hands as "unclaimed balances"; and, in due course, when such balances seemed unlikely ever to be claimed, they were transferred to the credit of the individual partners. It was held that these sums were not trading receipts of the firm. The following passage from the judgment of Sir Wilfrid Greene M.R. shows clearly the basis of the decision:

---

[330] (1938) 21 T.C. 608 (Ct. of Sess.). See also *Elson v James G. Johnston Ltd.* (1965) 42 T.C. 545; *Fleming v Bellow Machine Co. Ltd.* (1965) 42 T.C. 308.

[331] See *London & Thames Haven Oil Wharves Ltd. v Attwooll* (1966) 42 T.C. 491 (C.A.); *Rajas Commercial College v Gian Sing* [1977] A.C. 312; S.T.C. 282 (J.C.); *I.R.C. v Biggar* [1982] S.T.C. 677 (C.S.); *Lang v Rice* [1984] S.T.C. 172 (C.A., N.I.).

[332] (1938) 22 T.C. 51 (C.A.).

> I invited Mr. Hills to point to any authority which in any way supported the proposition that a receipt which at the time of its receipt was not a trading receipt could by some subsequent operation *ex post facto* be turned into a trading receipt, not, be it observed, as at the date of [105]receipt, but as at the date of the subsequent operation. It seems to me, with all respect to that argument, that it is based on a complete misapprehension of what is meant by a trading receipt in income tax law ... It seems to me that the quality and nature of a receipt for income tax purposes is fixed once and for all when it is received.

This case was distinguished in *Jay's the Jewellers Ltd* v *I.R.C.*,[333] where a company of pawnbrokers had unclaimed balances representing the proceeds of sale of unredeemed pledges. Some of these balances became the property of the pawnbroker after a period of time by virtue of the Pawnbrokers Act 1872, and these were held to have become trade receipts when they became the pawnbroker's property. The statute had changed the character of the balances. Other unclaimed balances were outside the Pawnbrokers Act but they became statute-barred after six years under the Statutes of Limitation. Atkinson J. decided that these also became trade receipts of the pawnbroker. It is not clear from the report whether this part of the case was fully argued but, in the author's view, this part of the decision cannot be reconciled with the decision of the Court of Appeal in *Tattersall's* case.[334]

In *Elson v Price Tailors Ltd.*,[335] the defendant tailors took "deposits" from customers who ordered garments. Where garments were not collected, the deposits were eventually transferred to an "Unclaimed Deposits Account" and would ordinarily be returned to dissatisfied customers. It was held:

a) that the payments were true deposits and were therefore strictly irrecoverable by the customers;
b) that they were trading receipts because they were paid to the defendant company subject to the consequence that they would used in the company's business, and they were receipts of the year when payments were made (following *Smart* v *Lincolnshire Sugar Co.*,[336]).

   Morley v *Tattersall* and *Jay's the Jewellers Ltd* v *I.R.C.* were distinguished because in those cases the balances in the trader's hands were originally their clients' property and y were not receipts of the trade.

---

[333] (1947) 29 T.C.274.

[334] Although the debts in Tattersall's case might not have been technically statute-barred, it is not thought that this is sufficient grounds of distinction.

[335] (1962) 40 T.C. 671.

[336] (1937) 20 T.C. 643 (H.L.) where Government advances to sugar manufacturing companies were repayable in certain contingencies and it was held that they became trade receipts in the year of payment and not in the year when the contingency of repayment ceased. What was decisive was that these payments were made in order that the money might be used in the business: Lord Macmillan at p. 670.

Released, remitted or forgiven debts. In *British Mexican Petroleum Co Ltd* v *I.R.C.*,[337] it was held that where a trade debt is incurred in an accounting period and the creditor later releases or forgives the debt (or part of it) (a) the accounts for the earlier period cannot be reopened and (b) no assessment can be made in the year of release, for there is then no trade receipt. This decision was nullified by section 36 of the Finance Act 1960 (now s.136 of the Income and Corporation Taxes Act 1970), as respects releases effected after April 5, 1960. Now, where a deduction has been allowed for any debt incurred for the purposes of a trade and the whole or part of that debt is thereafter released, the amount released is treated as a trading receipt of the period in which the release is effected.[338] The section does not apply to debts incurred on capital account which are later released.

c) *Post cessation receipts*: These are receipts paid to an individual or his personal representatives after taxpayer has ceased to carry on his trade, business, profession of vocation and are deemed to have been received on the last day on which the trade, etc., was carried on, PITD 1993, s. 31 and are hence taxable accordingly.

(b) Payments

Two tests must be satisfied before an item of trading expenditure can be allowed as a deduction and therefore not all payments may be included in the computation of the net income chargeable to tax.

1) The payment must be an income or revenue expense and not a capital expense.
2) The payment must be allowed as a deduction by the PITA or CITA.

In *Vallambrosa Rubber Co. Ltd* v *Farmer*,[339] Lord Dunedin suggested that expenditure which is made once and for all is normally capital expenditure, whereas recurrent expenditure (or Expenditure which is likely to recur) is revenue expenditure. In *British Insulated and Helsby Cables Ltd.* v *Atherton*,[340] Viscount Cave L.C. carried the matter a stage further:

> But when an expenditure is made, not only once and for all, but with a view to bringing into existence an asset or an advantage for the enduring benefit of

---

337 (1932) 16 T.C. 570 (H.L.)

338 This can have important repercussions when shares of a tax-loss company are purchase. It is not uncommon in such a case for trade creditors who are associated with the company to release their debts in order to facilitate the sale of the shares to outsiders.

339 (1910) 5 T.C. 529 (Ct. or Sess.).

340 [1926] A.C. 205 at p. 214; 10 T.C. 155 at p. 192. *Cf. Heather v P-E Consulting Group Ltd.* [1973] Ch. 189; 48 T.C. 293 (C.A), in which annual payments made by a company to establish a fund to acquire shares for the benefit of the employees were held to be of a revenue nature and deductible in computing profits (C.A.). See also *Strict v Regent Oil Co. Ltd.* (1965) 43 T.C. 1 (H.L.).

> a trade, I think that there is very good reason … for treating such an expenditure as properly attributable not to revenue but to capital.

The expenditure in that case was of £30,000, to form the nucleus of a pension fund which would endure throughout the life of the company. Whether an item of expenditure is capital or revenue expenditure is ultimately a question of law for the court; and in one case[341] Lord Greene M.R. remarked that "in many cases it is almost true to say that the spin of a coin would decide the matter almost as satisfactorily as an attempt to find reasons." The procedure by coin-spinning has not as yet commended itself to the Commissioners, however, so the quest for legal principles must continue. The passage form the speech of Viscount Cave L.C. (above) indicates that there are two elements which determine whether expenditure is capital expenditure. First, it must be made "once and for all." Secondly, it must be made "with a view to bringing into existence an asset or an advantage for the enduring benefit of the trade." This second "limb" has been said to be inappropriate as concentrating too much attention on the *reason* why the expenditure was incurred rather than on the *subject-matter* that acquired by means of the expenditure.[342] The courts seem now to have accepted an "identifiable asset test," making the obtaining of or the enrichment of some capital asset as the key factor in capital expenditure. The test is: can a capital asset be identified for which the payment was made?[343]

In *Tucker* v *Granada Motorway Services Ltd.*,[344] the taxpayer company had a lease of a motorway service area for 50 years from 1964. The rent payable consisted of two elements: a fixed rent of £15, 000 per annum and an additional rent equal to a percentage of the previous year's gross takings. The gross takings included tobacco duty in the selling price of tobacco. As tobacco duty increased, the rent increased and it became difficult to operate the service area profitably. A variation of the terms of the lease was accordingly negotiated. In consideration of a lump sum payment of £122,220 made by the taxpayer company in 1974 (being six times the additional rent due on tobacco duty in the year ended July 31, 1973) the lessor agreed to exclude this duty from the additional rent.

The House of Lords held that the lump sum payment was capital expenditure: it was expenditure on a capital asset (namely the lease) and it made the lease a more valuable asset. Lord Wilberforce said:

---

[341] *British Salmon Aero Engines Ltd.* v *I.R.C.* [1938] 2 K.B. 482; 22 T.C. 29 (C.A.). "*… reported cases are the best tools that we have, even if they may sometimes be blunt instruments*": Lord Wilberforce in *Tucker v Granada Motorway Services Ltd.* (1979) 53 T.C. 92 at p. 107 (H.L.). See also Lord Radcliffe in *Comr. Of Taxes v Nchanga Consolidated Copper Mines Ltd.* [1964] A.C. 948 at 959.

[342] *Tucker v Granada Motorway Services Ltd.* (1979) 53 T.C. 92 at p. 115D (Lord Fraser).

[343] *Tucker v Granada Motorway Services Ltd.* (1979) 53 T.C. 92 at p. 108A (Lord Wilberforce) and see the dicta of Walton J. in *Watney Combe Reid v Pike* [1982] S.T.C. 733 at pp. 752C *et seq*…Also *Whitehead v Tubbs (Plastics) Ltd.* (1984) S.T.C. 1 (C.A.).

[344] (1979) 53 T.C. 92; [1979] S.T.C. 393 (H.L.).

> I think that the key to the present case is to be found in those cases which have sought to identify an asset. In them it seems reasonably logical to start with the assumption that money spent on the acquisition of the asset should be regarded as capital expenditure. Extensions from this are, first, to regard money spent on getting rid of a disadvantageous asset as capital expenditure and, secondly, to regard money spent on improving the asset, or making it more advantageous, as capital expenditure. In the latter type of case it will have to be considered whether the expenditure has the result stated or whether it should be regarded as expenditure on maintenance or upkeep, and some cases may pose difficult problems.

It is true that the object of the payment was to increase the taxpayer's share of profits: but this commercial objective could not obscure the fact that, both in substance and in form, the payment was to secure a variation in the lease.

The cost of an item from the resale of which a trader makes his profit is generally deductible: the item is part of the trader's "circulating capital." There is, however, an important distinction between the purchase of the raw material of a trade (revenue expenditure) and the purchase of an asset from which the trader obtains his raw material (capital expenditure).

Thus in *Stow Bardolph Gravel Co. Ltd. v Poole*,[345] the company who were dealers in sand and gravel claimed as a deduction the cost of a contract giving them the exclusive right to excavate gravel. The contract was unlimited in time and imposed no obligation on the company to excavate the gravel; the price was not related to the quantity of gravel excavated; and there were options to acquire other reserves of gravel. *Held* to be capital expenditure.

This distinction was maintain in *H.J. Rorke Ltd. v I.R.C.*,[346] notwithstanding evidence that the payments in that case were a normal and recurrent incident of the trade and that, since the purchase had a lease for one year only, no "enduring benefit" was obtained. "They were not payments made for the purchase of coal but payments to put the company into the position to get coal."

Examples of revenue expenditure

In *Mitchell* v *B.W. Noble Ltd.*,[347] a lump sum was paid to a director who, though liable to dismissal, agreed to retire to avoid undesirable publicity. *Held* to be deductible. "... a payment to get rid of a servant in the interests of the trade is a proper deduction." (*Per* Rowlatt J.) The payment was make "not in order to secure an actual asset to the company but to enable the company to continue to

---

345 (1954) 35 T.C. 459 (C.A.); see also *Golden Horse Shoe (New) Ltd. v Thurgood* [1934] 1 K.B. 548; 18 T.C. 280 (C.A.); *Saunders v Pilcher* (1949) 31 T.C. 314 (C.A.); *Hopewood v C.N. Spencer Ltd.* (1964) 42 T.C. 169.

346 (1960) 39 T.C. 194.

347 [1927] 1 K.B. 719; 11 T.C. 372 (C.A.) and see *Nevill & Co. Ltd. v Federal Commissioner of Taxation* (1936) 56 C.L.R. 290; "The purpose was transient and, although not in itself recurrent, it was connected, it was connected with the ever-recurring question of personnel" (per Dixon J.).

carry on, as it had done in the past ... un-imperilled by the presence of one who ... might have caused difficulty." (*Per* Hanworth M.R.)

Similarly in *Anglo-Persian Oil Co. Ltd.* v *Dale,*[348] a lump sum paid by a principal to his agent for the cancellation of an onerous long-term agency agreement, the payment being in the course of a change in the principal's business methods and to effect an economy in the business, was allowed as a deduction. "The agency contract was not a capital asset and the result of terminating it was simply to relieve the company of an obligation to make recurring payments under the contract."[349]

In *Southern* v *Borax Consolidated Ltd.,*[350] costs incurred by a company in defending its title to certain land were allowed as a deduction.

In *Morgan v Tate & Lyle Ltd* [351] T. carried on the business of sugar refiners. Threatened with the nationalization of the sugar refining industry, T. incurred expenses on a propaganda campaign designed to show that nationalization would harm "workers, consumers and stockholders alike." *Held*, that the expenses were deductible. The money was spent "to preserve the very existence of the company's trade."

In *I.R.C.* v *Carron*[352] Company the cost of obtaining a new charter which provided a better administrative structure for the company was held to be deductible "... what matters is the nature of the advantage for which the money was spent. This money was spent to remove restrictions, which the money was spent. This money was spent to remove restrictions, which were preventing profits from being earned. It created no new asset. It did not even open new fields of trading which had previously been closed to the Company." The "identifiable asset test" was not satisfied.

Examples of capital expenditure

Mallet v *Staveley Coal and Iron Co. Ltd.,*[353] where a colliery company with long-term mining leases found that some of the seams of coal it had contracted to work were unprofitable. The lessor agreed to release the company from its obligations under the leases on payment of a lump sum. *Held*, this was not deductible. The company was "getting rid of a permanent disadvantage or onerous burden, arising with regard to the lease which was a permanent asset of the business." (Per Sargant L.J.)

---

[348] [1932] 1 K.B. 124; 16 T.C. 253 (C.A.).

[349] *Tucker v Granada Motorway Services Ltd.* (1979) 53 T.C. 92 at p. 115H (Lord Fraiser).

[350] [1941] 1 K.B. 111; 23 T.C. 597.

[351] [1955] A.C. 21; 35 T.C. 367 (H.L).

[352] (1968) 45 T.C. 18 (H.L) . And see *Cooper v Rhymney Breweries Ltd.* (1965) 42 T.C. 509 (cost of publicity campaign to achieve Sunday opening in the Principality of Wales *held* to be revenue expenditure).

[353] [1928] 2 K.B. 405; 13 T.C. 772 (C.A.).

Associated Portland Cement Manufacturers Ltd. v *Kerr,*[354] where lump sum payments to retiring directors in consideration of covenants that they would not thereafter carry on a similar business were held to be capital expenditure.

Strick v *Regent Oil Co. Ltd.,*[355] where R. - in other to secure exclusive sales of its products at service stations – paid substantial sums to dealers for the benefit of "ties" ranging from 5 to 21 years. The form of the transaction was a lease from the dealer to Regent Oil for a lump sum calculated by reference to estimated petrol sales over the "tie" period, with a lease back from Regent Oil to the dealer for the same time less three days. The rent payable under both leases was nominal. *Held*, that the lump sums paid by Regent Oil were capital expenses, having regard to the nature of the asset which the expenditure secured.

The statutory test

The P.I.T.A. 1993 s.20 and the C.I.T.A. 1990 s. 20 specify the payments allowed as deductions in respect of the income of individuals and companies respectively. For the purposes of the profits of trade the following examples of permissible deductions should be noted:

i) Rent and premium the liability for which was incurred during the accounting period, in respect of land or buildings occupied for the purpose of earning profits;
ii) Any expense incurred for repair of premises, plant, machinery or fixtures employed in acquiring profits;
iii) Contributions to pension, provident or other retirement benefit funds societies or schemes approved by the Joint Tax Board: see P.I.T.A. s.20(1)(g) and 4th Schedule.
iv) Any other expense the liability for which was incurred "wholly exclusively necessarily of a company, business, profession or vocation."

Wholly and exclusively test

It must be emphasized that although the qualifying expenses must be incurred solely for the purpose of the business the total may be apportioned. Thus if part of a certain expense is incurred wholly, exclusively, necessarily and reasonably for the purposes of the taxpayer's trade that part is deductible even though the remainder of the expenditure was incurred for another purpose.[356]

[354] (1945) 27 T.C. 103 (C.A.).
[355] [1966] A.C. 295; 43 T.C. 1 (H.L.). The speeches in this case merit careful study. See also *B.P. Australia Ltd.* v *Comr. Of Taxation of the Commonwealth of Australia* [1966] A.C. 224 (J.C.).
[356] Abdulrazaq M.T. (1991) Deductibility of Legal and Accounting Expenses to Contest Tax

For example where a business or employment is run partly from a private house the cost of the telephone, electricity, rent, cleaning, etc., may be apportioned between business and private use provided it is within (iv) above.

Some examples of English cases may help to indicate the position. In *Simpson* v *Tate* [1925] 2 K.B. 214, a medical officer employed by a county council sought to deduct from his salary assessed to income tax subscriptions to certain medical and scientific societies. He justified these subscriptions on the grounds that he was obliged to expend in the performance of his duties and they were therefore necessarily incurred. In *Ricketts* v *Colquhoun* [1926] A.C. 1, a barrister in private practice in London who also held the salaried appointment of recorder of Portsmouth was held unable to deduct from his emoluments the expenses of travelling from London to Portsmouth. The reason being that there was nothing in the terms of his employment as Recorder of Portsmouth which necessarily involved him travelling from London.

Other examples of where expenses have not been deductible for tax purposes are:

a) The expense of purchasing textbooks and travelling to classes in preparation for a university degree the attainment of which the taxpayer was a condition of his employment.[357]
b) The expenses of running a car and household expenses in excess of those allowed to a full-time hospital consultant by his employer.[358]
c) The upkeep of a car and telephone at the residence of a pilot whose duties included attendance at the airport at short notice.[359]
d) The expense of paying subscriptions to a club by a bank manager where he met actual and potential customers, on the ground that this was not necessarily incurred in the performance of his duties.[360]
e) The expenses incurred by a Northern Irish company director in joining two clubs in London because he found that the accommodation provided by his clubs on his business visits was cheaper than hotel accommodation and thus saved the company money. The expense was held deductible.[361]

In the Nigerian income tax law, there is no distinction in the assessment of profits and emoluments as there is in English law. The same expenses rule applies to both. It is now doubtful whether subscriptions to the professional societies or journals are allowable for the taxpayer who is either self-employed or in employment. In England such subscriptions by employees are allowed by statute but there appear to be no such allowance in the Act applying the rule to all taxpayers neither has the expenses rule been fully appreciated in Nigeria.

Liabilities in Nigeria. *Nigerian Financial Review* Vol 14 No.2 p.25-34.

[357] *Blackwell v Mills* (1945) 26 T.C. 468; See also *Western Soudan Exporters v F.B.I.R.* 1 NTC 239.

[358] *Hamerton v Overy* (1954) 35 T.C. 73.

[359] *Nolder v Walters* (1930) 15 T.C. 380.

[360] *Brown v Bullock* [1961] 1 W.L.R. 1095.

[361] *Utitz v Elwood* [1965] T.R. 201.

Certain deductions are specifically disallowed by statute under section 21 P.I.T.A. and section 23 C.I.T.A.:

a) domestic or private expense;
b) capital expenditure of any kind;
c) sums recoverable under indemnity insurance contracts;
d) tax levied by foreign governments where no double taxation relief is given;
e) payments in respect of unauthorized retirement benefit schemes;
f) depreciation on any asset; or
g) allowances for bad or doubtful debts except as permitted by the P.I.T.A. 1993 or C.I.T.A. 1990.

(c) Adjustments

There are three types of adjustments necessary to arrive at the final computation of chargeable income:

i) Apportionment
ii) Stock in trade
iii) Bad debts

i) Apportionment

A receipt or payment may have to be spread over more than one accounting period and must therefore be apportioned under P.I.T.A. 1993, s.30, C.I.T.A. 1990, s.25(6). This is always required where assessment is made on an "earnings" basis which means that assessment for tax is made on the amount earned during an accounting period and not necessarily on what was actually received in cash or kind. Where assessment is made on "cash" basis this will not be necessary.

Section 30 P.I.T.A. provides that where in the case of a trade, business, profession or vocation it is necessary in other to arrive at the income of any year of assessment or other period to allocate or apportion to specific periods the income or loss of any period for which accounts have been made up, or to aggregate any such income or loss or any apportioned parts thereof, it shall be lawful to make such allocation, appointment or aggregation, and any apportionment under this section shall be made in proportion to the number of days in the respective periods.

For example, a ship builder may take three years to build a ship but receive payment in the last year of delivery of the completed ship. If the ship-builder is assessed on an earnings basis the payment received in the third year must be apportioned over the three years to find the amount earned for each of the years of building. Similarly also expenses incurred in the building of the ship will be spread over the three year period.

ii) Stock in trade

i) Stock in trade is not defined in P.I.T.A. 1993 or C.I.T.A. 1990. However generally, it consists of movable chattels or assets capable of severance which have been severed. For example, coal from a mine, timber from the land or a paw-paw from a tree. If chattels are purchased before being detached, the purchase is one of a capital asset and not stock in trade.

Stock must be valued at the beginning and end of the accounting year at either the cost or market prices, whichever is the lower. The trading account is prepared at the end of a year's trading and shows the gross profit for the accounting period. In preparing this account the stock at the beginning of the accounting year should be entered together with any stock purchased during the year on the debit side and any stock outstanding at the end of the year must together with sales for the year be entered on the credit side.

Example:

Maples & Temples Associates Trading Account
January 1, - December 31, 2002

2002	₦	K	2002	₦	K
Jan. 1 Opening Stock B/d	5000: 00	-	Sales		6000: 00
Purchases	7000:00	Dec. 31	Valuation of closing Stock		8000: 00
Gross Profit for Year to P/LA/c.	2000: 00				
	₦14000: 00				₦14000:00
2003					
Jan. 1 Opening Stock B/d.					

By crediting the valuation of stock at the end of the year it is ensured that the gross profit is not artificially reduced by the amount of stock as yet unsold. Since it is to the advantage of the taxpayer to keep the stock valuation at the end of the accounting year as low as possible, so as to show a low profit figure, the rule is that identical items of stock must be valued either at market or cost price whichever is the lower. Furthermore where stock has been purchased at varying prices the rule for tax purposes is that the stock must be valued on the assumption that those items first purchased wee the first sold. The taxpayer cannot "pick and choose" which items he has sold during the year and thereby selected those items of stock for valuation which were purchased at the lowest and therefore most favourable price, claiming to have sold the more expensive items. However, the taxpayer may "pick and chose" between valuation at market or cost price. Thus he may value some items at market price and others at cost price if this is lower. Stock valuations should naturally be kept as low as possible during the early years of the life of a business so that the tax advantage conferred by the "commencement" provisions can be used to the full.

ii) On discontinuance of a business stock is valued at market price unless sold to a purchaser who will be continuing the trade. This rule is designed to prevent a trader valuing a stock which increases in value with maturity at cost price and then selling it at a capital profit on discontinuance of the trade. If sold to another trader he will pay tax on the profits of any latter sales of the stock.

iii) A problem arises where a trader uses his own stock – e.g. the owner of a shop who takes his own stock off the shelf for his own use. Where this happens it has been held that the notional market price for the goods or stock removed must be brought into account in the books of the trader to off-set the deduction he will receive, for the cost of the goods or stock, from his total trading profits. In *Sharkey* v *Wernher*,[362] the rule is that where a trader disposes of part of his stock in-trade not by way of sale in the course of trade but for his own use, enjoyment or recreation, he must bring into his trading account for tax purposes as a receipt the market value of that stock at the time of such disposition. The facts of the case were as follows:

> Lady Wernher owned a stud farm, which was a trade assessed under Case I of Schedule D. She also owned racing stables where horses were trained and this activity was admitted to be merely recreational. Lady Wernher transferred five horses from the farm to the stables, having debited in the stud farm accounts the cost of breeding the horses. Some figure (it was admitted) had to be brought into the stud form accounts as a receipt. Held, that the figure to be brought in was the market value of the horses.

This case shows that a person can make a taxable profit by trading with himself; and that unrealized profits may be assessable to tax. The practical consequence of the decision is that a farmer or grocer who (for example) takes his own produce or stock for domestic consumption must credit his account as if he had sold it in the normal course of trade, at the retail market value. The same problem arises (said Viscount Simonds):

> whether the owner of a stud form diverts the produce of his farm to his own enjoyment or a diamond merchant, neglecting profitable sales, uses his choicest jewels for the adornment of his wife, or a caterer provides lavish entertainment for a daughter's wedding breakfast. Are the horses, the jewels, the cakes and ale to be treated for the purpose of income tax as disposed of for nothing or for their market value or for the cost of their production?[363]

The answer given by House of Lords (Lord Oaksey dissenting) was their market value.

---

[362] [1956] AC 58; 36 T.C. 275 (H.L.); See Pinson *op cit* p.46, 47.

[363] [1956] AC 58 at pp. 69-70; 36 T.C. 275 at p. 297.

It should be observed that the rule applies only to dispositions of trading assets such as stock-in-trade[364] property which never becomes part of such assets is outside the rule. The rule applies in all cases where a trader disposes of his stock otherwise than in the normal course of trade. Thus a sale at an under-value to secure some tax advantage is subject to review by Revenue, under section 18 of CITA and section 17 of PITA.

In *Petrotim Securities Ltd.* v *Ayres,*[365] Petrotim (a company dealing in securities) purchased War Loan which it sold four days later at less than one-tenth of its realizable market value at the date of sale. It was held that neither the purchase nor the sale was a trading transaction and that both should therefore be expunged form the company's accounts. Petrotim also sold for £205,000 securities forming part of its trading stock which it acquired some time previously for £478,573, and which had a market value of £835,505. It was held that the sale was not a trading transaction. It was further held in the *Petrotim* case[366] that the principle in *Sharkey* v *Wernher*[367] applied and that a figure equal to the market value of the securities at the date of disposal should be brought in as a receipt. These decisions were affirmed by the Court of Appeal.[368] In one case it was held that a sale of land at an under-value by a land-dealing company to its parent company was a sale otherwise than in the ordinary course of trade.[369]

(c) Adjustments for debtors

Where assessment is on earnings basis money owed to the business must be brought into account. A deduction is however allowed for debt proved to be bad and for those properly estimated to be doubtful under P.I.T.A. 1993 s. 20(1)(e) and C.I.T.A. 1990 s. 20(d).

In *Curtis* v *Oldfield,*[370] the managing director of a company had used the company's bank account to pay his own private bills. It was held that the loss so incurred by the company was not deductible. In this connection, the remarks of Rowlatt J. are important:

> If you have a business...in the course of which you have to employ subordinates, and owing to the negligence or the dishonesty of the subordinates, some of the receipts of the business do not find their way into the till, or some of the bills are not collected at all, or something of that sort,

---

[364] Thus a solicitor who gives advice without reward cannot be required to bring in as a receipt of his profession the fee he foregoes. In *Mason v Innes* [1967] Ch. 1079; 44 T.C. 326 (C.A.) the Revenue contended unsuccessfully that the rule applied to a gift by an author of his rights in an unpublished novel. Such a gift would now attract capital gains tax.

[365] (1963) 41 T.C. 389.

[366] Ibid. at p. 402.

[367] [1956] A.C. 58; 36 T.C. 275 (H.I.)

[368] (1963) 41 T.C. 405 (C.A.).

[369] *Skinner v Berry Head Lands Ltd.* (1970) 46 T.C. 337.

[370] (1925) 9 T.C. 319.

that may be an expense connected with and arising out of the trade in the most complete sense of the word.

(d) Adjustment for creditors
If taxed on an earnings basis an apportioned amount of the money owned may be allowed as a deduction for tax purposes, provided that it is a revenue expense incurred wholly, exclusively, necessarily and reasonably for the purpose of earning profits. If the assessment is made on cash basis no deduction can be allowed until the payment is made and the expense incurred.

Treatment of losses in connection with the profits of trade

In ascertaining the assessable income of a taxpayer for a year of assessment relief is given for the amount of any loss incurred by or in a trade, business, profession or vocation carried on by the taxpayer.

Relief is available either:

(a) against any assessable income of the taxpayer for the year of assessment in which the loss was incurred under P.I.T.A. s.36(2) (a) and C.I.T.A. s 27 (2)(a)(ii), or

(b) by way of carry forward against future assessable income from the particular trade in which the loss was incurred, (under s. 36(2)(b)(iv) P.I.T.A. and s.27(2)(a)(iii) C.I.T.A.

The first form of relief must be claimed within twelve months of the end of the year of assessment. The points to note about this relief are that it is given in respect of the year of assessment in which the loss was incurred and further that the relief is available against the total income of the taxpayer – i.e. not merely income from a trade, business, profession or vocation but also any other income such as investment income.

Where this relief is sought the whole amount of the loss must be set off so far as is possible. Any balance may be carried forward.

The second form of relief allows losses to be carried forward for four years against future income but only income of the trade, business, profession or vocation in question. Relief must be taken against the first available profits of the trade. This method of relief is illustrated by the following example:

Accounts to December 31 each year	*Year of Assessment*
2000 Profit ₦100, 000	2000/1
2001 Loss ₦60, 000	2001/2 N199, 000
2002 Profit ₦ 50, 000	
2002/2003 Nil	
2003 Profit ₦ 70, 000	

2003/2004 Nil
2004 Profit ₦ 8, 000 2004/5 ₦ 60, 000
2005/2006 ₦ 80, 000

Assessments have been made on the usual preceding year basis and losses carried forward until exhausted. Thus for the tax year 2002/3, there will be a nil assessment since no profit was made in the accounting year ending in the preceding year of assessment. For the tax year 2003/2004, there will be another nil assessment sin e no profit was made in the accounting year ending in the preceding year of assessment. For the tax year 2003/2004, there will be another nil assessment since the carry forward of the loss incurred in the accounting year ended December 31, 2001, cancels out the profit which would otherwise form the basis of assessment for the year. In the following year of assessment the outstanding proportion of the loss will be set off against the profit of the accounting year ended December 31, 2003 thus forming an assessment for that year of ₦60, 000 and not ₦70,000.

If relief were sought in the year of assessment in which the less was incurred the effect would be to reduce assessment for the year 1991/92 from ₦100, 000 to ₦40, 000.

Advantages and disadvantages of the two forms of relief

(a) Use the first method under s.36(2) (a) P.I.T.A. or s.27(2) (a)(ii) C.I.T.A. if relief I required immediately, where profits are falling or if the rates of taxation are likely to go down.
(b) Use the second method s.36 (2)(b)(iv) P.I.T.A. or s.27 (2)(b)(iii) C.I.T.A., if profits are increasing or if the rates of tax are likely to increase.

Capital allowances

An individual or company is liable to tax on total income, which *inter alia* is ascertained by the addition, or subtraction or the items referred to in the Fifth Schedule to the P.I.T.A. and the second schedule of the C.I.T.A. These schedules contain the provisions relating to capital allowances.

The allowances are provided so as to give tax relief for capital expenditure on wasting assets, one of the main objects of capital allowances being to encourage industry to develop, modernize and re-equip. the allowances are in effect a form of statutory depreciation and operate in reduction of a taxpayer's assessment for the year to which they relate. If the assessment for the year is less than the amount of the allowances claimed, the balance may be carried forward indefinitely and set against the first available profits of succeeding years. That differs from expenses which are allowed in computing profits, for expenses are deducted from receipts in order to arrive at the amount of profits to be assessed, and if the expenses exceed the receipts, the result is a loss to be dealt with

In accordance with the rules of a "basis period", normally the year of expenditure, but allowed against the current tax assessment. In other words, they are calculated for a particular year of assessment and not for an accounting year. They do not therefore appear in the final accounts prepared at the end of an accounting period.

Capital Allowances are granted as follows under paragraph 7 and 8 of the Fifth Schedule of PITA:

7(1) Subject to the provisions of this Schedule, where in his basis period for a year of assessment the owner of an asset has incurred in respect thereof qualifying expenditure wholly and exclusively for the purpose of a trade or business carried on by him, there shall be made to that individual for the year of assessment in his basis period for which that asset was first used for the purposes of that trade or business an allowance (in this Schedule called "an initial allowance") at the appropriate rate per annum, set forth in the Table 1 to this Schedule, of the expenditure.

(2) Where capital expenditure is incurred on the purchase of an asset and either the purchaser is a person over whom the seller has control, or some other person has control over both the purchaser and the seller, then, the amount of an initial allowances to be made in respect of the expenditure shall be such an amount as the relevant tax authority may determine to be just and reasonable having regard to all circumstances relating to the asset and control:

Provided that the amount shall not exceed the amount of the initial allowance which would have been allowable apart from the provisions of this sub-paragraph.

8(1) Subject to the provision of this Schedule, where in his basis period for a year of assessment the owner of an asset has incurred in respect thereof qualifying expenditure wholly, exclusively, necessarily and reasonably for the purposes of a trade or business carried on by him whether or not an initial allowance may be made to him in respect of that qualifying expenditure, there shall be made to that individual for each year of assessment in his basis period for which that asset was used for the purposes of that trade or business an allowance (hereinafter called "an annual allowance") at the rate specified in respect thereof in Table 11 of this Schedule of the expenditure after the deduction of initial allowance where applicable:

Provided that an amount of N10 shall be retain in the accounts for tax purposes until the asset is disposed of.

(2) In the case of an asset in respect of which an allowance has been granted before the commencement of this sub-paragraph, an allowance shall be made in respect of the asset for the number of years of assessment which, if added to the number of years of assessment for which allowance is to be made under the provision of sub-paragraph (1) of this paragraph:

Provided that if an allowance has been made for a number of years which equal to or more than the number of years specified under sub-paragraph (1) of this paragraph, a single allowance shall be made for an amount which is N10 less than the residue of the qualifying expenditure for the year of assessment in which this sub-paragraph takes effect.

Example:
Machinery is purchased for a business for N100, 000. This is plant and 15% initial allowance will be allowed on the qualifying expenditure. Thus an initial allowance of N15, 000 will be allowed. The annual allowances are then calculated on the balance of the qualifying expenditure at 10% per annum. Annual allowances will be as follow:

First year: 10% x N85, 000 (i.e. N100, 000 – N15, 000 initial allowance) = N85, 000
Second year: 10% x N76, 500 (i.e. N85, 000 – N8, 500) = N76, 000
Third year: 10% x N68, 800 (i.e. 76, 000 – 7, 600) = N68, 800
And so on each year 10% of the reducing balance.

Sale of building

Where capital expenditure has been incurred on the construction of a building, structure or works and thereafter the relevant interest therein are sold, any company which buys that interest shall be deemed, for all the purposes of this Schedule except the granting of initial allowances, to have incurred, on the date when purchase price became payable, capital expenditure on the construction thereof equal to the price paid by it for such interest or to the original cost of construction whichever is the less. Provided that where such relevant interest is sold more than once before the building, structure or works is used, the provisions of the foregoing proviso shall have effect only in relation to the last of those sales.[371]

Neither machinery nor plant is defined in the Act, and the question whether an item is plant or machinery depends on the facts of the case. It is clear that an item may be both plant and machinery and an industrial building[372] but in such an event it is likely that only the machinery allowance will be claimed.[373]

Different definitions have been suggested for specific instances. In *Yarmouth* v *France,*[374a] a claim was brought by a workman under the United Kingdom Employers' Liability Act 1880 for damages for injuries sustained due to a defect in his employer's plant, in that case a vicious horse. Lindley LJ said:[374b]

---

[371] Section 4 Second Schedule C.I.T.A.
[372] *IRC V Barclay Curle & Ltd.*.
[373] See Tiley *Op cit.* p. 284-286.
[374a] (1988) 19 QBD 647.
[374b] Ibid, at p. 658.

> in its ordinary sense (plant) includes whatever apparatus is used by a business man for carrying on his business – not his stock-in-trade, which he buys or makes for sale; but all goods and chattels, fixed or movable, live or dead, which he keeps for permanent employment in his business.

This test has been found helpful,[375] but not exclusive in capital allowance cases.

This test is viewed as covering fixtures and fittings of a durable nature. So railway locomotive and carriages[376] and tramway rails[377] have been held to be plant as have knives and lasts used in the manufacture of shoes,[378] but not the bed of a harbour[379] nor stallions for stud purposes.[380] By concession, films and master copies of records and tapes also qualify.[381]

It is now clear that machinery and plant is not confined to things used physically[382] but extends to the intellectual storehouse of the trade or profession e.g. the purchase of law books by a barrister as in *Munby* v *Furlong*.[383] Whether plant can include things lacking physical manifestation (e.g. computer software) is still unclear. It is not however necessary that the object be active; although a passive object may be less obviously plant.[384]

Plant does not include the place where the business is carried on, "plant" is that with which the trade is carried on as opposed to the setting in which it is carried on[385] but these categories are not necessarily mutual exclusive[386] and the different rates of allowance make correct classification of great practical importance. So it has been held that special partitioning used by shipping agents to sub-divide floor space to accommodate fluctuating office accommodation requirements were plant.[387]

While there is a clear distinction between the shell of a building and the machinery currently used in it, there are considerable difficulties where a large and durable structure is created for a specific purpose. This occurred in the leading case of *IRC* v *Barclay, Curle & Co Ltd.*[388] The taxpayer had constructed a dry dock, a process requiring the excavation of the site and the construction of a construction of a concrete lining. The Revenue agreed that such expenditure as

---

[375] Lord Donovan in *IRC v Barclay Curle & Co. Ltd* [1969] 1 All ER 732 at 751, 45 TC 221 at 249.
[376] *Caledonian Rly Co. v Banks* (1880) 1 TC 487.
[377] *LCC v Edwards* (1990) 5 TC 383.
[378] *Hinton v Maden and Ireland Ltd* [1959] 3 All ER 356, 38 TC 391 (expected to last only three years): noted [1959] BTR 454.
[379] *Dumbarton Harbour Board v Cox* (1918) 1 TC 487.
[380] *Earl of Derby v Aylmer* [1915] 3 KB 374, 6 TC 147.
[381] SP 9/79.
[382] Per Cross J in *McVeigh v Sanderson* [1969] 2 All ER 771 at 775, noted [1969] BTR 130.
[383] [1977] STC 232, [1977] 2 All ER 953; See also *Williams* v *Adelaja*. 1 NTC 141.
[384] *Jarrold v John Good & Son Ltd* [1963] 1 ER 141, [1963] 40 TC 681.
[385] per Pearson LJ in *Jarrold v John Good & Son Ltd* [1963] 1 All ER 141, 40 TC 681 at 696.
[386] *Jarrold v John Good & Son Ltd* (*supra*)
[387] Ibid.
[388] [1969] 1 All ER 732, 45 TC 237.

that incurred on the dock gate and operating gear, the cast iron keel blocks and the electrical and pumping installations related to plant, but argued that while the expenses of excavation and concreting might relate to industrial building they did not relate to plant and machinery. The Revenue lost.

The expenditure on the concrete lining was held to be in respect of plant because it could not be regarded as the mere setting in which the trade was carried on but was an integral part of the means required for the trading operation. Hence a structure which fulfils the function of plant is, *prima facie*, plant.[389]

The costs of excavation wee likewise held to be incurred in the provision of plant because what was indubitably plant, namely the dock itself, could not have been made before the excavation had taken place. This "but for" test is not however without limits and, by analogy with the express provision in relation to industrial buildings, cost incurred on the acquisition of the land could not fall within the allowance.

Where capital expenditure is incurred on alterations to an existing building incidental to the installation of machinery or plant for the purposes of trade, allowances may be claimed in respect of such expenditure just as if the works formed part of the machinery or plant.

The problem of the distinction between setting and plant, a problem exacerbated by the fact that the terms are not mutually exclusive,[390] depends in part upon the degree of sophistication to be employed in the concept of a setting.[391] The problem is acute when electrical apparatus and wiring are concerned. The matter has to be resolved by the use of the functional test and so, for example, lighting will not usually be plant unless it is of a specialized nature,[392] as where it is designed to provide a particular atmosphere in a hotel; this must be judged by reference to the intended market.[393] The Revenue have consistently refused to treat wiring leading to such apparatus as plant.[394]

The distinction between buildings and apparatus is thus indistinct. Recent cases have shown that a prefabricated building at a school used to accommodate a chemical laboratory[395] and a canopy over a petrol station,[396] a false ceiling in a restuarant[397] and a floating ship used as are restaurant[398] were not plant since

[389] Lord Reid, ibid at 740; at 239.

[390] Supra n. 2.

[391] *Imperial Chemical Industries of Australia and New Zealand v Taxation Comr of the Commonwealth of Australia* (1970) 120 CLR 396.

[392] *Cole Bros Ltd v Phillips* [1980] STC 518 upheld by CA [1981] STI 355.

[393] *IRC v Scottish and Newcastle Breweries Ltd* [1981] STC 50

[394] They rely strongly on *J. Lyons & Co Ltd v A-G* [1944] Ch 281, [1944] 1 All ER 477.

[395] *St. John's School (Mountford and Knibs) v Ward* [1974] STC 69; on appeal, [1975] STC 7 (note the astonishingly harsh refusal by Templeman J to allow an apportionment between the building and the equipment).

[396] *Dixton v Fitch's Garage Ltd* [1975] STC 480, [1975] 3 All ER 455.

[397] *Hampton v Forte Autogrill Ltd* [1980] STC 80.

[398] *Benson v Yard Arm Club Ltd* [1979] STC 266, [1979] 2 All ER 336.

they performed no function in the trade; further a support for plant is not necessarily plant. On the other hand it has been held that a silo used in the trade of grain importing was not simply part of the setting and could not be considered separately from the machinery and other equipment within it.[399] Likewise a swimming pool at a caravan site was held to be plant since it was part of the apparatus of the business.[400]

Partnerships

Where a trade, business, profession or vocation is carried on by a partnership, the partners are each treated separately for tax purposes so that profits and losses are apportioned amongst the partners and no assessment is made on the partnership as a whole.[401]

The Personal Income Tax Act in Section 8(1) states that the income of a partner shall be the sum of any remuneration, interest on capital, or the cost of passages to or from Nigeria wholly or mainly undertaken for the purposes of leave or recreation, which is charged in the partnership accounts in respect of that partner according to his agreed share of the profits. A partner's share in the partnership income will be included in his income after deduction of the charges mentioned above has been made from the income of the partnership as a whole.

Where the partnership accounts show a loss, a partner's share in the loss is deducted from remuneration, interest on capital or passage money for leave or recreation. Where his share in a loss exceeds his income from these sources he will be deemed to have incurred a loss under Section 8(2) PITA.

The commencement and cessation provisions of the Personal Income Tax Act will apply to partners individually as will the provision relating to relief for losses. Capital allowances will be granted in computing the partnership profits and personal allowance will be calculated in the normal way in respect of each individual partner's share of the net profits.

Under Section 29 of the PITA and upon the dissolution of a partnership, a partner will not be treated as ceasing his trade, business, profession or vocation. He will not therefore, normally be able to take advantage of the commencement provisions more than once – i.e. when he first starts his business – unless he is able to form a limited company to carry on the business.

---

[399] *Schofield v R. and H. Hall Ltd* [1975] STC 353.
[400] *Cooke v Beach Station Caravans Ltd* [1974] STC 402, [1974] 3 All ER 159.
[401] See *Mba v C.I.R.* 1 NTC p.106

Chapter 5

Employment income

Emoluments of offices and employment

Section 3(1)(b) P.I.T.A. charges to tax "any salary, wage, fee, allowance or other gain or profit from employment including compensations, bonuses, premiums, benefits or other perquisites allowed, given or granted by any person to an employee" other than:

- (i) so much of any such sums as may admitted by the relevant tax authority to represent reimbursement to the employee or expenses incurred by him in the performance of his duties, and from which is not intended that the employee should make any profit or gain;
- (ii) medical or dental expenses incurred by the employee,
- (iii) the cost of any passage to and from Nigeria incurred by the employee,
- (iv) any sum paid in respect of the maintenance or education of a child if any provision of this Decree provides that any sum received by the employee during a year of assessment shall be deducted from the personal relief to be granted to him for the next following year,
- (v) Deleted by 1996 No. 32.
- (vi) so much of any amount of rent the employee is treated as being in receipt equal to the annual amount deemed to be incurred by the employer under section 4 of this Decree,
- (vii) so much of any amount of rent the employee is treated as having received under the provisions of section 5 of this Decree,
- (viii) so much of the amount of rent subsidy or rent allowance paid by the employer to or on account, for the employee not exceeding ₦100,000 *per annum*,
- (ix) the amount not exceeding ₦15,000 *per annum* paid to an employee as transport allowance,
- (x) meal subsidy or meal allowance, subject to a maximum of ₦5,000 *per annum*.
- (xi) utility allowance of ₦10,000 *per annum*,
- (xii) entertainment allowance of ₦6,000 *per annum*,
- (xiii) leave grant, subject to a maximum of 10 *per cent* of annual basic salary.

Deductible expenses

Any expense to be deductible must have been incurred wholly, exclusively, necessarily and reasonably in the production of the income. This rule is almost identical with that governing the expenses of professions and trades and the illustrative cases set out there are equally relevant here.

Under section 20 of the P.I.T.A. and for the purpose of ascertaining the income or loss of an individual for any source chargeable to tax, there shall be deducted all outgoing and expenses, or any part thereof wholly, exclusively, necessarily and reasonably incurred during period and ultimately borne by that individual in the production of the income include:

(a) a sum payable by way of interest on money borrowed and employed as capital in acquiring the income;

(b) interest on loan for developing an owner occupier house;

(c) rent for that period, and premiums on liability for which was incurred during that period, payable in respect of land and buildings occupied for the purpose of acquiring the income; and

(d) expenses for repairs of premises, plant, machinery or fixtures employed in acquiring the income, or for the renewal, repair, or alteration of any implement, utensil or article so employed:

Provided that if the premises, plant, machinery, fixtures, implement, utensil or article are used in part for domestic or private purposes, so much or the expenses as relates to such use shall not be so deducted;

(e) bad debts incurred in any trade, business, profession or vocation, proved to have become bad during the period for which the income is being ascertained, and doubtful debts to the extend that they has become estimated to have become bad during the said period and notwithstanding that such bad or doubtful debts were due and payable prior to the commencement of such period:

Provided that:

(i) where in any period a deduction under this paragraph is to be made as respect any particular debt, and a deduction has in any previous period been allowed in respect of the same debt, the appropriate reduction shall be made in the deduction to be made in the period in question,

(ii) all sums recovered during the said period on account of amounts previously written off or allowed in respect of bad or doubtful of bad or doubtful debts shall for the purpose of this decree be deemed to be income of trade, business, profession or vacation of that period,

(iii) it is proved that the debts in respect of which a deduction is claimed either were included as receipt of the trade, business, profession or vocation in the income of the year within which they were incurred, or were advances not falling within the provisions of subsection (b) of section 21 of this Act made in the course of normal trading, business, professional or vocational operation;

(f) a contribution or an abatement deducted from the salary or pension of a public officers under the Pensions Act or under any approved scheme within the meaning of that Act, and any contribution, other than penalty, made under the provisions of any Act establishing a National Provident Fund or other retirement benefits scheme for employees throughout Nigeria;

(g) a contribution to a pension, provident or other retirement benefits funds society or scheme approved by the Board subject to the provisions of the Fourth Schedule to this Act and such conditions as the Board in its absolute discretion may prescribe;

Provided that the instrument establishing the funds, society or scheme contain, *inter alia*, a general power or duty of the trustees or managers thereof to invest the money of fund, society or scheme, and on the first day of any year of assessment commencement after thirty – first day of March 1962:

(i) in the case of a fund, society or scheme deemed to have approved under the provision of this decree, less than thirty-three and one third *per centum* of all monies which are so invested are invested in securities issued by.or under the authority of any Government in Nigeria; or

(ii) in the case of und, society or scheme approved under the provisions of this section, less than fifty per centum of all monies which are so invested are invested in securities issued by or under the authority of any Government in Nigeria,

(h) in the of income from trade, business, provision or vocation, any expenses or part thereof incurred for that period (whether the liability was met during that or any previous period) wholly and exclusively for the purpose of trade, business, profession or vocation unless those expenses or the same part thereof is deductible for that or any other period under the foregoing provisions or this section, and for the purpose of this paragraph an expense incurred during a period shall be treated as having been incurred for that period to the extent that it is not specifically referable to the income of any other period;

(i) any expenses which is proved to the satisfaction of the relevant tax authority to have been incurred by the individual on research for the period including the amount of levy paid by him to the National Science and Technology Fund.

(2) Where the income is chargeable only by reason of it being brought into or received in Nigeria, nothing in this section shall confer a right to any deduction from the amount of that income so brought into or received in Nigeria.

Also under section 21 of the P.I.T.A. and subject to the express provisions of this Act, no deduction shall be allowed for the purpose of ascertaining the income of an individual in respect of:

(a) domestic or private expenses;
(b) capital withdrawn from a trade, business, profession or vocation and any expenditure of a capital nature;
(c) any loss or expenses recoverable under an insurance or contract or indemnity;
(d) rent or cost of repairs to any premises or part of premises not incurred for the purpose of producing the income;
(e) taxes on income or profits levied in Nigeria or elsewhere except as provided in Section 13 of this Act;
(f) any unapproved payment to a pension, provident, savings or widows' orphan society, fund or scheme, except as permitted by paragraphs (f) and (g) of subsection (1) of section 20 of this Decree;
(g) depreciation of any assets;

(h) any sum reserved out of profits, except as permitted by paragraph (e) of subsection (1) of section 20 of this Act or as may be estimated by the relevant tax authority, pending determination of the amount, to represent the amount of any expenses deductible under the provisions of that section the liability for which was irrevocably incurred during the period for which the income is being ascertained;

(a) any expenses of any description incurred within or outside Nigeria for the purpose of earning management fees unless prior approval of an agreement giving rise to such management fees has been obtained from the Minister;

(b) any expense whatsoever incurred within or outside Nigeria as management fees under any agreement fees under any agreement entered into after the commencement of this paragraph except to the extent as to the Ministry may allow.

Assessment

Under Section 10 P.I.T.A.;
(1) the gain or profit from an employment shall be deemed to be derived from Nigeria if:

(a) the duties of the employment are wholly or partly performed in Nigeria, unless;
   (i) the duties are performed on behalf of any employer who is in a country other than Nigeria, and
   (ii) the employee is not in Nigeria for a period or periods amounting to 183 days or more in any twelve month period commencing in a calendar year and ending either within that same year or the following year, and
   (iii) the remuneration of the employee is liable to tax in that other country.

(b) the employer is in Nigeria, unless the duties of the employment are wholly performed, and the remuneration paid, in a country other than Nigeria except during a temporary visit to or leave in Nigeria.

(2) Notwithstanding the provisions of paragraph (b) of subsection (1) of this section, the gains or profits from an employment by a Government in Nigeria shall be deemed to be derived from Nigeria wherever the remuneration is paid if the employee performs the duties of that employment in a country other than Nigeria which employee from tax on those gains or profits.

(3) The gain or profit from any employment exercised in Nigeria shall be deemed to be derived from Nigeria whether the gains or profits from the employment are received in Nigeria or not.

(4) The gains or profits from any employment, the duties of which are wholly or mainly performed in Nigeria shall be deemed to be derived from Nigeria during any period of leave of the employee from the employment, and any period of his temporary absence on duty from Nigeria.

(5) Subject to the foregoing provision of this section, the gain or profit from any employment, the duties of which are mainly performed outside Nigeria, shall be deemed to be derived from Nigeria to the extent that those duties are performed in Nigeria.

(6) Notwithstanding any provision of this section, the gains or profits of an individual from any employment as a seafarer, other than any such employment in the Nigeria Navy or the Nigerian Ports Plc, shall be deemed to be derived from Nigeria only during any period in which the individual is serving under articles which he had signed in Nigeria or is performing stand-by duty on board a ship preparatory to his signing articles in Nigeria.

Meaning of employment

Sections 3(3)(d) P.I.T.A. defines employment as including "any service rendered by any person in return for any gains or profits."

The term "employment" signifies something in the nature of a "post." Where a person works for more than one employer it is often a difficult question whether there are a number of separate employments or whether the employments are mere vocation. Where the activities of the taxpayer do not consist of obtaining a post and staying in it but consist of a series of engagements treated as carrying on a profession.[1] In *Fall* v *Hitchin,*[2] it was held that the word "employment" is conterminous with the words "contract or service" and that income derived by a ballet dancer from a contract with a theatre having the attributes of a contract of service was taxable, notwithstanding the fact that the dancer carried on a profession as such and entered into the contract in the normal course of carrying on that profession. This decision narrows the scope of *Davies* v *Braithwaite*[3] to contracts entered upon in the course of carrying on a profession which are contracts for services. The two cases are, however, difficult to reconcile since the modern cases[4] show that the test for distinguishing a contract of service from a contract for services is whether the propositus carries on business on his own account, and *ex hypothesi* a person who carries on a profession does so. It is interesting to note that the Solicitor-General, arguing the case for the English Crown in *Davies* v *Braithwaite*, contented that the employment rules were not applicable to a person who carries on a profession whether or not the profit arises under a contract for services or a contract for services.[5] An individual may hold an office or employment and carry on a profession at the same time,[6] in which case the rules of employment apply to the office or employment.

Thus in *I.R.C.* v *Brander & Cruickshank,*[7] a firm of advocates in Scotland,

---

[1] *Davies v Braithwaite* [1931] 2 K.B. 628; 18 T.C. 198 (an actress).

[2] (1972) 49 T.C.. 433; [1973] S.T.C. 66.

[3] *Pinson on Revenue Law* (16th ed.) p. 77-82.

[4] *Ready Mixed Concrete (South-East) Ltd. v Minister of Pensions and National Insurance* [1968] 2 Q. B. 497; *Market Investigations Ltd. v Minister of Social Security* [1969] 2 Q.B. 173; *Global Plant Ltd. v Secretary of State for Social Services* [1972] 1 Q.B. 139.

[5] See [1931] 2 KB 628 at pp. 631-632.

[6] *Mitchell and Edon* v *Ross* [1960] Ch. 498; 40; 40 T.C. 11 (C.A.)

[7] (1971) 46 T C. 574 (H.L.) (H.L.Sc). See also *Ellis v Lucas, supra. Cf. Walker v Carnaby*

although not holding themselves out as professional registrars, acted as secretaries and registrars for companies and performed the duties imposed on the holders of such offices by the Companies Acts. The registrarships were acquired in the ordinary course of the firm's practice as advocates. It was held that the registrarships were offices and that a payment of £2,500 on the termination of a registrarship was a payment to which the rules applied, and being less than £5, 000 was accordingly exempt from tax.

In practice, and as a matter of convenience, receipts from offices held by persons carrying on a profession are often treated as receipts of the profession.[8] Hence accountants bring in their fees from auditorships in computing profits chargeable. A strict application of the law would require that each auditorship should be treated as a separate office in respect of which a separate claim for expenses should be made in accordance with the expenses rules; moreover, in the case of partners, once a partnership is not treated as a separate legal entity there is no provision for joint employment assessments in the partnership name,[9] the employment rules ought strictly to be applied to each partner's share of the employment income. In one case,[10] a company trading as merchant bankers entered into agreements with other companies to provide managerial and secretarial services for fees which was conceded were properly chargeable under the employment rules; nevertheless, it was held that compensation received by the banking company on the termination of one of its employment agreements was chargeable under trading profit rules on the ground that the banking company acquired the employment source of income in the course of its trade. The terminal payment was so linked to the trade as to be identified as one of its products; but this conclusion could be reached only in a case in which there was a clear finding that the trader sought the office as part of his profession.[11]

A "salaried partner" does not *qua* partner hold an office or employment and his "salary" is accordingly not assessable under the employment rules.

Emoluments

Emoluments or "personal emoluments" as defined in section 2(8)PITA "means wages and salaries and includes allowances, gratuities, super-annuation or pension schemes and any other income derived solely by reason of employment."

Harrower, Barnham & Pykett (1969) 46 T.C. 561.

[8] [1980], S.T.I. 128.

[9] See *Walker* v *Carnaby Harrower, Barnham & Pykett* (1969) 46 T.C. 561.

[10] *Blackburn* v *Close Brothers Ltd.* (1960) 39 T.C. 164.

[11] See Lord Donovan in *I.R.C.* v *Brander & Cruickshank* (1971) 46 T.C. 574 at p. 595.

Emoluments therefore includes salaries, fees, wages perquisites and profits whatsoever.[12] Not every payment made to an employee is made to him as a profit arising from his employment: "the payment must be made in reference to the services the employee renders by virtue of his office, and it must be something in the nature of a reward for services, present or future."[13] The office or employment must be the source of the payment.[14]

In *Hochstrasser* v *Mayes,*[15] I.C.I. established a housing scheme to assist those of their married male employees whose jobs demanded mobility. If the employee sold his house at a loss, I.C.I. (Subject to certain options reserved to I.C.I.) guaranteed him against the loss. Held that a sum paid to an employee in respect of such a loss was not an emolument from the employment.

This case shows that, to render a benefit chargeable to tax, the office or employment must be the *causa sine qua non.*[16] In another case, an employee was required, as a condition of entering upon his employment to enter into a restrictive covenant with his employer which was to take effect on leaving his employer's service; and it was held that a lump sum paid in consideration for such a restrictive covenant was not an emolument from the employment.[17]

---

[12] Statute may provide that something shall be chargeable as an emolument. See *FBIR* v *Nasr* 1 NTC 114

[13] *Hochstrasser* v *Mayes* [1960] A.C. 376 at p. 388; 38 T.C. 673 at p. 705, per Viscount Simonds quoting with approval from the judgement of Upjohn J. in [1959] Ch. 22 at p. 33. See also *Laidler* v *Perry* (1965) 42 T.C. 351 (H.L.), where Christmas gift vouchers given to employees were held to be assessable emoluments: the vouchers were a reward for services notwithstanding that they were given to all members of staff alike. In *Holland* v *Geoghegan* (1972) 48 T.C. 482, refuse collectors' compensation for loss of salvage was held to be an emolument of the employment: "... the main purpose of the Borough was to get the respondent back to work, and the money when received by him was a form of substituted remuneration for his former rights to share in the proceeds of sale of the salvage" (p. 492H). And see *Tyrer* v *Smart* (1978) 52 T.C. 533; [1967] S.T.C. 141 (C.A.), where employees of a group of companies with at least five year' service were given a right to subscribed for shares on preferential terms on the occasion of the group going public. Held, in the High Court and Court of Appeal, not an assessable emolument: the employees who subscribed for shares did so as private investors. This decision was reversed in the House of Lords: [1979] S.T.C. 34 (H.L.). See also *Beecham Group Ltd.* v *Fair* [1984] S.T.C. 15 where garage allowance to salesman who stored the employer's stock and the company car held to be an emolument.

[14] In *Pritchard* v *Arundale* (1972) 47 T.C. 680, a transfer of shares to a former partner in a firm of accountancts, in consideration of his undertaking to serve a company, was held not to be an assessanle emolument. It was an inducement to him to give up an established position and status and not a reward for future services.

[15] See note 13.

[16] But see the remarks of Lord Simon of Glaisdale on outmoded and ambiguous concepts of causation expressed in Latin, in *Brumby* v *Milner* (1976) 51 T.C. 583 at p.613 D (H.L.).

[17] *Beak* v *Robson* [1943] A.C. 352; 25 T.C. 33 (H.L.). The position is the same where the covenant is to take effect during the currency of the agreement: *Hose v Warwick* (1946) 27 T.C. 459. Payments for restrictive covenants are chargeable to higher rate income tax under I.C.T.A. 1970, s.34.

Another illustration of the principle under discussion is given by Lord Denning M.R. in his judgment in *Jarrold* v *Boustead*.[18]

> Suppose there was a man who was an expert organist but was very fond of playing golf on Sundays. He is asked to become the organist of the parish church for the ensuing seven months at a salary of 10 pound sterling a month for the seven months, but it is expressly stipulated by this strange parish council that, if he takes up the post, he is to give up Sunday golf for the rest of his life. Thereupon he says that, if he is to give up golf, he wants an extra 500 pounds sterling and they agree to pay it. In such a case the 500 pound sterling is not a payment for relinquishing what he considered to be an advantage to him.

An employee may receive a present in such circumstances that the employment is not its source. When a director wrongly directs moneys from a company into his own pocket and, by virtue of his fiduciary obligation to the company to preserve its assets, holds those moneys as trustee for the company, such moneys are not received as an emolument of the office.[19]

Basis of charge

Employment tax

Employment tax is charged on the full amount of the emoluments falling under the appropriate case, subject to such deductions only as are authorized by the Tax Acts.[20]

It seems that emoluments are not chargeable to tax unless they are received by or credited to or otherwise placed at the disposal of the employee. If an employee assigns his right to emoluments to a third person, they will be treated as having been received by the employee.[21] If the emoluments, when received, relate to services rendered in the past, they must be treated as income of the years in which the services were rendered.[22]

Thus in *Heasman* v *Jordan*,[23] a special bonus paid to an employee in 1945 for overtime during the war years (it being understood that the overtime would

---

[18] (1964) 41 T.C. 701 at p. 729. In this case, signing-on fee paid to Rugby League players on relinquishing amateur status were held not to be taxable.

[19] *Rose* v *Humbles* (1971) 48 T.C. 103, *per* Buckley J. at p. 117H.

[20] s.2(8) PITA 1993

[21] *Smyth* v *Stretton* (1904) 5 T.C. 36; *cf. Edwards* v *Roberts* (1935) 19 T.C. 618 (C.A.); *Hibbert* v *Fysh* (1962) 40 T.C. 305 (earnings of undischarged bankrupt)'

[22] *Heasman* v *Jordan* [1954] Ch. 744; 35 T.C. 518. *Quaere* if remuneration paid some years in advance can be "spread forward."

[23] [1954] Ch. 744; 35 T.C. 518.

not be "overlooked") was held to be taxable as an emolument of the years when the services were rendered.

Payments made to an employee after his employment has ceased are not chargeable[24] unless they are remuneration for past services or are expressly charged to tax, e.g. pensions[25] and "golden handshakes."[26] Tax under section 3(i)(b) of PITA is charged on the emoluments of the current year of assessment, e.g. the statutory income for the year 2001 - 2002 includes the total of the emoluments of that year. Income tax is collected under PAYE system.

Pension and retirement benefits schemes

Pensions, provident funds or retirement benefit funds or schemes must be approved by the Joint Tax Board subject to the conditions contained in the Fourth Schedule to the Personal Income Tax Act of 1993 and such other conditions as the Board may impose.

Under section 1 of the Fourth Schedule of PITA "pension fund" means a society, fund, contract or scheme the assets of which are held under irrevocable trusts and any scheme established by a law in Nigeria or elsewhere, the main objects of which are, in the opinion of the Board, the provision of non-assignable and non-commutable retirement pensions or annuities for an individual or his dependants after his death, or for any group or class of individuals and their dependents;

Also "provident fund" means a society, fund or scheme, not being a pension fund, established under irrevocable trusts or a law in Nigeria or elsewhere, the objects of which are the provision of retirement benefit for an individual or benefits for an individual or benefits for his dependents, after his death, or for any group or class of individuals and their dependents.

The fundamental tax principle behind these schemes is that contributions made by both employers and employees to approved schemes are deductible from the profits of the employer and the income of the employer. Any pension or annuity receivable after retirement will be taxable under section 3(i) (e) of PITA 1993.

Deductions are permitted in respect of contributions under section 20(1)(f) and (g) of PITA as follows:

(f) a contribution or an abatement deducted from the salary or pension of a public officers under the Pensions Act or under any approved scheme within the meaning of that Act, and any contribution, other than penalty, made under the provisions of any Act establishing a National Provident Fund or other retirement benefits scheme for employees throughout Nigeria:

---

[24] See, e.g. *Cowan* v *Seymour* [1920] 1 K.B. 500; 7 T.C. 372.

[25] s.21(f) PITA, see also s.26 PITA

[26] Ibid., s. 3(i)(e).

(g) a contribution to a pension, provident or other retirement benefits funds society or scheme approved by the Board subject to the provisions of the Fourth Schedule to this Decree and such conditions as the Board in its absolute discretion may prescribe;
provided that the instrument establishing the funds, society or scheme contain, *inter alia*, a general power or duty of the trustees or managers thereof to invest the money of fund, society or scheme, and on the first day of any year of assessment commencing after thirty-first day of March 1962 –
   (i) in the case of fund, society or scheme deemed to have been approved under the provision of this decree, less than thirty three and one third *per centum* of all moneys which are invested in securities issued by or under the authority of any Government in Nigeria, or
   (ii) in the case of a fund, society or scheme approved under the provisions of this section, less than fifty *per centum* of all moneys which are so invested are invested in securities issued by or under the authority of any Government in Nigeria.

Chapter 6

Companies income tax

Cap 60 LFN 1990 provides an Act to consolidate the provisions of the Companies' Income Tax Act 1961 and to make other provision relating thercto.

Administration

Section 1 of the Companies Income Tax Act (CITA) establishes the Federal Board of Inland Revenue whose operational name shall be called and known as Federal Inland Revenue Service (FIRS). This board is charged with the duty to administer the taxation of companies in regard to income tax, to make assessments, collect tax and account to the Government. To assist the Board in relation to income tax, the C.I.T.A. provides in s.1A for the establishment of Technical Committees.

Part 1 of CITA provides as follows:

Establishment and constitution of the board

Section 1 provides:

(1) There shall continue to be a Board of which the official name shall be the Federal Board of Inland Revenue (hereinafter referred to as "The Board") whose operational arm shall be called and known as the Federal Inland Revenue Service (hereafter in this Act refereed to as "the service")

(2) The Board shall comprise-

- (a) an Executive Chairman, who shall be a person within the Service experienced in taxation to be appointed by the president;
- (b) the Directors and Heads of Departments of the Service;
- (c) the officer from time to time holding or acting in the post of Director with responsibility for planning, research and statistics matters in the Federal Ministry of Finance;
- (d) a member of the Board of the National Revenue Mobilisation Allocation and Fiscal Commission;
- (e) a member from the National Petroleum Corporation, not lower in rank than an Executive Director;
- (f) a Director from the National Planning Commission;
- (g) a Director from the Nigerian Customs Service;
- (h) the Registrar – General of the Corporate Affairs Commission; and
- (i) the Legal Adviser to the Service;

  (1) Any seven members of the Board, of whom one shall be the Chairman or a

Director of a Department within the Service shall constitute a quorum.
(2) The Secretary (who shall be an-officio member of the Board) shall be nominated by the Board from within the Service.
(3) Notwithstanding that the Legal Adviser to the Board is at any time a member of the Board, he may appear for the represent the Board in his professional capacity in any proceedings in which the Board is a party; and the Legal Adviser shall not in such circumstances given evidence on behalf of the Board.
(4) The secretary shall summon a meeting of the Board whenever the business requiring its attention so warrants, or upon any request of a member; or a majority decision of the members on any matter obtained by him in written correspondence shall be treated in all respects as though it were a decision of the Board in actual meeting unless any member has requested the submission of that matter to such meeting.

Establishment of technical committee of the board

Section 1A provides that:

(1)There shall be a Technical Committee of the Board (hereinafter referred to as "the Technical Committee") which shall comprise-
(a) the executive chairman of the Board as Chairman;
(b) all the Directors and Heads of Departments of service;
(c) the Legal Adviser in the Federal Inland Revenue Service; and;
(d) the Secretary of the Board.
(2) The Technical Committee may co-opt from the Service such staff as it may require for the discharge of its functions.

Powers and duties of the board

Section 2 provides that:

(1) The due administration of this Act and the tax shall be under the care and management of the Board who may do all such things as may be deemed necessary and expedient for the assessment and collection of the tax and shall account for all amounts so collected in a manner to be prescribed by the Minister.

Signification and execution of powers and duties

Under section 3:

(1) Anything required to be done by the Board, in relation to the powers or duties specified in the First Schedule, may be signified under the hand of the Chairman or of the Chairman or of the Secretary.
(2) Any authorization given by the Board under or by virtue of this Act shall be signified under the hand of the Chairman unless such authority is notified in the

Federal Gazette.

(3) Subject to Subsection (1) of this section, any notice or other document to be given under this Act, or under any subsidiary legislation made thereunder, shall be valid if;

(a) it is signed by the Chairman or by person authorized by him; or

(b) such notice or document is printed and the official name of the Board is duly printed or stamped thereon.

(4) Everything notice, authorization or other document purporting to be a notice, authorization or other document duly given and signified, notified or bearing the official name of the Board, in accordance with the provision of this section, shall be presumed to be so given and signified, notified or otherwise without further proof, until the contrary is shown.

Power to amend the first schedule

Section 4 provides that the Minister may at any time by Order delete any of the powers or duties specified in the First Schedule of the Act or include therein additional powers or duties or otherwise amend such Schedule or substitute a new Schedule therefore.

Official secrecy

Under section 5:

(1) Every person having any official duty or being employed or have any official duty in the administration of this Act shall regard and deal with all documents, information, returns, assessment list and copies of such lists relating to profit or items of profits of any company, as secret and confidential.

(2) Every person having possession of or control over any documents, information, returns or assessment lists or copies of such lists relating to the income or profits or losses of any person, who at any time communicates or losses of any person, who at any time communicates or attempts to communicate such information or anything contained in such documents, returns lists, or copies to any person-

(a) other than a person to whom he is authorized by the Minister to communicate it; or

(b) otherwise than for the purposes of this Act or any enactment in Nigeria imposing tax on income of persons other than companies shall be guilty of any offence against the Act.

(3) Any proceedings for an offence against this section may be taken by the name of the Board but not by any other person except with the consent of the Attorney-General of the Federation.

(4) No person appointed under or employed in carrying out the provisions of this Act shall be required to produce in any court any return, document or assessment; or to divulge or communicate to any court any matter or thing coming under his notice in the performance of his duties under this Act except as may be necessary for the purpose of carrying into effect the provisions of this Act, or in order to institute a prosecution, or in the course of a prosecution for any offence committed in relation

to any tax on income or profits in Nigeria.

(5) Where under any law in force in any Commonwealth country provision is made for the allowance of relief from income tax in respect of the payment of income tax in Nigeria, the obligation as to secrecy imposed by this section shall not prevent the disclosure to the authorized officers of the Government in that country of such facts as may be necessary to enable the proper relief to be given in cases where relief is claimed form the tax in Nigeria or from income tax in that country

(6) Where any agreement or arrangement with any other country with respect to relief for double taxation of income or profits includes provisions for exchange of information with that country for the purpose of implementing that relief or preventing avoidance of tax, the obligation as to secrecy imposed by this section shall not prevent the disclosure of such information to the authorized officers of the Government of such country.

(7) Notwithstanding anything contained in this section, the Board may permit the Auditor-General of the Federation or any officer duly authorized by him to have assess to any records or documents as may be necessary for the purpose of carrying out his official duties in this circumstances he shall be deemed to be person employed in carrying out the provision of this Act.

Forms

Under section 6, the Board may, from time to time, specify the form of returns, claims, statements and notice under the Act.

Service and signature of notices

Section 7 provides that -

(1)Except where it is provided in the Act that service shall be effected either personally or by registered post, the provisions of section 26 of the Interpretation Act (which relates to service by post) shall apply to the service of a notice if such notice is addressed in accordance with the provision of subsection (3) of this section.

(2)Where a notice is sent by registered post it shall be deemed to have been served on the day succeeding the day on which the addressee of the registered letter containing the notice would have been informed in the ordinary course of events that such registered letter is awaiting him at a post office, if such notice is addressed in accordance with the provisions of subsection (3) of this section.

Provided that a notice shall not be deemed to have been served under this subsection if the addressee proves that no notification informing him of the fact that the registered letter was awaiting him at a post office, was left at the address given on such registered letter.

(3)A notice to be served in accordance with sub section 1 and 2 shall be addressed-

(a) in the case of company registered in Nigeria, to the registered office of the company or any other known address of the company; and

(b) In the case of a company incorporated outside Nigeria, either to the individual authorized to accept service of process under the Companies and Allied Matters

Act at the address filed with the Registrar-General of Companies, if any, or to the registered office of the company wherever it may be situated; and

(c) In the case of an individual or body of persons to the last known business or private address of such individuals or body of persons.

(4) Without prejudice to section 50 and 65 (1)(b) of this Act, in any case where the service or any notice under this Act has proved impossible the notice may be served by being left at the appropriate office or address as determined in subsection (3) above or by pasting it at the office or address or by publishing it in one issue of the Federal Gazette

(5) Any person who obstructs any officer of the Board in the exercise of this functions under this Act or who uses violence on such officer shall be guilty of an offence and shall on conviction-

(a) in the case of a first offence, be liable to imprisonment for six months or to a fine of not less than ₦2,000.00 or to both such fine and imprisonment; and;

(b) in case of a second and subsequent offence and in any case where violence is used on any such officer, be sentenced to imprisonment for six months without option of a fine.

Categories of companies

The C.I.T.A. divides companies into two categories, Nigerian companies and non–Nigerian companies. A Nigerian company is one the control and management of whose activities are exercised in Nigeria under s. 11. All other companies fall into the remaining category. This distinction is important in relation to profits, which are deemed to be derived from Nigeria, and is therefore subject to Nigerian tax under s. 8(1). Thus the profits of a Nigerian company are deemed to accrue in Nigeria wherever they arise and whether or not they have been brought into or received in Nigeria. On the other hand the profits of a company, other than a Nigerian company, are only deemed to be derived from Nigeria to the extent that they are attributable to some part of the operations of the company carried on within Nigeria under s. 1(2))[1]

Apart from the basic division into Nigerian and non-Nigerian companies further sub-categories arise to which special rules apply. These sub-categories are:

(i) *Shipping and Air Transport Companies* which, broadly speaking, are taxed only in respect of profits deemed to be derived from the carriage of passengers, mails, livestock or goods, shipped or loaded into an aircraft in Nigeria under s. 12;[2]

(ii) *Cable and Wireless Companies* i.e. companies carrying on businesses of transmitting messages are taxed on profits derived from messages

[1] *Karam v Commissioner of Income Tax* 12 WACA 331

[2] *Alitalia Airlines Ltd v FBIR* HCL Suit No. M'213'70 of March 1, 1971.

transmitted from or within Nigeria on principles similar to shipping companies under s. 13;

(iii) *Insurance Companies* under s. 14 other than a life insurance company are taxed by ascertaining the gross premiums and interest and other income receivable in Nigeria less any premium returned to the insured and premiums paid on reinsurance. In the case of life insurance the profits on which tax may be imposed shall be the investment income less the management expenses, including commission.

Rate of tax

As a general rule, income tax is payable by companies at a standard fixed rate of 30k in the naira on their profits under C.I.T.A., S. 29. No personal reliefs are given and there are no reduced rates.

The charge to income tax (C.I.T.A., s.8)

Income tax are payable for each year of assessment upon the profits of any company[3] *accruing in, derived from, brought into or received in Nigeria* in respect of:

(a) any trade or business for whatever period of time such trade or business may have been carried on;

As we have seen above, the Companies Income Tax Act 1990 does not define "trade."[4] Even the English Acts, which define "trade" do so in a rather circular way for as Lord Macmillan observed in *Van Den Berghs* v *Clark,*[5] the definition

> only informs us with disregard of logic, that it 'includes every trade, manufacture, adventure or concern in the nature of trade.'

His Lordship then provided a valuable guide when he continued,

> Consequently it is to the decided cases that one must go in search of light. While each case is found to turn upon its own facts and no infallible criterion emerges, nevertheless the decisions are useful as illustrations and as affording indications of the kind of consideration which may relevantly be borne in mind in approaching the problem.

---

[3] CITA., s.8

[4] Orojo, *Company Tax Law* p.17, 18, 19, 20. (Sweet & Maxwell) (1979)

[5] (1935) 19 T.C. 390.

Since the Nigerian statute does not define "trade, "the Nigerian courts have treated the question of trade as one of fact and have decided that it should be given its ordinary meaning where the statute does not restrict such meaning. When the appeal in *Arbico Ltd.* v *F.B.I.R.*[6] was argued in the Supreme Court, it was contended on behalf of the appellant that as there was no definition of the word in the Companies Income Tax Act, the court should apply its ordinary dictionary meaning, namely, "the practice of some occupation, business, or profession habitually carried on, especially when practiced as a means of livelihood..." The Supreme Court rejected the suggestion that it was necessary to establish that the business must be one habitually carried on since one single transaction can amount to trade. Their Lordships then said:

> We do not see that because there is no definition of 'trade' in our own law we must give that word a more restrictive meaning than has been given in the United Kingdom where by the definition trade includes any 'adventure or concern in the nature of trade.' It is of course not every sale under a power of sale, which is clearly an ancillary power to a main purpose of a company, that is a transaction by way of trade. It is not only necessary to show that such a sale has been made at a profit, but it is necessary to go further and to show that the profit is attributable to a trading transaction rather than to merely capitalizing a portion of the business which in this regard is not otherwise trading..."[7]

Unfortunately, the Court refused to give a general definition of the word trade for it said:

> We do not consider that for the purpose of this appeal it is necessary for us to define 'trade' in section 17(a) of the Companies Income Tax Act 1961, save to say that we think it can be given a wide interpretation in order to include clearly what is in the contemplation of the section.

Another case, which in recent years has given some strong indications of the attitude of Nigerian courts as to what is or is not trade, is *Aderawo's Timber Trading Co. Ltd.* v *Federal Inland Revenue Service.*[8] In that case, the applicant company who had a concession to exploit a timber forest for 25 years entered into an agreement to supply another company, A.T. & P Ltd., with timber for five years. At the end of the four years, the agreement was modified and A.T. & P. Ltd. paid £30,000 to the applicant and agreed to pay 5½d per cubic foot of timber instead of 4½d in the original agreement. As consideration for these, the applicant agreed not to terminate the contract before the end of five years from the time of the second agreement. The respondent assessed the sum £30,000 to

[6] ibid. at p. 428.
[7] Ibid. at p. 273.
[8] [1966] L.L.R. 195.

tax of £7,000 on the ground that the amount was a trading and not capital receipt. The applicant appealed to the respondent unsuccessfully and thereupon applied for an order of certiorari to quash the decision on the ground that the assessment did not come under any of the items in section 17 of the Act. Ikpeazu J., relying on English authorities,[9] held that:

> the structure of the applicant's business was not destroyed and no serious dislocation of the normal organization of their business took place and nothing was lost by them and the payment cannot in my view be categorized as a capital receipt. It is income.

He further held that:

> It is clear... in the light of the evidence and the authorities that it is incidental to the Applicants' trade or business to enter into ordinary commercial and beneficial contract which would include the grant of licenses to other persons to cut timber from their timber estate and to modify such contract, and the original agreement...as also the subsequent one modifying the original arrangements is one entered into by the Applicants in the ordinary course of their trade or business and any sum received for such modification, which was not destructive of the Applicants' profit-making machinery, is a sum which would go into ordinary trading receipt of the company.[10]

On appeal to the Supreme Court, the judgment was affirmed and the Court observed that:

> The applicants thought that it was a good bargain in their trading activities in timber to get a certain immediate large sum plus an extra penny per cubic foot in return for forgoing the possibility of achieving a modification, by given six months' notice to terminate if it was refused, by the new term of five years certain. We don not think that this therefore was a single capital transaction, but was, though in a lump sum, in fact, profit derived from the trading activity of selling timber.[11]

Arbico Ltd v *Federal Board of Inland Revenue*[12] was a case where this issue was squarely before the court. There, the company acquired land at 213A Igbosere Road, Lagos and erected a building which they intended to use for housing their staff. The property was later bought by the Federal Government for use as the Nigerian Law School at a price of £87,500 whereby the company

---

[9] Especially *Murray v Commissioner of Inland Revenue* (1923) 32 T.C. 238; *Kelsall-Parsons & Co. v Commissioner of Inland Revenue* 21 T.C. 608 and *Commissioner of Inland Revenue v Fleming & Co. (Machinery) Ltd.* (1951) 33 T.C. 57.

[10] *Aderawo's Timber Trading Co. Ltd. v F.B.I.R.* [1966] L.L.R. 195 at p. 206.

[11] S.C. 398/1967, of June 13, 1969, unreported.

[12] [1968] 1 All N.L.R. 263.

made a profit of £23,000. The company was assessed to tax of £7,211.12 on the profit after deducting capital allowances. The objects in the memorandum of association of the company included the acquisition and sale of property. The company appealed to the Appeal Commissioners contending that transaction was not a trade activity but a realization of capital. The appeal was dismissed and the company appealed to the High Court, which again dismissed the appeal. On further appeal to the Supreme Court, it was held, affirming the judgment of Sowemimo J:

(1) That the fact that the memorandum of association of a company contains a power to sell property is an important consideration in determining whether profit from such an isolated transaction is trading profit, the tax payer's purpose or object cannot prevail over what he does, if what he does has all the characteristics of trading; but if what he does is equivocal, his purpose or object may become very material;
(2) That the fact that the memorandum of association of a company contains a power to sell property is an important consideration in determining whether the company's intention on a sale of property is to make a trading profit, but it is not conclusive; and where the power is exercised on a single occasion only, or where it is ancillary to the main purpose of the company and has not been used often enough to have become a main purpose itself, there is no presumption that a sale under a power is a trading activity rather than a mere capitalization of portion of the business.
(3) That there was no reason to upset the finding of the Appeal Commissioners that on the facts which they found established there was a transaction by way of trade within section 17(a) of the 1961 Act.

b) Rent or any premium arising from property;
This is "rent or any premium arising from a right granted to any other person for the use or occupation of any property: (s.8 (b)), for example, under a lease, a tenancy, or a right of occupancy.[13]

Rent is the periodical payment by the tenant for the exclusive possession of land.[14] Such payment must be certain or capable of being ascertained. Thus, as is usual, it is so much per month or per annum, but it maybe fluctuating provided it is certain or ascertainable. It may be paid in money or in money's worth or in kind. If a payment is in fact rent, it will be taxed as such no matter how disguised or described. In *I.R.C.* v *Baillie*,[15] X & Co. took a lease of the coal and other minerals on an estate. In addition to a fixed rent, it was bound, while coal was being worked, to furnish free to the lessor all coal (not exceeding 200 tons a

[13] Under the Land Use Decree 1978
[14] Orojo J.O. (1979) *Company Tax Law in Nigeria*. p. 24,25,
[15] (1936) S.C. 438; 21 T.C. 740.

year) which he might require for the use of his establishment on the estate. It was held that the free coal was rent paid in kind and therefore assessable to tax. Similarly, in *House and Property Investment Co. Ltd.* v *Kneen*[16] where, in addition to fixed rent" a yearly sum equal to the premium for insurance of the premises, it was held that the further sum was properly.

As we have seen, it is sufficient if the right is for the "use or occupation" of the property. In *Francis Jackson Development Ltd.* v *Stepm*,[17] a person agreed to purchase a house but, before completion, he was let into possession as tenant at will and he paid a sum for such "occupation and use." It was held that the payment was rent. However, money paid by a prospective purchaser to meet mortgage outgoings or the rates and insurance will not be rent; neither will a payment for a collateral agreement which contains no demise;[18] but where a person occupies and uses a market stall or stand and pays a periodic sum, such sum will be rent and chargeable. As Lord Coleridge C.J. said, in *Hall* v *Metcalfe*:[19]

> The holding of an ascertainable piece of land from a person who is entitled to let it at a fixed payment constitutes ... at least a tenancy at will.[20]

The above relationships must be distinguished from those of a licencee and a lodger. Although section 8(b) of the Companies Income Tax Act 1990 refers to the "use or occupation of any property," what is chargeable is rent which implies a tenancy. Thus a licence to enter the precincts of a theatre for the purpose of selling cigarettes, etc., to the members of the audience will not create the relation of landlord and tenant. Similarly, a lodger is not a tenant in that, although he may have exclusive occupation, he does not have exclusive Possession which is an indispensable element in a tenancy.[21] In both cases of licences, the sum paid for such use and occupation is not rent and not chargeable under section 8(b). Such profits may be charged either under the residuary provisions of section 8(d) or even under section 8(a) if it is established that the owner of the premises is carrying on a business in this regard. Although rent is normally payable monthly or annually, it often happens that rents are paid in advance for several years. To deal with such rent and spread the charge over a number of years instead of assessing it on the normal preceding year basis.

Where any payment on account of such a rent as is mention in paragraph (b) of section 8 of the Companies Income Tax Act 1990, is made before the expiration of the period to which it relates and is included for the purpose of that section in the profits of a company then, so much of the payment as relates to

---

[16] [1943] 2 All E.R. 601.
[17] [1943] 2 All E.R. 601.
[18] *See Duke of Westminster v Store Properties Ltd.* [1844] Ch.129, 131.
[19] [1892] 1 Q.B. 208 at p. 212.
[20] See also *Joel v International Circus and Christmas Fair* (1920) 124 L.T. 459.
[21] See *Edwardes v Barrington* (1901) 85 L.T. 650.

any period beginning with the date on which the payment is made shall be from day to day over the last mentioned period or over the five years beginning with that date, whichever is the shorter."[22]

Example

Thus, if a property is let for 10 years at a rent of ₦30,000 per annum beginning from January 1, 1998 and the sum of ₦180,000 is paid on January 1, 1998 the rent for six years paid in advance, then the sum of ₦180,000 will be spread over five years beginning from January 1, 1998 and income will be calculated as follows:

Year of assessment

1998/99: 3 months (1/1/98–1/3/98) @ ₦36,000.00 …………	₦ 9000.00
1999/00: 12 months (1/4/98–31/3/99) @ ₦360,000.00 ………	₦36,000.00
00//01: 12 months (1/4/99-31/3/00) @ ₦360, 00.00 …………	₦36,000.00
2001/02: 12 months (1/4/00-31/3/01) @ ₦36,000.00…………	₦36,000.00
2002/03: 12 months (1/4/01-1/4/02) @ ₦36,000.00…………..	₦36,000.00
2003/04: 9 months (1/4/02-31/12/02) @N36,000.00…………	₦27,000.00
5 years	₦180,000.00

On the other hand, a premium is payment other than rent made as consideration for the grant of a lease. It is normally expense of a capital nature.

c) Dividends, interest, discounts, charges or annuities:
This has been described as "a reward or consideration or recompense for the actual or notional use of one person's money by another person."[23] In *Westminster Bank Ltd* v *Riches*,[24] Lord Wright explained the general characteristics of interests as follows:[25]

> The essence of interest is that it is a payment which becomes due because the creditor has not had his money at the due date. It may be regarded either as representing the profit he might have made if he had the use of the money, or conversely, the loss suffered because he had not that use. The general idea is that he is entitled to compensation for the deprivation.

With straightforward cases of lending of money, for example, by a bank, a finance company or professional moneylenders, there is no difficulty in determining whether or not money paid is interest. As the Companies Income

---

[22] CITA Section 8(b)
[23] Hannan, *The Principles of Income Taxation* (1952), p. 118
[24] [1947] A.C. 390; 28 T.C. 353
[25] Orojo, *Company Income Tax Law in Nigeria*(1979), p.30-34

Tax Act 1990 does not define interest, we are obliged to give to it the ordinary and natural meaning and for this purpose we may draw inspiration from the attitude of the English courts in their interpretation of the word in a similar context.

Sometimes, it is difficult to determine whether a payment is in fact interest or not. For example, in *Lomax* v *Peter Dixon & Sons Ltd.*,[26] a company made a loan to another company secured by notes at a discount of 6 *per cent.* Interest was agreed and the notes were to be payable at specified times and to bear premium at 20 *per cent.* It was held that the discount and the premium were capital payments and not chargeable interest. Similarly, a loan agreement may provide for the payment of a premium. Such a payment will normally be an accretion to capital and, therefore, not interest; but in some cases, it may be in the nature of additional interest. Thus, in *I.R.C.* v *Thomas Nelson & Sons Ltd.*,[27] the respondent company lent a sum of money to an Indian Company under an agreement which provided that the interest would be paid at 3 *per cent* per annum and that on repayment of the principal sum or any part thereof, there would also be paid a premium varying with the date of repayment. The full amount of the loan was ultimately repaid to the respondent company, together with the accrued interest and the premiums payable under the agreement.

The question was whether the premiums were part of the principal sums repaid and therefore capital payments, or were income and it was held that they were income from the foreign possessions.

Where a loan is granted at a discount and repayable at a premium, both being capital sums, the income derived thereby would be part of the capital sums and, therefore, not interest.[28] In determining the true nature of a discount or premium where it is not determined by the contract, one has to consider the surrounding circumstances and also *"the term of the loan, the rate of interest expressly stipulated for, the nature of the capital risk, the extent to which, if at all, the parties expressly took or may reasonably be supposed to have taken the capital risk into account in fixing the terms of the contract."*[29]

Another distinction which must be made is between what is compensation and what is interest. Where an amount was paid as interest for a certain sum which is in the form of damages or compensation, e.g. for a tortuous act or misfeasance, and the award on which the interest is based is mainly given as damages, such interest will be part of damages and, therefore, not chargeable interest.[30] Where a judgment is given on a debt or similar claims and an award is made together with compound interest, such interest is not in the nature of

---

[26] a[1943] 1 K.B. 671; 25 T.C. 353

[27] (1938) S.C. 816; 22 T.C. 175

[28] *Lomax v Peter Dixon & Sons Ltd.*, ante.

[29] *Ibid.* at p. 263

[30] See *I.R.C. v Ballantine* (1924) 8 T.C. 595; *Simpson v Maurice's Executors* (1929) 45 T.L.R. 581; 14 T.C. 580

damages but of interest in the true sense.[31]

The determining factor in these cases is whether the payments were payments of profits, that is, were income, or were payments on capital account estimated in terms of interest. In *Westminster Bank Ltd.* v *Riches*,[32] the House of Lords reviewed previous relevant cases and, in his judgment, Lord Wright explaining the position, stated as follows:

> The distinction through these cases is whether the payments were payments of profits, that is, were income, or were payments on capital account estimated in terms of interest. The latter type of case is less frequent in the books, but a good illustration is to be found in *Glenboig Union Fireclay Co. Ltd* v *I.R.C.* (1922) 12 T.C. 427, in which it was held that the sum there awarded was in truth, though described as interest, only a method of determining the value of the fireclay sterilized in the hands of the company for which it was entitled to compensation. That was a payment on capital account; it was for the destruction of a capital asset, which was indeed the source of profit but could not be regarded as income. On the other side of the line is *I.R.C.* v *Barnator* (1936) 20 T.C. 455 where the payment was a sum of compound interest which had been made to the taxpayer in commutation of his share of profit in a partnership. It was a sum of profit, not capital.

Finally, where in the repayment of a loan, a payment is made covering both principal and interest, the interest so included represents true interest for, unless otherwise agreed, the general rule is that when such payments are made, they are appropriated to interest in priority to principal.[33]

Under the Companies Income Tax Act interest is deemed to be derived from Nigeria in any of the following circumstances:

i) If there is a liability to payment of the interest (s.8(2)(a))

In *F.B.I.R.* v *Aluminium Industries Akitichgeschischaff*,[34] the respondent company advanced to a Nigerian subsidiary company, namely, Alumaco, a loan of £100, 000 at 5 per cent. Interest per annum which was duly paid to the foreign company. The question was whether the interest so earned was subject to tax under section 17(c) and section 17(i) of the Companies Income Tax Act 1961. The loan agreement provided that Alumaco would pay the interest in Swiss Francs and in Switzerland. Rejecting the majority decision of the Appeal Commissioners in favour of the minority judgment, Sowemimo J. held that although the interest was to be paid in Switzerland, in case of default in payment, the company had a right to sue Alumaco in Nigeria and recover the interest. Furthermore, the Court found that Alumaco was both agent and

---

[31] See *I.R.C. v Barnato* (1936) 155 L.T. 211; 2 T.C. . 454; and also *Barlow v I.R.C.* (1937) 21 T.C. 354 and *Schulze v Bensted* (1915) 53 S.L.R. 176; 7 T.C. 30 at p. 34

[32] [1947] A.C. 390; 28 T.C. 159 at p. 191

[33] See *Benefit Building Society v Mallandaine* [1897] 2 Q.B. 402; 3 T.C. 577

[34] High Court of Lagos, Suit No. LD/7A/69 of November 2, 1969, unreported.

subsidiary and accordingly held that since this foreign company had decided to invest money in a subsidiary company in Nigeria, it cannot escape payment of tax on the interest derived from profits made on the investment in the subsidiary company merely because the "deeming" provisions of section 17 speaks of a right to a payment of interest in Nigeria.

As the minority judgment of the Appeal Commissioners rightly pointed out, "the right of payment of interest in Nigeria exists independently of a similar right which the Swiss company has in Switzerland."

i) If the interest accrues to a foreign company regardless of whichever way the interest may have accrued (s.8(2)(b) [35]

Interest on foreign loans

Section 9 of the Companies Income Tax Act 1990[36] grants some exemptions in the case of any loan not less than ₦150,000 granted by a foreign company to any person carrying on any trade, business profession or vocation in Nigeria for the purposes of that trade, business, profession or vocation. It provides that if the loan is not repayable by the borrower until after the expiration of a period of not les than 10 years, the interest on the loan is exempted from tax. If, on the other hand, the loan is repayable in less than 10 years but not less than five years, the interest is chargeable to tax at half the normal rate (s. 9(1))(b). If in the former case the loan is repaid within a period of less than eight years or in the latter case within a period of less than four years, then the exemption or relief as the case may be is inapplicable and if such exemption or relief has been granted or made, it will be withdrawn (s. 9(2), (3)).

A foreign company is defined by the section as "any company or corporation (other than a corporation sole) established by or under any law in force in any territory or country outside Nigeria" and a foreign loan is one granted by a foreign company with moneys brought into Nigeria from any territory or country outside Nigeria, or a loan granted by that company in any territory or country outside Nigeria in a currency other than Nigeria currency (s. 9(8)(c).

Discounts

This has been interpreted in England to cover all profits on security bought at or involving a discount.[37] The discount must, however, be an income profit such as discount by a bank, a broker or an issuing house, but not a capital profit such as

[35] See Section 60 CITA 1990.

[36] Section 9 CITA 1990.

[37] *Brown v National Provident Institution* [1921] 2 A.C. 222 (H.L.) at p. 239; 8 T.C. 57 at p. 80 and 87; see also definition at p. 251-152 and 94 respectively.

the discount between the cash and credit price of an article allowed by a seller.[38]

Charges and annuities

These are sums payable annually or at other regular intervals and either charged on property or secured by covenant. Examples are a periodical benevolent contribution secured to a charity,[39] payment of amounts equal to interest and sinking fund under a contract,[40] and the payment of a percentage of gross receipts from the sale of articles manufactured under secret process.[41]

d) any profits or gains not falling within the preceding categories;
e) any amount deemed to be income or profits under a provision of the C.I.T.A.; or so regarded in connection with any benefit arising from a pension or provident fund approved under the P.I.T.A.

Section 36 of CITA provides that a company shall be chargeable to tax:

(a) in its own name; or
(b) in the name of a principal officer, attorney, factor, agent or representative in Nigeria in like manners and like amount as such company would chargeable; or
(c) in the name of a receiver or a liquidator, or of any attorney, agent, or representative thereof in Nigeria, in like manner or like amount as such company would have been chargeable if no receiver or liquidator had been appointed.

Taxation of dividends received by companies

Special provisions are laid down for the taxation of dividend income which forms part of the total profits of a company. The basic rule is that a recipient company receives dividend income from another Nigerian company net after deduction of income tax under section 16(b) C.I.T.A. by the paying company although it is treated for the purpose of calculating the total profits of the recipient company as having been received gross.

The recipient company is entitled to a certificate from the paying company setting out particulars or the gross amount and the income tax deducted by the paying company under C.I.T.A; s. 62(5) is not charged again to income tax on such part of its profits as have already been taxed by deduction at source.[42]

---

[38] *Brown v National Provident Institution* 8 T.C. 57 at p. 66
[39] See *I.R.C. v London Corporation* [1953] 1 W.L.R. 652 (H.L.)
[40] *Surbiton U.D.C. v Callender Cable and Construction Co. Ltd.* (1910) 74 J.P. 88
[41] *Delage v Nugget Polish Co. Ltd.* (1905) 92 L.T. 682
[42] *Pool v Guardian Investment Trust Ltd* [1922] 1 KB 347; 8 TC 167; See also sections 62(3) 15, 15A and 17 of CITA; See section 14A CITA for Authorized unit trust scheme.

A company paying a dividend is entitled to retain the tax deducted from any dividend paid by it and thus recoup itself for the income tax which it pays on its own profits. It follows that income tax is only paid on the profits of a company once and where those profits are distributed to shareholders, whether corporate or individual, by way of dividend the burden of income tax is ultimately passed on to the shareholders.

Profits exempted from income tax

The following are exempted from tax under C.I.T.A.; s. 19(1):

(a) the profits of any company which is a statutory or registered friendly society in so far as profits are not derived from a trade or business carried on by the society;
(b) the profits of any company which is a registered co-operative society registered under any enactment or law relating to a co-operative societies not being profits form any trade or business carried on by that company other than co-operative activities solely carried on by that company other than co-operative activities solely carried out with its members or from any share owned or other interest possessed by that company in a trade or business in Nigeria carried on by some other persons or authority;
(c) the profits of any company engaged in ecclesiastical, charitable or educational activities or a public character in so far as profits are not derived from a trade or business carried on by the company;
(d) the profits of any company formed for the purpose of promoting sporting activities where the profits are wholly expendable for these purposes; subject to such conditions as the Board may prescribe.
(e) the profits of any company registered as a trade union registered under any Trade Union Act in so far as such profits are derived from trade or business carried on by such trade union;
(f) dividend distributed by Unit Trust;
(g) dividend derived by a company from another incorporated in Nigeria; provided that: the equity participation of the recipient of the dividend in the company paying the dividend is either wholly paid for in foreign currency or by assets brought or imported into Nigeria between 1st January 1987 and 31st December, 1992 and the company receiving the dividend is the beneficiary owner or not less than ten *per cent* of the equity share capital of the company paying the dividend. For the purpose of this subsection, the dividend tax-free period shall commence from the year of assessment following the year in which the new capital is brought into Nigerian for the purpose of the trade or business in Nigeria of the company paying the dividend and shall continue for five years if the company paying the dividend is in the agricultural trade or business as defined in section 9(8) of this Act or is engaged in the petrochemicals or liquefied natural gas. In any other case, the dividend tax-free period shall be limited to three years;
(h) the profits of any company engaged in petroleum operations within the meaning of section 2 of the Petroleum Profits Tax Act, shall in so far as those

profits are derived form such operations and liable to the tax under that Act, be exempt from the tax imposed under this Act; the foregoing provisions of this paragraphs shall be deemed to have come into effect on 1st January, 1958;

(i) the profits of any company being a body corporate established by or under any Local Government Law or Edit in force in any State of Nigeria;

(j) the profits of any body corporate being a purchasing authority establishment an enactment and empowered to acquire any commodity for export from Nigeria for the purchase and sale (whether for the purposes of export or otherwise) of that commodity;

(k) the profits of any company or any corporation established by the law of the State for the purpose of fostering the economic development of the state, not being profits derived form any trade or business carried on by that corporation or from any share or interest possessed by that corporation in trade or business in Nigeria carried on by some other person or authority.

(l) any profits of a company other than Nigerian company which, but for this paragraph, would be chargeable to tax by reason solely of their being brought into or received in Nigeria;

(m) dividends, interest, rent, or royalty derived by a company from a country outside Nigeria and brought into Nigeria through Government approved channels;

For the purpose of this subsection, "Government approved channel", means the Central Bank of Nigeria, or any bank, or other corporate body appointed by the Minister as authorized dealer under the Second Tier Foreign Exchange Market Act;

(n) nothing in this section shall be construed to exempt from deduction at source, the tax which a company making payments is to deduct under section 60, 61, 62 of this Act, such that the provisions of sections 60, 61, and 70 of this Act, shall apply to a dividend, interest, rent or royalty which is a part of the profits or income referred to in subsection (1)(a) to (f), (1)(h) to (l) of this section.

(o) the interest of deposit accounts of a foreign non-resident company provided the deposits into the account are transfers wholly of foreign currencies to Nigeria on or after 1st January 1990 through Government approved channels;

(p) dividend received from small companies in the manufacturing sector, in the first five years of their operation;

(q) dividend received from investments in wholly export oriented businesses;

(r) the profits of any Nigerian company in respect of goods exported from Nigeria provided that the proceeds from such export are repatriated to Nigeria and are used exclusively for the purchase of raw materials, plants, equipment and spare parts;

(s) the profits of a company whose supplies are exclusively inputs to the manufacturing of products for export provided that the exporter shall give a certificate of purchase of the input of the exportable goods to the seller of the supplies.

A few points concerning the exemptions mentioned above may be emphasized. First to ensure an exemption under section 19 C.I.T.A. careful drafting of the memorandum of association of the company will be needed. Thus the objects of the company should be so drawn as to restrict the company to objects which are within the exemption. In most cases, this will involve prohibiting trading. Secondly, it should be noted that paragraph (c) applies only where the activity, be it ecclesiastical, charitable or education, is of a public character although on the other hand it is not merely limited to charitable activities but could apply to a non-charitable educational activity provided it was of a sufficiently public character. Paragraph (d) which relates to companies formed for the purposes of promoting sporting activities is quite separate and apparently it is not it is not necessary to show either a charitable or a public element and moreover all profits are exempt (even though derived from a trade or business) provided they are wholly expendable for the sporting purposes for which the company was formed. Again the drafting of the memorandum of association will be critical in this respect as well as the manner in which the activities are carried out.

Returns

As in the case of individuals, companies are required to make tax returns under Part VIII of C.I.T.A. which must be made for each year of assessment to the Federal Board of Inland Revenue. The Board has wide powers in connection with returns and may call for a return under s. 42[43], require delivery to it of books of accounts, documents and other information (s. 43)[44] and may by notice require a company to keep such records, books and accounts as it considers adequate for the purposes of income tax.[45]

The need of the demand for returns as a pre-requisite for assessment was emphasized in the case of *F.B.I.R.* v *Joseph Rezcallah & Sons Ltd.*[46] where Bairamian F.J. said:

> the request to render a return is a condition precedent to assessment; the waiting for the time allowed in the request to pass is also a condition precedent; both conditions are intended to protect a person by affording him an opportunity of stating his income and other relevant matters; and an assessment which does not fulfil either of those conditions is made without jurisdiction, and is null and void.[47]

Assessments

By section 47 of the C.I.T.A., the Board is charged with the duty of assessing

[43] *FBIR v Joseph Rezallah & Sons Ltd* [1962] 1 All NLR 1
[44] *FBIR v Doherty Ltd* (1971) N.M.L.R. 162
[45] *Mandaria v Commissioners of Income Tax* [1959] A.C. 114 (P.C.)
[46] [1962] 1 All N.L.R. 1
[47] *Ibid.* at p. 11. See also *ibid.* p. 9 and *F.B.I.R.* v *J.H. Doherty Ltd.* (1971) N.M.L.R. 162

companies to tax which it may do on the basis of a return made to it or if it considers the return to be inaccurate it can use its judgment to determine the total profits of the company and make an assessment accordingly. In the case of *F.B.I.R. v Omotesho,*[48] Belgore, J. (as he then was) stated the factors to consider in making the best of judgment assessment as follows:

(1) (Citing the decision in the case of *Income Tax Commissioners* v *Badridas Ramrai Shop, Akola).* In making an assessment to the best of judgment against a person who defaulted as regards supply of information, the tax authority must not act dishonestly or vindictively or capriciously. The assessment must be a fair estimate of the proper figure of assessment and must take into consideration local knowledge and repute in regard to the assessee's circumstances as well as the previous returns and other matters which the tax authority thinks will assist in arriving at a fair and proper estimate.

(2) Reasons should be given for differences in reliefs granted between two years where the circumstances were similar.

Also in *F.B.I.R.* v *Azigbo Brothers Ltd.*, the company, having failed to deliver the return of income, was assessed to tax on the *best of judgment* basis. The assessment was based on the experience of the Acting Senior Inspector of Taxes of mining companies where the defendant company carried on its mining operations and also on the tax of the company relating to previous years. No capital allowances were granted because none was claimed as required by law. The defendant contended that the assessments wee arbitrary and not made to the best of the Board's judgment in that they excluded capital allowances having regard to capital allowances which had been permitted to the company. Smith S.P.J. held this was a matter that should have been raised on objection and/or appeal and not in a matter for recovery of the tax and on the evidence, he concluded that "*the view of the Board in ignoring capital allowances until they were claimed was prima facie reasonable.*"[49] In *Chairman Board of Inland Revenue* v *Joseph Rezcallah & Sons Ltd.,*[50] the assessment was made without demand having been made for a return and it was held that the Chief Inspector of Taxes did not, on the facts, exercise his discretion "*to the best of his judgment*" in making the assessments. The same issue was considered in *Federal Board of Inland Revenue* v *Nigerian General Insurance Co. Ltd.*[51] There, the Board raised a "*best of judgment*" assessment and while capital allowance was made for the year 1962-1963, it was not made for the year 1963-1964 and 1964-1965, it was held that although the allowance ought to be claimed, the court could not ignore the provision of paragraph 22 of Schedule 3

---

[48] 1 NTC 57
[49] *Ibid.* at p. 202
[50] (1961) N.N.R. 32
[51] [1966] L.L.R. 88

of the Companies Income Tax Act 1961 that such allowances should be made "*where the Board is of opinion that it would be reasonable and just so to do*" and it accordingly set aside the assessments.

An assessment must be made under some section of the Act,[52] and cannot be made under the Companies Income Tax Act generally.[53] If no return is made the Board may make an arbitrary assessment if it considers the company to be liable to pay tax. Where a company has been assessed on too little of its profits the Board is entitled to make an additional assessment within six years of the end of the year of assessment at any time.[54]

The Board is required to prepare lists of companies assessed to income tax under s. 49, C.I.T.A.

Basis of assessment

The profits for the accounting year ending in the preceding year of assessment form the basis of assessment for a company's liability to tax under C.I.T.A., s. 25(1) in accordance with principles similar to those applicable to unincorporated trade or businesses. Furthermore, the special rules which apply in the case of new and discontinued trades or businesses also apply to companies under s.25 (3) and (4). However, it should be noted that these rules will not apply if a business is sold or transferred to a subsidiary company or where the sale is between two companies both of which are controlled by the same person under s.25(9).

Service of notice of assessment

Under section 50 of CITA 1990, the board shall cause notice of the assessment to be served on or sent by registered post to each company, or person in whose name a company is chargeable, whose name appears on the assessment lists (s.49).[55] With regard to service of notices generally, section 50 of the Companies Income Tax Act 1990 provides that such notice shall be address, in the case of a company incorporated in Nigeria, to the registered office of the company.[56] In

---

[52] e.g., under C.I.T.A., s.49

[53] See *F.B.I.R. v Joseph Rezcallah & Sons Ltd.* [1962] 1 All N.L.R. 1 at p. 8

[54] *John Khawam Ltd. v F.B.I.R.* 1 NTC 407; Where it was held that the tax authorities was not permitted to review previous years assessment beyond six years in the absence of fraud wilful default or negligence. See also *F.B.I.R. v Azigbo Brothers Ltd.* [1963] 2 All NLR 198; *F.B.I.R. v Nigerian General Insurance Co. Ltd.* [1966] LLR 88

[55] Orojo, *Company Income Tax Law in Nigeria*(1979), p. 167-169, *op. cit.*

[56] If the Company is incorporated outside Nigeria, the notice is served either on the individual authorized to accept service on behalf of the company at an address filed with the Registrar or sent to the registered office of the Company wherever it may be situated (C.I.T.A., s.36(c))

F.B.I.R. v *Nigerian General Insurance Co. Ltd.*,[57] notices requiring the defendants to make tax returns were sent to them at their registered office and there being no returns, the plaintiff raised a "*best of judgment*" assessment and claimed payment from the company. It was established in evidence, first, that in previous years, the plaintiff were in the practice of sending notices to the company's accountants at a different address as instructed by the company; secondly, that the notice addressed to the registered office of the company did not come to their attention in good time. Omololu J. took the view that in spite of the provision of section 16(3)(a) of the 1961 Act, requiring service at the registered office of the company, the Board itself was in the practice of sending notices to some other address as instructed by the company and that in now addressing notice to the registered office, it ought to know that the notices were being addressed to a place which through their experience and previous practice was not the normal place. He accordingly held that the service of the notice was bad. This decision is of doubtful authority in that it tends to create an estoppel against the Revenue, and also because the words of section 16(3)(a) are unambiguous and it will be going too far to say that the taxpayer and the Board can by agreement vary its provisions. It is submitted that a variation of the section by agreement cannot bind either party. Although this case went on appeal to the Supreme Court,[58] it is unfortunate that the point as to the service of notice was not allowed to be raised in that no notice of it was given as required by the rules.

Another case on this point is *F.B.I.R.* v *J.H. Doherty Ltd.*[59] There, the Board addressed a demand note to the company as follows:

> The Managing Director, J.H. Doherty Ltd. c/o Messrs G. Gikoonu & Co., 15 Bamgbose Street, Lagos.

The registered office of the company was 35, Kosoko Street, Lagos and there was no evidence that the company had requested notices to be sent to 15, Bamgbose Street, the address of the company's accountants.

In his judgment, Adefarasin J. (as he then was) commented on the validity of the service of the demand note as follows:[60]

> In any event it is my view that notices of request to furnish returns and assessment notices must be served on a company incorporated in Nigeria at its registered office. Service of such notices must in my view, be strictly in accordance with the provisions of section 16(3) of the Companies Income Tax Act...While the authorities are entitled to discuss with the accountant the tax position of his client, they must, when it comes to the services of statutory

[57] [1966] L.L.R. 88
[58] Sc 60/68, unreported
[59] (1971) 1 N.M.L.R. 162
[60] Ibid. at p. 169

> notices under section 44 of the Act, serve it in accordance with the laid down procedure.

Earlier in the judgment, he said:

> When notices are served requesting a person or company to render a return or having rendered a return, he is to be served with notice of assessment; my view is that it must be served on the tax paying company itself and at its registered offices. Service by any other means is, I think, invalid.[61]

He found that the notice in this case had not been properly served. That the position of the plaintiffs was not helped by the fact that the defendants themselves held out Messrs G. Gikoonu & Co. to be their accountants and, consequently, that any income tax assessments made on such notice were without jurisdiction and, therefore, null and void.

It submitted that on a proper construction of section 16(3)(a) of the Companies Income Tax Act 1961, this is the correct view.

Final and conclusive assessment

Under section 58 of CITA 1990 where no valid objection or appeal has been lodged within the time limited by section 51, 54, or 57 of this Act, as the case may be, against the assessment as regards the amount of total profits assessed thereby or where the amount of the total profits has been agreed to under subsection (3) of section 51 of this Act, or on appeal, as the case may be, shall be final and conclusive for all purposes of this Act as regards the amount of such total profits, and if the full amount of the tax in respect of any such final and conclusive assessment is not paid within the appropriate period or periods prescribed in this Act, the provisions thereof relating to the recovery of tax, and to any penalty under section 65 of this Act shall apply to the collection and recovery thereof subject only to the set-off of the amount of any tax repayable under any claim, made under any provision of this Act, which has been agreed to by the Board or determined on any appeal against refusal to admit any such claim:

Provided that:

(a) where an assessment has become final and conclusive any tax overpaid shall be repaid.

(b) nothing in section 51 or in Part X of this Act shall prevent the Board from making any assessment or additional assessment for any year which does not involve re-opening any issue, on the same facts, which has been determined for that year of assessment under subsection (3)

---

[61] Ibid. at p. 168

of section 52 of this Act by agreement or otherwise on appeal.

In *F.B.I.R.* v *Joseph Rezcallah & Sons Ltd.*, the Board, without giving notice to the company to deliver a return of income, proceeded to assess it to tax. The company did not object or appeal and the Board brought an action to recover the tax assessed and penalties. At the trial, the company contended that the assessments were not properly made in that no notice to deliver return of income was served as required by law. This contention was upheld by the High Court which accordingly dismissed the action. The Board then appealed to the Federal Supreme Court and contended that since the company had neither objected to nor appealed against the assessment, the High Court had no jurisdiction to pronounce on the merit or legality of the assessment because in the words of the Act, the assessment was "final and conclusion..." The court rejected this contention and held that while the assessment was final and conclusive as to other matters, and the court in subsequent proceedings can inquire into the validity of the assessment except in so far as it is restricted by any other provisions of the Act.[62] In his judgment, Bairamian F.J., as stated earlier,[63] said that:

> the request to render a return is a condition precedent to assessment; the waiting for the for the time allowed in the request to pass is also a condition precedent; both conditions are intended to protect a person by affording him an opportunity of stating his income and other relevant matters; and an assessment which does not fulfil either of those conditions is made without jurisdiction and is null and void.

It is only if those conditions are fulfilled that the assessment can be final and conclusive even as regards the amount of the chargeable income. The aim of an objection and appeal to the Appeal Commissioners is to review or revise the assessment "on the presupposition that the assessment was made with jurisdiction: they do not...contemplate a case where it was made without jurisdiction.[64] He then went on to say that while under the section an assessment becomes final and conclusive as to the amount of the chargeable income:

> that presupposes that it was made with jurisdiction; for if it was null and void '*ab inito*,' it must remain null and void ... as the assessments were made outside the provisions of the Act, they could not result in anything final and conclusive against the defendants.[65]

---

[62] Ibid., Per Unsworth F.J. at p.8

[63] *Ante*, p.164

[64] [1962] 1 All N.L.R. 1 at p.13

[65] *Ibid.* at p. 13 and 14; see also *F.B.I.R. v J.H. Doherty*, ante, where *Rezcallah's Case* was referred to. *Cf Aboud v Regional Tax Board* (1966) N.M.L.R. 100 where the Supreme Court held that since the purpose of the appellant's action was to reduce the amount of tax on the chargeable income, it could not be entertained, the assessment being "final and conclusive ... as regards the amount of

Computation of profits

Saved where the provisions of subsection (2) and (3) of section 12 or of 14 of this Act apply, for the purpose of ascertaining the profits or loss of any company of any period from any source chargeable with tax under this Act, there shall be deducted all expenses wholly, exclusively, necessarily and reasonably incurred in the production of those profits including but without otherwise expanding or limiting the generality of the following:

(a) any sum payable by way of interest on any money borrowed or employed as capital in acquiring the profits.

(b) rent for that period, and premiums, the liability for which was incurred during that period, in respect of land or building occupied for the purpose of acquiring profits, subject, in the case of residential accommodation occupied by employees of the company, to a maximum of 100% of the basic salary of employees.

(bb) In the case of any property-holding company

(i) expenses attributable to the maintenance of the property concerned; and

(ii) director's remuneration, which shall not exceed ₦10, 000.00 *per annum* in respect of each director, and he number of directors to be so remunerated shall in no case exceed three;

(bbb) Any outlay or expenses incurred during the year in respect of:

(i) salary, wages or other remuneration paid to the senior staff and executives;

(ii) cost to the company of any benefit or allowance provided for the senior staff and executives;

which shall not exceed the limit of the amount prescribed by the collective agreement between the company and the employees and approved by the Federal Ministry of Employment, Labour and Productivity and the Productivity, Prices and Income Board, as the case may be.

(c) any expenses incurred for the repairs of premises, plant machinery or fixtures employed in acquiring the profits, or the renewal, repairs, or alteration of any implement, utensil or article employed;

(d) bad debt incurred in the course of trade or business proved to have become bad during the period for which the profit are being ascertained and doubtful debts so the extend that they are respectively estimated and doubtful debts to the extend that they are respectively estimated to the satisfaction of the Board to have become bad during the said period notwithstanding that such bad or doubtful debts were due and payable before the commencement of the said period;

Provided that:

(i) where in any period a deduction under this paragraph is to be made as respect any particular debt, and a deduction has in any previous period been allowed in respect of the same debt, the appropriated reduction shall be made in the deduction to be made for the period in

---

such chargeable income."

question;

(ii) all sums recovered during the said period on account of amounts previously written off or allowed either under the companies income tax Act 1979 or this Act in respect of bad and doubtful debts shall for the purpose of this Act be deemed to be profits of the trade or business of that period;

(iii) it is proved to the satisfaction of the Board that the debts in respect of which is claimed either were included as a receipt of a trade or business in the profits or the year within which they were incurred or were advances not falling within the provisions or paragraph (a) of section 23 made in the course of normal trading or business operation;

(e) any contribution to a pension, provident or other retirement benefits funds, society or scheme approved by the Joint Tax Board under the powers conferred upon it by paragraph (g) of section 20 of the Personal Income Tax Act 1993 subject to the provisions of the fourth schedule to that Act and other provision imposed by the Board; and any contribution other than penalty made under the provisions of any enactment establishing a national provident fund or other retirement benefits scheme for employee throughout Nigeria;

(f) in the case of the Nigeria Railway Corporation such deductions as are allowed under the provisions of the Authorized Deductions (Nigerian Railway Corporation) Rules 1959, which rule shall be in force for all purposes of this Act;

(g) in the case of profits from a trade or business any expense or part thereof;

(i) the liability of which was incurred wholly, exclusively, necessarily and reasonably for the purpose of such trade or business and which is not specifically referable to any other period or periods; or

(ii) the liability of which was incurred during any previous period wholly, exclusively, necessarily and reasonable for the purpose or business and which is specifically referable to the period of which the profit are being ascertained;

which is not deductive under any other provision of this section;

(iii) the expenses proved to the satisfaction of the Board to have been incurred by the company on research and development for the period including the amount of levy paid by it to the National Science and Technology Fund.

(h) such other deduction as may be prescribed by the Minister by any rule.

Treatment of losses

The amount of loss that the board is satisfied has been incurred by the company in any trade or business during any preceding year of assessment shall be deducted under section 27 (2)(a), (3) and (4) of CITA provided that:[66]

---

[66] See *FBIR v Adenubi* 1 NTC 92; where the Supreme Court held that losses sustained from one source of income could only be dedicated from profit earned at a future date from that particular source of income.

(i) in no circumstances shall the aggregated deduction from assessable profit or income in respect of any such loss exceed the amount of such loss, and

(ii) a deduction under this section for any particular year of assessment shall not exceed the amount, if any, of the assessable profits, included in the total profits for that year of assessment, from the trade or business in which the loss was incurred and shall be made as far as possible from the amount of such assessable profits of the first year of assessment after that in which the loss was incurred and, so far as it cannot be so made, then from such amount of the assessable profits of the next year of assessment, and so on;

(iii) the period for carrying forward any loss in subparagraph (ii) of this paragraph shall be limited to four years after which period any unrelieved loss shall become laps.

Capital allowances

The rules relating to capital allowances for companies are contained in Second Schedule to the C.I.T.A.

1) *Initial allowances*: Under C.I.TA. Second Schedule s.6 (1) where in its basis period for a year of assessment a company owning any asset have incurred in respect thereof qualifying expenditure wholly, exclusively, necessarily and reasonably for the purposes of a trade or business carried on by it, there shall be made to that company for the year of assessment in its basis period for which that asset was first used for the purpose of trade or business an allowance (in this Schedule called "an initial allowance") at the appropriate rate per centum, set forth in Table 1 to this Schedule, of such expenditure.

   The rates *per cent* are as follows:

	Table I: Initial Allowances rate per cent	*Table II: Annual Allowances rate per cent*
Building (industrial and non-industrial)	15	10
Mining	95	Nil
Plant: Agricultural Production	95	Nil
Others	50	25
Furniture and Fittings	25	20
Motor Vehicles: Public transportation	95	Nil
Others	50	25
Plantation Equipment	95	Nil
Housing Estate	50	25
Ranching and Plantation	30	50
Research and Development	95	Nil

When the expenditure is exhausted by the sale or abandonment of assets balancing allowances or balancing charges may apply. If the written down value of the expenditure exceeds the amount (if any) realized on sale, a balancing allowance is made equal to the excess. If on the other hand the proceeds of sale exceed the written down value, the excess is added to income by way of a balancing charge, restricted however to the total of the allowances made on the asset.

In total, therefore, a trade, business or profession is given tax allowances equal to the net cost of an asset, spread over the life of the asset.

Relief from tax

Section 28 C.I.T.A. provides that:[67]

(A)(1) Notwithstanding any other provisions of this Act, where in any year of assessment the ascertainment of total assessable profits form all sources of a company results in a loss or where a company's ascertained total profits results in no tax payable or tax payable which is less than the minimum tax there shall be levied and paid by the company the minimum tax as prescribed in subsection (2) of this section.

(2) For the purpose of subsection (1) of this section, the minimum tax to be levied and paid shall:

- (a) if the turnover of the company is N500, 000.00 or below and the company has been in business for at least 4 calendar years, be:
  - (i) 0.5 *per cent* of gross profits; or
  - (ii) 0.5 *per cent* of net assets; or
  - (iii) 0.25 *per cent* of paid up capital; or
  - (iv) 0.25 *per cent* of turnover of the company for the year whichever is the highest.
- (b) a company with at least 25 *per cent* imported equity capital; and
- (c) any company for the first four calendar years of its commencement of business.

(4)(a) Nothing in this section shall be construed as preventing the Board from levying tax on a company by an assessment based on the profits of the company in any year of assessment at the rate specified in section 29 of this Act and the tax so levied shall be paid or payable by the company, so however, that the tax payable under subsection (1) of this section shall be the amount by which the amount computed under subsection (2) of this section exceeds the amount that is levied and payable under section 29 of this Act.

(b) For the purpose of this section and the Second Schedule to this Act, the capital allowance for any assessment year in which a minimum tax is payable shall be computed and the amount so computed, together with any

---

[67] See Industrial Development (Income Tax Relief) Act Cap 179 LFN 1990

unabsorbed allowance brought forward from the previous year, shall be deducted as far as possible from the assessable profits of the assessment year and, so far as it cannot be completely deducted, the amount by which the total amount of the capital allowance exceeds the amount of assessable profit of the assessment year shall be carried forward to the next assessment year.

28B (1) Where a company incurs capital expenditure on the provision of facilities such as electricity, water, tarred road or telephone for the purpose of a trade or business which is located at least 20 kilometres away form such facilities provided by Government there shall be allowed to such company as addition to initial capital allowance under Second Schedule to this Act. An allowance (herein this section called Rural Investment Allowance) at the appropriate rate per centum as set forth in subsection (2) of this section, of the amount of such expenditure.

Provided that where any allowance has been given in pursuance of this section, no investment allowance under section 28 of this Act shall be due to be given in respect of the same assets or in addition to the allowance given under this section:

(a) no facilities at all -------------------- 100%
(b) no electricity ------------------------ 50%
(c) no water ----------------------------- 30%
(d) no tarred road ----------------------15%
(e) no telephone ------------------------5%

(3) For the purpose of this section rural investment allowance shall be made against the profit of the year in which the date of the completion of such facilities fall and the allowance and any fraction thereof shall not be available for carry forward to any subsequent year whenever full effects cannot be given to the allowance owing to their being no assessable profits less than the total allowance for the year the investment was made.

28C (1) A company which has incurred an expenditure in its qualifying building and plant equipment in an approved manufacturing activity in an Export Processing Zone shall be granted 100% capital allowance in any year of assessment.

(2) A company granted capital allowance under subsection (1) of this section shall not be entitled to an investment Allowance under this Act.

(3) No Provision, See Section 19 of 1998 No. 18.

(2) The profit or gain of a 100% export oriented undertaking established within and outside an Export Free Zone shall be exempted from tax for the first three consecutive assessment years provided that :

(i) the undertaking is 100% export oriented;
(ii) the undertaking is not formed by splitting or breaking up or reconstructing a business already in existence;
(iii) it manufacturers, produces and exports articles during the relevant year and the export proceeds from 75% of its turnover;
(iv) the undertaking is not formed by transfer of machinery or plants previously used for any purpose to the new undertaking or where machinery or plant previously used for any purpose is transferred does not exceed 25% of the total value of the machinery or the undertaking;
(v) the undertaking repatriates at least 75% of the earnings to Nigeria and

places it in a domiciliary account in any registered and licensed bank in Nigeria;

(5) For the purpose of section 28C (4), only the tax written down value of the assets shall be carried forward at the end of the tax holidays.

28D. A new company going into the mining of solid minerals shall be exempted from tax for the next three years of its operation.

28E. 25% of incomes in convertible currencies derived from tourists by a hotel shall be exempted from tax provided that such income is put in a reserved fund to be utilized within fives years for the building expansion of new hotels, conference centres and new facilities for the purpose of tourism development.

28F(i) A company which engages wholly in the fabrication of spare parts, tools and equipment for local consumption and export shall be allowed 25% investment tax credit on its qualifying capital expenditure.

(iii) A company which purchases a locally manufactured plant, machinery or equipment for use its business shall be allowed 15% investment tax credit on such fixed asset bought for use.

(G)(1) A company engaged in gas utilization (downstream operations) shall be granted the following incentives, that is:

(a) an initial tax free period of three years which may, subject to the satisfactory performance of the business, be renewed for an additional period of two years;

(aa) as an alternative to the initial tax free period granted under granted paragraph (a) of this subsection, an additional investment allowance of 35 % which shall not reduce the value of the value of the asset, so however that a company which claims the incentive provided under paragraph (b) (ii) of this subsection;

(b) accelerated capital allowances after the tax free period, as follows, that is:

(i) an annual allowance of 90% with 10% retention, for investment in plant and machinery,

(ii) an additional investment allowance of 15% which shall not reduce the value of the asset;

(c) tax free dividend during the tax free period, where:

(i) the investment for the business was in foreign currency, or

(ii) the introduction of imported plant and machinery during the period was not less than 30% of the equity share capital of the company;

(d) interest payable on any loan obtained with the prior approval of the Minister for a gas project, shall be deductible.

(2) The tax free period of a company shall start on the day the company commences production as certified by the Ministry of Petroleum Resources.

(3) In this section:

"Gas utilization" means the marketing and distribution of natural gas for commercial purpose and includes power plant, liquefied natural gas, gas to liquid plant, fertilizer plant, gas transmission and distribution pipelines;

"tax free period" means the tax free period referred to in subsection (1)(a) of this section.

Acceptance certificate

The position of the CITA 1990 as amended to date is that for qualifying capital expenditure whose value is not less than ₦500,000 an acceptance certificate must be obtained from the inspectorate division of the Federal Ministry of Industries.[68]

There is often some confusion as to the correct interpretation of this requirement as to the significance of the threshold of ₦500,000. Indeed, up to the end of 1994 year of assessment, this threshold was a paltry ₦20,000.

In any case, capital allowance may be claimed on all qualifying capital expenditures but the Revenue will require the acceptance certificate in respect of assess in excess of ₦500,000. Where an acceptance certificate is not obtained for qualifying capital expenditure for the class of assets costing M500.000 capital allowance computed may not be accepted by the Revenues. This is not to say that in practice, the Acceptance certificate must be presented at the point of presenting between the claim of capital allowance and the issuing of acceptance for one or all of the following reasons:

(a) the procession of the Acceptance Certificate for qualifying capital expenditure for any particular tax year takes time to complete;
(b) the Inspectorate Division of the Federal Ministry of Industries often complain of lack of adequate manpower;
(c) the taxpayer may not be able to satisfy the complete requirement of the inspectors at once.

The processing of an Acceptance Certificate may be tasking and so the tax manager must be patient. Even with his patience, a complete approval may not be given at once but he persists. Let us quickly review the things that need to be done to hasten the processing of an acceptance certificate.

Responsibilities of the tax administrator

(a) A formal application must be made to the Inspectorate division of the Federal Ministry of Industrial stating clearly the value of the qualifying capital expenditure and the classes. This application is by way of any intention to incur capital expenditure;
(b) This application is responded to by the Federal Ministry of Industries with the provisions of the relevant forms to be completed;
(c) The form is completed according to the class of each qualifying capital expenditure. In completing the form, all the assets involved must be collated

[68] Seyi Ojo (1998), *Elements of Tax Management & Practice in Nigeria,* Sagibra Tax Publications. pp 92, 93, 94.

with the relevant supporting documents such as invoices, payment vouchers, architect's papers, valuation reports, certificate of occupancy etc. as applicable. These documents are maintained in a form that allows for easy reference by the inspectors. Where the assets are not in the same location, the files for inspection purpose should be maintained by location.

(d) The inspector will normally visit the locations where the assets are located not only for verification but to examine the records to satisfy themselves of the existence and valuation of the assets for which the acceptance certificate is to be issued. The administrator should assist the inspectors in the identification of the assets. Where the files containing the records have been properly prepared, it will hasten the completion of the inspection. At the completion of the inspection, the office work involves writing of reports and the review of the reports of inspection before the acceptance certificate is eventually issued.

The practical problem in practice especially in a situation where the assets are located in several locations that are for apart from each other, test-inspection may be carried out by those on field which may not be satisfactory to the desk officer who reviews the report and issues the final report. This results in an unnecessary cost to the taxpayer. More often than not, the inspectors will request to be accommodated, provided with transportation to and from their location in Abuja and be fed. This could be sometimes huge that a repeat inspection is not desirable in respect of the same exercise.

A way out of this is to file an application for the acceptance certificate of a subsequent year so that the inspection of the new year can be carried out with the old ones.

Petroleum profits tax

Petroleum companies are not subject to tax at the standard rate under the Petroleum Profit Tax Act 1959, re-enacted under cap 354 LFN 1990 (P.P.T.A). This tax is also administered by the Federal Board of Inland Revenue.

The main distinguishing features between this profits tax and the orthodox income tax on companies are as follows:

(1) By section 19 of the Petroleum Profits Tax Act the assessable tax for any accounting period of an oil company is equal to 85% of its chargeable profits of that period. Deductible from this assessable tax are such liabilities as royalty payments, rates, imports and fees payable to the Federal or State Governments. The effect of this is that the Government bears these outgoings out of its share of the chargeable profits. Subject to the foregoing all "outgoings and expenses wholly and exclusively incurred, whether within or without Nigeria" are

deductible from the oil company's gross profits[69] under section 10 PPTA.

(2) The above arrangement of, in effect, splitting the chargeable profits evenly between the company and the Revenue affects dividend payments payable by the company out of its slice of profits. These are payable without deduction of tax at source and the taxpayer is neither entitled to claim any repayment on their grossed up basis nor is he liable to pay income tax on the amount received under s. 12 P.I.T.A.

(3) Petroleum profits tax is payable by twelve equal instalments under S. 42 (1) of PPTA, the first instalment being payable on an estimated basis not later than the third month of the relevant accounting period.

In *Shell-BP Petroleum Development Company Nigeria Ltd.* v *F.B.I.R.*,[70] the question was whether or not a sum of ₦151,996.00 demurrage or dead freight charges incurred by the Appellants in its sales of crude oil should be deducted in computing the Appellant's tax under section 10 of the Petroleum Profits Tax Act 1959. This depends on whether or not the sale of crude oil is a petroleum operation is defined by the Act. It was contended on behalf of the Appellant that on the proper interpretation of the definition of petroleum operations, "sale of or any disposal of chargeable oil by or on behalf of the company" is included. The contention was rejected by the Appeal Commissioners who held that it is excluded. They accordingly decided that the expenses incurred on dead freight and demurrages were not deductible. On further appeal to the Federal High Court, the decision was reversed and it was held that on the true construction of section 10(1) of the Act, the sale of crude oil is included in the definition of petroleum operations and the expenses incurred on dead freight and demurrage, having been incurred wholly, exclusively and necessarily on the sale, are deductible.

"Petroleum" is defined as:

> any mineral oil or relative hydro-carbon and natural gas existing in its natural condition in Nigeria, but does not include coal or bituminous shales or other stratified deposits from which oil can be extracted by destructive distillation.

And "chargeable oil" is defined as:

> any one or more of the following, namely, casinghead petroleum spirit,[71] crude oil[72] or natural gas as the case may be, won or obtained by the company from such operations (s.3).

---

[69] *Shell – BP v FBIR*; FRC/L/IA/25 Of 5/11/79; See Abdulrazaq M.T. (1997) An Analysis of the Supreme Court of Nigeria Decision in the case of Shell Petroleum Development Company of Nigeria Limited and the Federal Board of Inland Revenue. *Journal of International and Comparative Law* (University of Ilorin) p. 120-139.

[70] No. FRC/L/1A/25 of November 5, 1976, unreported

[71] i.e. any liquid hydro-carbons obtained in Nigeria from natural gas by separation or by any

Like the companies income tax, petroleum profits tax is administered by the Federal Board of Inland Revenue as a federal tax (s.3).

Anti-avoidance

The C.I.T.A. contains two important anti-avoidance provisions in sections 17 and 18. The former provides for the taxing in certain cases of undistributed profits earned by a company which are not paid over to shareholders by way of dividend and the latter gives the Federal Board of Inland Revenue power to disregard "artificial" transactions involving companies.

Taxation of undistributed profits

Section 17 C.I.TA. provides as follows:

(1) Where it appears to the Board that a Nigerian company controlled by not more than five persons, with a view to reducing the aggregate of the tax chargeable in Nigeria on the profits or income of the company and those persons, has not distributed to it's shareholders as dividend, profits made in any period for which accounts have been made up by such company, which profits could have been distributed without detriment to the company's business as it existed at the end of that period, it may direct that such undistributed profits of such period be treated as distributed.[73]

(2) Any amount of profits treated as distributed under the provisions of the foregoing subsection shall, for the purposes of Act and any enactment in Nigeria imposing tax on the incomes of persons other than companies, be deemed to profits or income from a dividend accruing to those persons who are shareholders in the company in proportion to their shares in the ordinary capital thereof on such day, and the amount of such profits or income to be taken for assessment in the hands of each such person shall be his due proportion thereof increased by such amount in respect of tax deemed to be deducted at source, as the Board may determine.[74]

(3) Any direction by the Board under this section shall be made in writing and be served upon the company, and shall specify:

---

chemical or physical process but before the same has been refined or otherwise treated (P.P.T.A., s2)

[72] i.e. "any oil (other than oil extracted by destructive distillation from coal, bituminous shales or other stratified deposits) won in Nigeria either in its natural state or after the extraction of water, sand or other foreign substance therefrom but before any such oil been refined or otherwise treated." (P.P.T.A., s2).

[73] *Willingale v Islington Green Investment Co* [1972] 1 All ER 199, 48TC 547; See Goldberg [1971] *British Tax Review* 380

[74] *CHW (Huddersfield) Ltd v IRC* [1963] 2All ER 952, 41TC 92; See *R v IRC, exparte Newfields Developments Ltd.* [1999] STC 373; where it was held that if the Revenue forms the view that those other persons are indeed associates, then it has a duty to attribute those rights to the other persons; it has no discretion in the matter.

(a) the day to be taken for the purposes of the preceding subsection;
(c) the net amount of those profits so deemed to be distributed;
(d) the rate of tax deemed to be deducted, being the rate prescribed in subsection (2) of section 62 f this Act, and
(e) the gross amount which after deduction of tax at the said rate leaves such net amount of those profit.

(4) For the purposes of this section, the Board may give notice to any company which it has reason to believe is controlled by not more than five persons requiring it to supply within such reasonable time limited in such notice, full particulars of its shareholders on any day.

(5) Any direction by the Board under this section with respect to the profits of any accounting period of a company, shall be made not later than two years after the receipt by the Board of the duly audited accounts of the company for that period.

(1) A company in respect of which any direction is made under this section shall have a right to appeal in like manner as though for the purposes of Part X of this Act, such direction were an assessment.

Artificial transactions

Section 18 C.I.T.A. provides power to the Board:

(1) Where the Board is of the opinion that any disposition is not in fact given effect to or that any transaction which reduces or would reduce the amount of any tax payable is artificial or fictitious, it may disregard any such disposition or direct that such adjustments shall be made as respects liability to tax as it considers appropriate so as to counteract the reduction of liability to tax affected, or reduction which would otherwise be effected, by the transaction and any company concerned shall be assessable accordingly.

(2) For the purpose of this section:
   (a) "disposition" includes any trust, grant, covenant, agreement or arrangement;
   (b) transactions between persons one of whom either has control over the other or, in the case of individuals, who are related to each other or between persons, shall be deemed to be artificial or fictitious if in the opinion of the Board those transactions have not been made on terms which might fairly have been expected to have made by persons engaged in the same or similar activities dealing with one another at arm's length.[75]

(3) a company in respect of which any direction is made under this section shall have a right of appeal in like manner as though for the purposes of Part X of this Act such direction were an assessment.

---

[75] Abdulrazaq M.T.(1991) Legislation Against Tax Avoidance: The Nigerian Experience; *JUSTICE – Journal of Contemporary Legal Problems* (Federal Ministry of Justice) JUS Vol. 2 No. 9 p.33-46; See also *Akinsete Syndicate v Senior Inspector of Taxes* 1 NTC 109; *Aboud v Regional Tax Board* 1 NTC 124

This section is aimed at transactions which include and are generally referred to as (a) stock stripping; (b) bond washing (c) dividend and stripping.[76]

(a) Stock stripping

This is a device whereby on a sale of assets, the Revenue is deprived of its tax. This was of considerable importance before April 1, 1972 when under the Finance (Miscellaneous Taxation Provisions) Decree 1972 gains from a disposal of stocks and shares, became chargeable to tax. Before then, such gains were not chargeable and so where the assets of a company had appreciated, the company could, instead of selling the assets, sell the shares. Since the gains therefrom would attract no tax unless the company was not dealing in shares or was chargeable to tax under section 10 of the Capital Gains Tax Decree 1967, the company would have successfully avoided paying any tax at all.

Ever since April 1, 1972 it is possible to employ this device with some advantage in the sale of stock-in-trade. Gains from a sale of stock-in-trade should normally be revenue profits taxable as income. Where, however, there is an appreciation of the stock-in-trade and, therefore, of the value of shares of the company, a sale of the shares at the enhanced value will ensure that the company gets the full benefits of the sale but pays the capital gains tax of only 10 *per cent.*

Again, where a company which does not deal in shares sells shares to another company, it will not pay any income tax on the profits of the sale and if the purchasing company is an associate of the seller, then the profit is retained in the group without any liability to income tax even if the purchasing company is a dealer in shares.

(b) Bondwashing

Where shares or stocks are sold, the sale maybe with or without dividend or interest. Where a person sells stocks or shares, income is deemed to accrue when the dividend is due. When they are sold cum-dividend, the dividend belongs to the buyer who has paid a capital sum for it whereas if sold ex-dividend it belongs to the sellers and if the buyer receives it, he holds it in trust for the seller.[77] Where a company sells shares, stocks or other securities cum-dividend or interest before the due date, it has sold the dividend or interest for a capital sum thus avoiding payment of income tax on the dividend which would normally have been chargeable under section 8(1) of the Companies Income Tax Act 1990.

(c) Dividend stripping

A company that has made substantial profits on which it has paid tax may

---

[76] Orojo, *Company Income Tax Law in Nigeria* (1979), p. 40-41. (Sweet & Maxwell)

[77] *I.R.C. v Roberts* (1927) 13 R.C. 277; *Thompson v Trust and Loan Co. of Canada* [1932] 1 K.B. 517 16 T.C. 394 (C.A.).

plough the balance back into new assets for the business. The company, if it had cash, may decide to pay dividends. If the shareholder is exempt from tax, the dividend will be worth its gross amount to him and if a person with high rate of tax purchases the shares, and dividend is then declared, he may resell the shares to the original shareholders at a lower price. The original shareholder thereby receives the difference between the sale and repurchase prices as capital profit and, in addition, gets his shares back after they have been stripped of their dividends. The other party will reclaim tax on the dividend so that against his loss on purchase and repurchase he benefited to the extent of the gross dividend.

Suppose, for example, that X Ltd. pays a company tax of 40 *per cent*. While Y Ltd. is a pioneer company in its tax free year and that X Ltd. owns securities which were shortly to make an income payment. X Ltd can then agree to sell the securities to Y Ltd. on condition that X Ltd. will repurchase after the interest or dividend has become due to Y Ltd. and that the difference between the sale and repurchase price be worth more to X Ltd. than the income. Alternatively, the buyer may be a dealer in securities who in computing his trading profits would be entitled to deduct his loss on the transaction which could be set off against the income he received from securities so as to reclaim part of the tax deducted from the income.[78] In this way, X Ltd. will make a capital profit of the difference between the sale price and the repurchase price while Y Ltd. would make a taxable profit of the gross income less such difference.

Objections and appeals

Section 51 C.I.TA. states that:

(1) If any company disputes the assessment it may apply to the Board, by notice of objection in writing, to review and revise the assessment made upon it.

(1A) An application under subsection (1) of this section shall:

(a) be made within thirty days from the date of service of the notice of assessment; and

(b) contain the ground of objection to the assessment, that is:

(i) the amount of assessment and total profits of the company for the relevant year of assessment; and

(ii) the amount of tax payable for the year, which the company claims should be stated on the notice of assessment.

(1B) If the Board is satisfied that, owing to the absence from Nigeria, the person in whose name an assessment is made is unable to make an application within the thirty days specified in subsection (1A) of this section, it shall extend the time for making the application to such time as may be reasonable in the circumstances.

---

[78] Whiteman and Wheatcroft, *op. cit.* p.691

(2) On receipt of the notice of objection referred to in subsection (1) of this section, the Board may require the company giving the notice of objection to furnish such particulars as the Board may deem necessary and to produce all books or other documents relating to the profits of the company, and may summon any person who may be able to give evidence respecting the assessment to attend for examination by an officer of the Federal Inland Revenue Services on oath or other otherwise.

(3) In the event of any company assessed, which has objected to an assessment made upon it, agreeing with the Board as to the amount at which it's liable to be assessed, the assessment shall be amended accordingly, and notice of the tax payable shall be served upon such company:

Provided that if an application for revision under this provisions of subsection (1) of this section fails to agree with the Board the amount at each the company is liable to be assessed, the Board shall give notice or refusal to amend the assessment as desired by such according to the best of its judgement, determine and give notice of its revised assessment and of the tax payable together with the notice of refusal to amend the revised assessment and, whichever requisite, any reference in this Act to an assessment or to an additional assessment shall be treated as a reference to an assessment or to an additional assessment as revised under the provision of this proviso.

Section 54 C.I.T.A. provides that:

(1) Any company which being aggrieved by an assessment made upon it, has failed to agree with the Board in the manner provided in subsection (3) of section 51 of this Act, may appeal against the assessment of the Appeal Commissioners upon giving notice in writing to the Board and to the secretary to such appeal co Commissioners within thirty days after the date of service upon such company of notice of the refusal of the Board to amend the assessment.

(2) A notice of an appeal against an assessment, to be given under subsection (1) of this section shall specify the following particulars:

(a) the official of the assessment and the year of assessment for which it was made;
(b) the amount of the tax charged by such assessment;
(c) the amount of the total profits upon which such tax as charged as appearing in the notice of assessment; as desired.
(d) The date upon which the appellant was served with notice or refusal by the Board to amend the assessment as desired.
(e) The precise grounds of appeal against the assessment but such grounds shall be limited to the grounds stated by the appellant in its notice of of objection; and
(f) An address for service of any notice, precept or other documents to be given to the appellant by the secretary to the Appeal Commissioners;

Provided that at any time, the appellant may give notice to such secretary of the Board, by delivering the same or by registered post, of a change such address but any such notice shall not be valid until delivered or received.

(3) All notices or documents to be given to the Appeal Commissioners shall be addressed to the Secretary to the Appeal Commissioners in writing at any time before the hearing of such appeal.

(4) A company may discontinue any appeal by it under this section, on giving notice to the Secretary to the Appeal Commissioners in writing at any time before the hearing of such appeal.

(5) Notwithstanding the notice of appeal against an assessment has been given by a company under this section, the Board may revise the assessment in agreement with the company, and upon notice of such assessment being given in writing by the Board to the secretary of the Commissioners at any time before the hearing of the appeal, such appeal shall be treated as being discontinued.

(6) Upon the discontinuance of any appeal under provisions of this section, the amount or revised amount of the assessment, as the case may be, shall be deemed to have agreed between the Board and the company under the provisions of subsection (3) of section 51 of this Act.

In section 57 (1) CITA and subject to section 56(2) of this Act, any company which, having appealed against an assessment made upon it to the Appeal Commissioners under section 61 of this Act, is aggrieved by the decision on such body may appeal against such decision on point of law to the Federal High Court upon giving such decision on point of law to the Federal High Court upon giving notice in writing to the secretary to the Appeal Commissioners within thirty days after the date on which such decision was given. Such notice shall set out all the grounds of law on which the decision is being challenged.

Under section 58 CITA, where no valid objection or appeal has been lodged within the time limited by section 51, 54, or 57 of this Act, as the case may be, against the assessment as regards the amount of total profits assessed thereby or where the amount of the total profits has been agreed to under subsection (3) of section 51 of this Act, or on appeal, the assessment as made, agreed to, revised or determined on appeal, as the case may be, shall be final and conclusive for all purposes of this Act as regards the amount of the tax in respect of any such final and conclusive assessment is not paid within the appropriate period or periods prescribed in this Act, the provisions thereof relating to the recovery of tax, and to any penalty under section 65 of this Act shall apply to the collection and recovery thereof subject only to the set-off of the amount of any tax repayable under any claim, made under any provision or this Act, which has been agreed to by the Board or determined on any appeal against refusal to admit any such claim:

Provided that:

(a) where an assessment has become final and conclusive any tax overpaid shall be repaid.

(b) nothing in section 51 or in Part X of this Act shall prevent the Board from making any assessment or additional assessment for any year which does not involve re-opening any issue, on the same facts, which has been determined for that year of assessment under subsection (3) of section 52 of this Act by agreement or otherwise on appeal.[79]

Collection and recovery

Section 59 C.I.T.A. provides that:

(1) Notwithstanding any other provision of this section, every company shall not later than three months from the commencement of each year of assessment pay provisional tax of an amount equal to the tax paid by such company in the immediately preceding year of assessment in one lump sum.

(2) Tax charged by any assessment which is not or has not been the object of any objection or appeal by the company shall be payable (after the deduction of any amount to be set by the purposes of collection under the provisions of this Act) or the place stated in the notice of assessment within two months after the service of such notice upon the company.

Provided that:

(a) if such period of two months expires after the 14th day of December within the year of assessment for which the tax has been charged, the aggregate tax to be set-off, and of any tax paid for that year within such period, amount to less than the tax charged, then the payment of any balance of such tax may be made not later than that day

(b) where the assessment notice is served on the company within the approved period of provisional tax, the tax shall be paid within two months after the end of the approved period, but if such period of two months expires within the 14th day of December within the year of assessment for which the tax has been charged, then the payment of any balance of such tax may be made not later than that day;

(f) the board may exercise its discretion to extend the period in which payment should be made;

(3) Subject to the provisions of subsection (3) of section 56 of this Act, collection of tax in any case where notice of an objection or appeal has been given by the company shall remain in abeyance until such objection or appeal is determined save that the company shall have paid the provisional tax as provided in subsection (1) of this section or the tax not in dispute, whichever is higher.

(4) Upon the determination of any objection or appeal, the Board shall serve upon the company a notice of the tax payable as so determined, and that tax shall be payable within one month of the date of service of such notice upon the company.

Provided that if such period of one month expires after the 14th day of December within the year of assessment for which the tax has been charged and the condition specified in the proviso (a) to subsection (2) of this section are satisfied with respect to the amount of tax charged as so determined, then any balance of the tax payable may be paid not later than that day.

---

[79] *Mobil Oil Nig. Ltd. v F.B.I.R.* (1) 1 NTC 424; *John Khawam v F.B.I.R.* (1) 1 NTC 354; *Queen v Port Harcourt Tax Authority* 1 NTC 44; *Archibong v Commissioner of Inland Revenue* 1 NTC 62; See also Abdulrazaq M.T. (1996) An Analysis of Income Tax Appeal (Appeal Commissioners) Rules in Nigeria. *Nigerian Tax Notes* September. Vol. 2 (Malthouse Press Ltd.)

(5) A company filing self assessment shall pay the tax due within two months from the date of filing the assessment in one lump sum or such number of monthly instalments (not being more than six) as may be approved by the Board:

(a) Provided further that where a request for instalments expires after the 30th day of November within the year of assessment for each the tax have been charged, the payment of any balance of such tax may be made not later than that day.

(b) Provided further that where a request for instalmental payment has been made, the request shall be accompanied with proof of payment of the first instalment to the designated bank.

(6) The provisions of subsection (1) of this section shall not apply to a company that files self-assessment for the year of assessment.

(7) Where a company is required to file a return within the time allowed under section 40A or specified under section 41 of this Act tax as computed or shown in the return when filed shall be payable within two months from the date of filing the return, and the provisions of section 65 of this Act shall apply to the collection of the tax.

(8) Notwithstanding anything to the contrary in any laws, income tax payable under section 40A, 40B and 41 of this Act shall be paid to the Board in the currency in which the income giving rise to the tax derived and paid to the company making the return.[80]

Offences and penalties

Under Section 71 C.I.TA.:

(1) Any person guilty of an offence against this Act or any person who contravenes or fails to comply with any of the provisions of this Act or of any rule made thereunder for which no other penalty is specifically provided, shall be liable on conviction to a fine of N200.00, and without prejudice to section 41(4) or (5), where such offences is the failure to furnish a statement or information or to keep records required, a further sum of N40 for each and every day during which such failures continues, and in default of payment to imprisonment for six months the liability for such further sum to commence from the day following the conviction, or from such day thereafter as the court may order.[81]

---

[80] See Abdulrazaq M.T. (1997) *Shell Petroleum Development Company v FBIR op cit.* The rules outlined in this case was a judicial response to the treatment accorded to exchange gains and losses under the normal application of the principles of income and capital gains taxes. See also John Tiley (2000) *Revenue Law* (Hart Publishing) p. 842, 846. In the same way that Nigerian Courts cannot enforce the revenue law of another country it is unconstitutional to request that Nigerian tax be paid in any other currency than Nigerian currency. See also *Government of India v Taylor* [1955] 1 All ER 292 [1955] AC 491; *A-G for Canada v William Schulze & Co* 1901 9 SLT 4; *Aluminium Industries v F.B.I.R.* 1 NTC 202

[81] *R v Charlton* [1996] STC 1418; See Abdulrazaq M.T. (1993) *Nigerian Tax Offences and Penalties* (Batay Law Publications); See also Abdulrazaq M.T. (1999) Aspects of Tax Criminality in Nigeria. *The Judicial Voice: Law and Practice Journal* (Magistrates Association of Nigeria) Vol. 2 p. 58-70.

(2) Any person who-
   (a) fails to comply with the requirements of a notice served on him under this Act; or
   (b) without sufficient cause fails to attend in answer to a notice or summons served on him under this Act or having attended fails to answer any question lawfully put to him, shall be guilty of an offence against this Act.

(3) Notwithstanding any provisions of the Criminal Procedure Act or other applicable law, a magistrate may dispense with personal attendance of the defendant if he pleads guilty in writing or so pleads by a legal practitioner.

(4) In the case of failure by a company to comply with the requirements of any notice given by the Board under the provisions of section 41 or 42 of this Act for the purpose of the tax to be charged upon the company for any year of assessment, the Board may, in lieu of the institution of proceedings under subsection (2) of this section, impose a penalty upon the company of an amount equal to the tax chargeable upon the company for the preceding year of assessment:

   Provided that:
   (a) written notice of penalty shall be served upon the company; and
   (b) any amount of such penalty remaining unpaid thirty days after service of such notice may be sued for and recovered in a court of competent jurisdiction by the Board in its official name with full costs of action from the company liable thereto as debt due to the Government of the Federation; and
   (c) a certificate signed by an officer of the Federal Inland Revenue Service duly authorized by the Board setting out the name, and address of such company, the date of service of the said notice, and the amount of the penalty remaining unpaid, shall be sufficient authority for the court to give judgement for that amount; and
   (e) the Board may remit the whole or part of such penalty, whether before or after judgement, for any reason which appears to it to be adequate.

The Act also subsequently provides for penalties for making incorrect return under Section 72, false statement and returns under section 73 and for offences by authorized and unauthorized persons under section 74.

No prosecution in respect of the above offences may be commenced except at the instance of or with the sanction of the Board. Under Section 76, the imposition of any penalty does not relieve any company form liability to payment of any tax under section 75 neither shall it affect any criminal proceedings under any other enactment.

Chapter 7

Income from settlements, trusts and estates

Under section 16 P.I.T.A., the income of an individual or of a trustee or executor from a settlement, trust or estate of deceased person, made, created or administered in Nigeria, or in the case of a settlement or trust made, created or administered in Nigeria, shall be ascertained in accordance with the provisions of the Second Schedule to this Act.

Section 27 P.I.T.A. states that:

> Notwithstanding the foregoing provisions of this part of this Act, the assessable income of a trustee, or of an executor of the estate of a deceased individual, or of a beneficiary or a trust or estate for any year of assessment shall be the income of that person as determined under the provisions of the second schedule to this Decree of the year preceding that year.

Settlements and trusts

Under paragraph 8 of the Second Schedule of P.I.T.A. "Settlement" includes any disposition, trust, covenant, agreement, arrangement or transfer of assets.

In relation to settlement on infant children the term also includes a transfer of assets.[1]

The word "settlement" is not a dominating word which colours the others and the word arrangement is not a term of art.[2] Many acts have been held to be settlements as the following cases show. The limiting factor is that a transaction can only be a settlement if it contains an element of bounty.[3]

Two cases

In *F.B.I.R.* v *Nasr,*[4] the respondent was assessed to tax on an income which

---

[1] See Abdulrazaq M.T. (1990) Tax Planning Considerations under the Special Provisions as to Settlement of Unmarried Children in the Nigerian Income Tax Management Act of 1961. *Journal of Private and Property Law* (Unilag) p. 15-23.

[2] Greene MR in *IRC v Payne* (1940) 23 TC 610 at 626. Cf. *Shop and Store Developments Ltd v IRC* [1967] 1 All ER 42, [1967] 1 AC 472 (Stamp duty); See Tiley (1981) (op. cit) p. 379.

[3] *IRC v Plummer* [1979] STC 793, [1979] 3 All ER 775; see *Moodie* v *IRC* [1993] STC 188

[4] 1 NTC 114

included rental income of a property on which trust deed of gift had been created. The trust deed, created by the respondent, vested the ownership of the property on the respondent and six other beneficiaries equally, and it was created with terms, which excluded the tax authority from taxing the rental income in the hands of the respondent only. It was however established on evidence that the respondent was in position to make use of the income of the trust property as he pleased.

The respondent contended that the assessments were excessive in so far as they included the rental income of the trust property, and that the deed of gift and its terms were valid. The appellant contended that notwithstanding the validity of the trust deed, the rental income was subject to tax in the hands of the respondent in accordance with the second schedule paragraph 1 (i) of the Income Tax Management Act, 1961 since the respondent could use the income directly or indirectly.

Another issue of £500 which arose by way of Director's fees to the respondent was also argued. The respondent contended that the fees, being income from employment, should have been taxed on current year and not preceding year basis, in accordance with Section 20(5) of the Income Tax Management Act, 1961.

It was held that (i) the onus of proving excessive assessment and how much it was excessive rested with the taxpayer. The income from the trust property was available for the use of the respondent directly or indirectly. The respondent did not therefore discharge the onus; (ii) income from employment should be taxed on current year basis in accordance with the Income Tax management Act, 1961.

In *Aboud* v *Regional Tax Board,*[5] the appellant was assessed to pay income tax in respect of certain property. The property in question was transferred by the appellant to his wife, and he brought an action seeking a declaration that he was not liable to pay income tax in respect of the property and that the assessment was null and void.

The respondent treated the transfer as an artificial or fictitious transaction under Section 15 of the Income Tax Law (Cap. 48) of Western Nigeria, and assessed the appellant to tax on an income which included rent from the property. The High Court of Western Nigeria which heard the case considered the claim on its merit and dismissed the action without considering whether it could properly entertain the declaration sought by the appellant.

The Supreme Court of Nigeria raised the matter on its own motion as a preliminary issue having regard to Section 55 of the Income Tax Law (Cap. 48) which provided for a time limit for appeals against assessment, the appellant not having exercised his statutory right of appeal.

The appellant contended that even if he could no longer maintain an appeal against the assessment, the court could give a declaratory judgment and an

[5] 1 NTC 124

authoritative interpretation of Section 15 of the Income Tax law of Western Nigeria (cap. 48).

It was held that (i) where no appeal had been lodged against an assessment within the statutory time permitted by the law, the assessment should be final and conclusive for all-purpose of the Law as regards the amount of the chargeable income; (b) The court would not give a declaratory judgment where no useful purpose would be served.

The court will however look at the transaction as a whole. In *Chinn* v *Collins*[6] trustees exercised a power of appointment in favour of a beneficiary who later assigned his contingent interest under that exercise as part of a scheme to avoid tax. It was argued that there was no element of bounty about the appointment or the subsequent transaction however the House of Lords held that the appointment and the subsequent activities made an arrangement and that the benefit accrued to the tax payer as a result of the original act of bounty by the settlor in creating the settlement; the settlor's bounty remained incomplete until the appointment was made and the trustees then conferred bounty on the beneficiary.

The term settlement is so widely defined that the more crucial question[7] is to determine what property is comprised in the settlement. In *Chamberlain* v *IRC*,[8] the settlor transferred assets to a company which he controlled and trustees acquired ordinary shares issued by the company. The trustees paid for the shares with money given them by the settlor. The settlor later gave them more money with which to buy further shares. It was held that the property comprised in the settlement was the money given by the settlor and the shares purchased with that money. The assets of the company did not constitute the settled property.

The word "settlement" for the purpose of other provisions, also includes "a transfer of assets."[9] Although this definition is sufficiently wide to include commercial transactions, the House of Lords has confirmed that the settlement provisions apply only to transactions in which there is an element of bounty.[10] Lord Wilberforce stated the position as follows:

> My Lords, it seems to me to be clear that it is not possible to read into the definition an exception in favour of commercial transactions whether with or without the epithet 'ordinary' or 'bona fide.' To do so would be legislation not interpretation: if Parliament had intended such an exception it could and must have expressed it ... my lords, it can, I think, fairly be seen that all these

---

[6] [1981] STC 1, [1981] 1 All ER 189.

[7] Per Lord Thankerton in *Chamberlain v IRC* [1943] 2 All ER 200 at 203, 25 TC 317 at 329.

[8] Supra.

[9] Para 8 Second Schedule PITA 1993

[10] *IRC v Plummer* [1980] A.C. 896 54 S.T.C. 793 (H.L.). See also *Bulmer v IRC* 41 T.C. [1967] Ch. 145; 44 T.C. 1; following *Copeman v Coleman* (1939) 22 T.C. 594 and *IRC v Leiner* (1964) 41 T.C. 589. And see *IRC v Levy* [1982] S.T.C. 442. The exercise by trustees of a power of appointment is an exercise of bounty by the settlor: *Chinn v Collins*, 54 T.C. 311; [1981] S.T.C 1 (H.L.).

> provisions, in have a common character. They are designed to bring within the net of taxation dispositions of various kinds, in favour of a settlor's spouse, or children, or of charities, cases, in popular terminology, in which a taxpayer gives away a portion of his income, or of his assets, to such persons, or for such periods, or subject to such conditions, that Parliament considers it right to continue to treat such income, or income of the assets, as still the settlor's income. These sections, in other words, though drafted in wide, and increasingly wider language, are nevertheless dealing with a limited field, one far narrower than the field of the totality of dispositions, or arrangements, or agreements, which a man may make in the course of his life. Is there any common description which can be applied to this? The courts which, inevitably, have had to face this problem, have selected the element of 'bounty' as a necessary common characteristic of all the 'settlements' which Parliament has in mind. The decisions are tentative, but all point in this direction.

The House of Lords thus rejected the contention that the definition applied to all transactions that did not have a bona fide commercial reason, including a transaction the sole reason for which was to avoid tax.

The expression "arrangement" is extremely wide. A scheme to secure a particular objective may constitute an "arrangement" from its inception even though, at its inception, the final steps have not been worked out.[11] Further, an arrangement may include a combination or series of transactions, some of which may be for consideration or of a commercial character.[12]

A court order can constitute a "settlement" and in *Yates* v *Starkey*[13] (a divorce case) it was held that an order directing the husband to make payments in trust for each of his children was settlement of which the husband was settlor. It was (the court held) immaterial that the order was not a consent order and that the husband was acting under compulsion in making the payments due under the order. Where the court orders that the payments be made directly to the child, it is Revenue practice not to treat the order as constituting a settlement. Where, however, there is a consent order and the amount ordered is excessive in relation to the legal obligations of the father to maintain his child, the Revenue may contend that there is a settlement.

Also in paragraph 8 Second Schedule P.I.T.A., "Settlor" in relation to a settlement, includes a person by whom the settlement was made or entered into directly or indirectly, and in particular (but without prejudice to the generality of the foregoing) includes a person who has provided or undertaken to provide fund s directly or indirectly for the purpose of the settlement, or has made with any other person a reciprocal arrangement for that other person to make or enter into the settlement.

---

[11] *Crossland v Hawkins* (1961) 39 T.C. 493 (C.A.).

[12] *Chinn v Collins* [1981] S.T.C. 1, per Lord Wilberforce at p.7 H.L.

[13] [1951] Ch. 465; (1981) 54 T.C. 32 T.C. 38 (C.A.).

The Act imposes severe limits on the usefulness of this device by laying down that the income of a settlement or trust shall for tax purposes "be deemed to be the income of the settlor or person creating the trust" in the following cases (under section 1 of the Second Schedule P.I.T.A.).

(a) that settlor or person retains or acquires an immediately exercisable general power of appointment over the capital assets of the settlement or trust or over the income derived there from; or

(b) that settlor or person makes use, directly or indirectly, by borrowing or otherwise, or any part of the income arising under the settlement or trust; or

(c) the settlement or trust is revocable in circumstances whereby that settlor or person, or the spouse thereof, resumes control over any part of the income or assets comprised therein:

Provided that a settlement or trust shall not be regarded as revocable solely by reason of the fact that an income or asset comprised therein may revert to that settlor or person or the spouse thereof, in the event of a beneficiary predeceasing that settlor or person, or of the happening of an uncertain event upon which the settlement or trust is limited.

Computation of income

Under paragraph 2 Second Schedule, the amount of the income (in this Schedule referred to as the "computed") of each period of twelve months ending on the thirty-first day of December in each year shall be ascertained as though the provisions of Part 1 and 11 of this Act applied thereto and:

(a) there shall be deducted:

   (i) any expenses of the trustee or executor relative to the settlement, trust or estate which is authorized by the terms of the deed of settlement or trust or of the will as the case may be;

   (ii) any annuity of fixed annual amount paid out of the income of the settlement, trust or estate in accordance with the provisions of the deed or will; and

      (a) if the income includes any gain or profit from a trade, business, profession or vocation, or a rent or premium, there shall be added or deducted, as the case may require, any sum which would have been added or deducted for the next following year of assessment under the provisions of Part IV of this Act if the income from those source had been the assessable income of an individual for that year of assessment under the provisions of section 36 of this Act.

Also under paragraph 3 of the Second Schedule of P.I.T.A. the computed income of a year of a settlement, trust or estate shall be apportioned for the assessment in the following manner:

(a) Where:
  (i) the terms of the deed of settlement or trust or of a will provided that the whole income of the settlement, trust or estate after deduction of any authorized expense or annuity of fixed amount is to be divided in specific proportions among the beneficiaries entitled thereto, from time to time, or
  (ii) by operation of law, on an intestacy, the income of an individual is to be divided in the manner referred to in sub-paragraph (a) (1) of this paragraph, the income of each beneficiary of any year from the settlement, trust or estate shall be his similarly apportioned share of the computed income;

(b) Where a trustee or executor has discretion to make any payment (other than a payment on account) to a beneficiary out of the income of a settlement, trust or estate in such amount as he sees if, from time to time, then:
  (i) the amount of the payment to a beneficiary made in the cause of a year shall be treated as income of that year which is assessable to tax in the hands of that beneficiary, and
  (ii) out of the remainder of the computed income after deducting the aggregate amount of all the payments during any year, there shall be apportioned to each beneficiary who has any specified proportional interest in the income of the settlement, trust or estate, so much thereof as is obtained by applying the proportion to that remainder:

  Provided that if the aggregate amount exceeds the computed income, the amount of each payment to be treated as income in the hands of a beneficiary under this sub-paragraph shall be reduced proportionally so that the aggregate of the amount as so reduced does not exceed the computed income;

(c) any remainder of the computed income of a settlement, trust or estate of any year after deducting all amount apportioned to beneficiaries, or treated as income in the hands of beneficiaries under the provisions of sub-paragraph (b) of this paragraph shall be apportioned to the trustee or executor for assessment in his name as trustee or executor for assessment in his name as trustee of the settlement or trust or as executor of the estate.

Assessment

Pursuant to paragraph 3 of the Second Schedule of PITA 1993 and under Paragraph 10 Part III of the Second Schedule an individual in receipt of an annuity of fixed annual amount paid out of the income of a settlement, trust or an estate shall be assessable to tax on the full amount of the annuity.

Also, under paragraph 3(c) Part 1 of the Second Schedule of PITA 1993 any remainder of the computed income of a settlement, trust or estate of any year after deducting all amount apportioned to beneficiaries, or treated as income in the hands of the beneficiaries shall be apportioned to the trustee or executor for assessment in his name as trustee of the settlement or trust or as executor of the estate.

The income arising from a settlement, trust or an estate assessable to tax under paragraph II Part III of the Second Schedule PITA is the amount of the income ascertained in the year preceding the year of assessment.

Income which has already borne tax may be reclaimed by the beneficiaries or trustees.

Deceased persons

The income arising to a deceased person are taxable under section 2(6) of PITA 1993 and payable by the executor from his estate.

In *F.B.I.R.* v *Gbolahan Benson & Ors,*[14] the plaintiff was claiming from the defendants the sum of N41, 626.56 being the arrears of income tax and penalties covering 1961/62 to 1965/66 assessment years.

The amount of the tax due for those years were based on the audited accounts presented by the auditors of the defendant and the defendant died after entering into correspondence and negotiation on terms of payment of the tax due.

On the death of the defendant, his personal representatives were substituted by order of the court. The personal representatives did not dispute the tax liability but pleaded for further opportunity to enable them to reach some settlement with the plaintiff as to the terms of payment.

It was held that the defendants having been properly substituted for the deceased defendant as his personal representatives, and having not raised any valid defence to the claim, the plaintiff was entitled to judgment. The estate of the deceased was therefore liable.

[14] 1 NTC 335

Chapter 8

International taxation

International tax is concerned with the tax system as soon as it moves beyond the purely domestic scene. It is concerned with the taxation of non-Nigerian source income accruing to residents and with Nigerian source income accruing to non-residents.[1]

International tax has developed its own criteria and when a national government examines its international tax rules it wants to achieve three things:

(1) to get a reasonable share of tax from international business
(2) to maintain horizontal equity between its people; and
(3) to encourage its own business or at least see that they are not unfairly discriminated against.[2]

The charge to tax in section 3(1) P.I.T.A. 1993 and section 8(1) C.I.T.A. 1990 catches all varieties of income "*...brought into, or received in Nigeria.*" Thus, *prima facie*, any foreign income remitted from abroad to Nigeria is taxable.

However tax is normally only charged in respect of residents although the income of an employee even though paid abroad can be assessed to Nigerian tax if the employee is resident in Nigeria for more than 183 days in any year of assessment. [3]

The profits of non-Nigerian companies are assessed to Nigerian tax to the extent to which they are attributable to any part of their operations carried on inside Nigeria.[4]

Foreign income tax

Relief is given in certain cases where income is liable both to foreign tax and Nigerian income tax. There are broadly speaking two forms of relief granted:

(i) Relief in respect of Commonwealth income tax[5]
(ii) Relief under double taxation agreements[6]

---

[1] See Tiley (2000) *Revenue Law* 4th ed. (Hart Publishing) pp.991, 992.
[2] See, generally, *Taxing Profits in a Global Economy* (OECD, Paris, 1991)
[3] *Section 10 (1) (ii) P.I.T.A..,* 1st Schedule PITA; *Potter's Case* 1 NTC 10; *Lasbrey's Case* 1 NTC 13
[4] *C.I.T.A. 1990, s.1(2); Aluminium Industries A.G. v F.B.I.R.* 1 NTC 202; *Offshore International S.A. v F.B.I.R.* 1 NTC 384
[5] *Section 33 C.I.T.A.*
[6] *Section 34 C.I.T.A.*

The first consists of relief in respect of income tax charged under the laws of commonwealth countries or the Republic of Ireland on income which is also liable to Nigerian tax. The relief is given by setting off the tax already paid in the Commonwealth country concerned against the tax due in Nigeria.

The following conditions should be noted:

(i) Relief is only available to Nigerian residents;
(ii) Relief is only given where the other country concerned has passed reciprocal legislation in respect of Nigerian income; and
(iii) Relief is limited to half the Nigerian tax rate applicable.

The second form of relief stems from agreements reached with foreign governments whereby certain classes of income are exempted altogether and foreign tax on other classes of income forms a credit against tax in Nigeria.

Determination of residence

The word "reside" is not statutorily defined, and it is clear that it has no technical or special meaning.[7] Thus, the determination of the residence of an individual in a tax case will be made in accordance with the ordinary meaning of that word. That meaning was considered by Viscount Cave L.C. in *Levene* v *I.R.C.*:[8]

> My Lords, the word, 'reside' is a familiar English word and is defined in the Oxford English Dictionaries as meaning 'to dwell permanently or for a considerable time, to have one's settled, or usual abode, to live in or at a particular place.' No doubt this definition must for present purposes be taken, subject to any modification which may result from the terms of the Income Tax Act and Schedule; but, subject to that observation, it may be accepted as an accurate indication of the meaning of the word 'reside.'

The question whether an individual is or is not resident in a particular year of assessment is a question of degree and therefore one of fact; that general principle and its necessary corollary are to be found in the judgment of Lord Buckmaster in *I.R.C.* v *Lysaght:*[9]

> The word 'reside' or 'residence' [is used] in the Income Tax Acts ... in its common sense [meaning] and it is essentially a question of fact whether a man does or does not comply with its meaning ... the matter must be a matter

[7] See per Lord Warrington of Clyffe in *Levene v I.R.C.* [1929] A.C. 217, at p. 232; 13 T.C. 486, at p. 509.
[8] *Ibid.* at p. 222 (A.C.) and at p. 505 (T.C.).
[9] [1928] A.C. 234, at p. 248; 13 T.C. 511, at p. 534. See also the judgment of Lord Warrington, *ibid*, at p. 249 (A.C.0 and at p. 536 (T.C.).

> of degree, and the determination of whether or not the degree extends so far as to make a man resident or ordinarily resident here is for the Commissioners and it is not for the Courts to say whether they would have reached the same conclusion.

The determination of an individual's residence must be made for each relevant year of assessment. However, the court may have regard to the tax payer's conduct in years both previous, and subsequent to, the year of assessment in question in considering whether the tax payer was resident in that year. Viscount Sumner enunciated that general principle in *Levene* v *I.R.C.* as follows:[10]

> It is suggested that the Commissioners misdirected themselves in point of law because they took into account, with regard to earlier years, conduct which only occurred subsequently. I agree that the taxpayer's chargeability in each year of charge constitutes a separate issue even though several years are included in one appeal, but I do not think that any error of law is committed if the facts applicable to the whole of the time are found in one continuous story. Light may be thrown on the purpose with which the first departure... took place, by looking at his proceedings in a series of subsequent years. They go to show method and system and so remove doubt which might be entertained if the years were examined in isolation from one another.

There appear to be five main factors, which if one or more is present, ought to be taken into account in deciding whether a particular individual is or is not resident in a country.

First, the period of physical presence in that country in the year under question. Secondly, whether he was or was not, resident in that country in the year of assessment previous to that under consideration. Next, the regularity or otherwise of his visits in successive years. Fourthly, the reason for those visits and finally, whether there is a place available for his domestic use during the year in question.

The rules for the determination of residence in Nigeria are contained in the First Schedule of the Personal Income Tax Act of 1993, paragraphs 1–10 which provides as follows:

1. In this schedule, unless where the context otherwise requires -
   "earned income" in relation to an individual, means income derived by him from a trade, business, profession, vocation or employment carried on or exercised by him and a pension derived by him in respect of a previous employment;
   "foreign employment" means an employment the duties of which are wholly performed outside Nigeria save during any temporary visit of the employee to Nigeria;
   "Nigerian employment" means any employment, not being a foreign employment,

[10] [1928] A.C. 217, at p. 226-227; 13 T.C. 468, at p. 501

the duties of which are wholly or partly performed in Nigeria;

"Nigerian pension" means a pension in respect of past service under, and payable by, a Government or Governments in Nigeria;

"place of residence" in relation to an individual, means a place available for his domestic use in Nigeria on a relevant day, and does not include any hotel, rest-house or other place at which he is temporarily lodging unless no more permanent place is available for his use on that day;

"Principal place of residence" in relation to an individual with two or more place or residence on a relevant day, not being both within any one territory means –

(a) in the case of an individual with no source of income other than a pension in Nigeria, that place of those place in which he usually resides;

(b) in the case of an individual who has a source of earned income other than a pension in Nigeria, that place of those places which on a relevant day is nearest to his usual place of work;

(c) in the case of an individual who has a source of unearned income in Nigeria, that place of those places in which he usually resides.

2. An individual not being a person to whom subsection (1)(b) of section 2 of this Act applies, who holds a foreign employment on the first day of January in a year of assessment, or who first becomes liable to income tax in Nigeria for that year by reason of his entering that employment during that year, shall be deemed to be resident for that year in the territory in which the principal office of his employer is situated on that day or on the day his foreign employment commences, as the case may be.

3. An individual who holds a Nigerian employment on the first day of January in a year of assessment, or who first becomes liable to income tax in Nigeria for that year by reason of his entering that employment during that year, shall be deemed to be resident for that year in the territory in which he has a place or principal place of residence on that day or, as the case may be, on the day on which he enters upon the full duties of that employment in Nigeria.

Provided that if the individual is on leave from a Nigerian employment on the first day of January in a year of assessment he shall be deemed to be resident for that year by reference to his place or principal place of residence immediately before his leaves began.

4. An employee whose remuneration is subject to income tax in Nigeria for a year of assessment, but who is not deemed to be resident in a territory for that year under the provisions of paragraph 3 of this schedule, shall be deemed to hold a foreign employment, and if he has no territory of residence for that year under the provisions of paragraph 2 of this schedule, he shall be deemed to be a person to whom subsection (1)(b) of section 2 of this Act applies.

5(1) An individual whose only source of earned income arising in Nigeria on the 1st day of January in a year of assessment was a pension, and who had a place or principal place of residence on that day shall be deemed to be resident for that year in the territory in which that place or principal place was situated on that day.

(2) An individual whose only source of earned income arising in Nigeria on the 1st day of January in a year of assessment was a pension, and who had no place of residence on that day, shall be deemed to be resident for that year -

(a) if the pension is a Nigerian pension wholly payable by Government on one territory, not being a Nigerian pension in respect to which the subsection (1) of section 2 of this Act applies, in that territory;

(b) if the pension is not a Nigerian pension, in the territory in which the principal office in Nigeria of the pension fund or other person authorizing payment of the pension is situated.

(3) An individual whose only source of earned income arising in Nigeria on the 1st day of January in a year of assessment was a Nigerian pension, and who had no place of residence on that day shall, if the pension is payable by more than one Government or if there are two or more pensions arising in different territories to the individual on that day, be subject to subsection (1)(b) of section 2 of this Act.

6. An individual (other than a corporation sole or body of individuals) who has a source of earned income in Nigeria for a year of assessment, other than an employment or a pension shall deemed to be resident for that year in the territory in which he had a place or principal place of residence on the 1st day of January in that year.

Provided that -

(a) if the source of the income is first acquired by the individual during the year of assessment, and he had no place of residence on the first day of that year, he shall be deemed to be resident for that year in the territory where he first establishes a place of residence during that year; and

(b) in any other case, the individual shall be deemed to be resident for that year in any territory from which any part or the whole of his earned income arising in Nigeria is derived, if the income is derived from more than one territory.

7. An individual (other than corporation sole or body of individuals) who has no source of earned income in Nigeria for a year of assessment but who has one or more source of unearned income in Nigeria for that year shall be deemed to be resident for that year in the territory in which he has a place or principal of residence on the 1st day of January of that year;

Provided that -

(a) if all the unearned income of the individual for that year arises in one territory, and he has no place of residence on that day, he shall be deemed to be resident for that year in that territory;

(b) if the unearned income of the individual arises for that year in more than one territory, and he has no place of residence on that day, he shall be deemed to be resident for that year in the territory from which any part of the unearned income arises.

8. (1) Where the territory of residence of an individual for a year of assessment may be determined under more than one of the preceding paragraphs of this Schedule, it shall be determined by the first numbered paragraph which is applicable to his circumstances.

(2) If, by reason of sub-paragraph (1) of this paragraph, or otherwise, a determination of residence an individual for a year of assessment falls to be revised by a tax authority, other than that of the territory in which the individual is finally determined to be resident for that year, it shall discharge any assessment by it on the income of the individual for that year.

9. A corporation sole or body of individuals other than a family or community shall be deemed to be resident for a year of assessment in the territory in which its principal office in Nigeria is situated on the 1st day of January in that year or, if it has no office in Nigeria on that day, in a territory in which any part or the whole of its income liable to tax in Nigeria for that year.

10. (1) In an objection to an assessment which is or includes, an objection to the determination of an individual's territory of residence by any tax authority, the individual shall set out all the grounds on which he relies to refute that determination, and those grounds together with the observations thereon by that tax authority shall be referred by it to the Board.

(2) Where a dispute arises as to the territory of residence of an individual for a year of assessment, either between two or more tax authorities or between a tax authority and an individual before he has been assessed to tax by that authority for that year, the facts may be referred to the Board by any tax authority which is a party to the dispute.

(3) Where a dispute arises between two or more tax authorities with respect to the territory of residence of an individual for a year of assessment and that individual has already been assessed to tax in Nigeria for that year, the fact of that dispute may be referred to the Board by any tax authority.

(4) The Secretary to the relevant tax authority shall give notice of any grounds, observations or fact referred to the relevant tax authority under the provisions of sub-paragraphs (1),(2) or (3) of this paragraph to those parties, including the individuals who are affected or likely in his opinion to be affected by a determination of residence by the relevant tax authority, and shall afford the parties a period being not less than forty days from the issue of the notice in which to reply thereto.

(5) The Secretary to the Board may, call for further information to be given by any party, including an individual, to an objection or dispute within such time as may appear to him to be reasonable, and after the expiry of that period or to the period mentioned in sub-paragraph (4) of this paragraph, whichever is the later, the Board shall proceed to determine the territory of residence of the individual for the relevant year of assessment.

(6) Written notice of a determination by the Board shall be given by its Secretary to the individual and to each tax authority affected thereby, and an assessment which has been made on that individual otherwise than in accordance with the determination of the board shall be discharged.

(7) Pending a determination by the Board, the tax authority which has referred an objection to the Board under the provisions of this paragraph shall not determine that objection unless that objection in-so-far as it concerns the territory of residence of the individual, is previously withdrawn by him in writing.

(8) A determination of the Board this paragraph shall be binding on all tax authorities and on appeal tribunal or other body established under a law of a territory for the purposes of income tax within that territory, but may be questioned by the individual in the High Court of the territory of the tax authority which has made the relevant assessment.

(9) It shall not be competent for an appellant in an appeal against an assessment, to enter a ground concerning his territory of residence which he has not disclosed on a valid objection to the relevant assessment.

(10) An appeal from a decision of a High Court in respect of the territory of residence of an individual shall lie to the Court of Appeal.

Domicile

People are domiciled where they have or are deemed by law to have their permanent home.[11] They must have a domicile, but may not have more than one. "Domicile of origin" is the domicile which the law attributes to every individual at birth. If a child is legitimate, this is the domicile of the father at the date of the child's birth; if the child is illegitimate, this is the domicile of the mother.[12]

"Domicile of Choice" is the domicile which people may acquire by leaving the country of their domicile of origin and taking up residence in another country with the intention of making their permanent home there. However, until there is both the intention to change the domicile and also the establishment of residence in the new territory, the domicile of origin remains. Mere length of stay in a country is not sufficient to establish a domicile of choice in that country. A domicile of choice is acquired by the combination of residence and intention of permanent or indefinite residence.[13] Thus, civil servants, missionaries and other persons whose domicile of origin was in one of the constituent States of Nigeria and who reside abroad for vocational or business reasons, even for the greater part of their lives, retain that domicile unless they have abandoned the intention of ultimately returning to live in the country of their domicile of origin and have formed the definite settled intention of taking up permanent residence in the particular country in which they reside.

Change of domicile

The domicile of origin continues until a domicile of choice is acquired. On the other hand, a domicile of choice is lost by departure from the country of such domicile without the intention of returning there to live; in that event, the domicile of origin revives unless and until a new domicile of choice is acquired.[14] The onus of proof of abandonment of the domicile of origin is upon those who seek to establish the acquisition of a domicile of choice, and very strong evidence is required for this purpose.[15]

---

[11] *Whisker v Hume* [1858] 7 HL Cas. 124, 160, per Lord Cranworth; See Tiley (2000) (Hart) p.1002.
[12] *Udny v Udny* [1869] LR 1 Sc. & Div. 441, 457.
[13] On nationality as a factor, see *Bheekhun v Williams* [1999] 2 FLR 229; noted by Stibbard (1999) Private Client Business 360.
[14] See *Bell v Kennedy* [1868] LR 1 Sc. & Div. 307.
[15] For example *F. and F. v IRC* [2000] STC (STD) 1.

Tax havens

A tax haven is simply a place with a favourable tax climate. Among the favourites are the Channel Islands, the Isle of Man or, with greater tax advantages, the Bahamas, the Turks and Caicos Islands, the Cayman Islands and Liechtentein. All depend on the local rules with regard to tax, trust and company law. Even Nigeria has tax advantages for foreigners. One country's tax incentive cause another country to brand it as a tax haven. Some countries need overseas earnings and may accept it in fees for financial services rather than the profits of polluting plant and machinery. If other countries tax so highly as to encourage the flight of fiscal refugees they have to take the consequences.

Foreign revenue laws

In *Government of India* v *Taylor,*[16] the House of Lords held that the UK courts would decline to exercise jurisdiction to entertain a suit for the enforcement of the revenue law of another country, whether by direct or indirect means.[17] A foreign judgment for a sum payable in respect of taxes cannot be registered in any Nigerian Court.[18] Following the same approach it has been held that such a judgment is not a civil matter.[19] Where a foreign government had successfully sued in its own courts for tax due to it and recovered the tax but not the costs, it was not able to sue for the costs.[20]

What is a revenue law is a matter for the *lex fori.* It has extended to compulsory contributions to a state insurance scheme since a compulsory contribution levied by a state organization is a revenue matter.[21] A payment for services supplied by the state would, however, seem to fall outside this definition, at least where there is some choice over whether to accept the services.

In the *Taylor* case the UK House of Lords also held that the foreign tax liability was not an allowable liability under the company's legislation. The matter arises where X is insolvent in one state, owing tax there, but has assets in another state. The legislation, as interpreted by the courts in other countries,

---

[16] [1955] AC 491, [1955] 1 All ER 292; noted in 3 *ICLQ* 161, 465; 4 ICLQ 564, See, generally, Carter [1989] CLJ 417; Smart, *Cross-Border Insolvencies* (2nd ed., Butterworths, 1998), 197-211; Baker [1993] BTR 313; and Baker, in *Tolley's International Tax Planning* (4th ed.). ch. 33; See Tiley (2000) pp1013-1016.

[17] [1955] AC 491, 510; on indirect enforcement, see Smart (1986) 35 *ICLQ* 706.

[18] See Tiley (2000) *op cit.* p.1015.

[19] See *QRS* 1 *Aps and others v Fransden* [1999] STC 616.

[20] A.-G. for *Canada v William Schulze & Co.* (1901) 9 SLT 4.

[21] *Metal Industries (Salvage) Ltd. v ST Harle (Owners)* 1962 SLT 114 (employer's contribution); issues which have been held not to be revenue matters include exchange control (*Kahler v Midland Bank Ltd.* [1950] AC 24, [1949] 2 All ER 621) and a legal aid contribution (*Conor v Connor* [1974] 1 NZLR 632).

allows the trustee in bankruptcy or the receiver to get at the assets in the other country; however, it should be noted that none of these cases concerns the situation in which the only creditor is the tax authority.[22a] UK case-law establishes that an assignee acting as nominee for a foreign tax gathering authority may obtain the assistance of the English court in gathering evidence, but may not sue in England or otherwise recover assets in England.[22b]

The now lapsed European Convention on Insolvency Proceedings, Article 39 would have abolished the common law approach and allowed the enforcement of a claim by a foreign Revenue authority.[23] In one common law jurisdiction, a judge has declined to apply the basic principle in bankruptcy proceedings.[24]

The principle probably originates in a dictum of Lord Mansfield in 1775[25] where, upholding a vendor's claim for the purchase money due on goods sold in France and which the purchaser intended, to the vendor's knowledge, to smuggle into England, he said that "no country ever takes notice of the revenue laws of another." The proper law of the contract being French, English law was irrelevant.

An attempt to enforce a foreign revenue law indirectly was made in the Irish case of *Peter Buchanan Ltd. and Macharg* v *McVey.*[26] The taxpayer, a director of a Scottish company, had disposed of his shares in two other companies and, after full disclosure to the UK Inland Revenue, was assured that the deal did not involve excess profits levy. Subsequently, the levy was retrospectively applied to the taxpayer. He therefore arranged to transfer his stock of whisky and his private assets to safe hands in Ireland, followed his wealth to Ireland and thought that "he might safely snap his hands in the face of the disgruntled Scottish Revenue". The liquidator of Peter Buchanan Ltd., a man chosen by the Revenue because of his potentialities as a financial Sherlock Holmes, then sued in the Irish courts on the ground that the stripping of the company's assets was *ultra vires* the company and a breach of his duty as director. The action was dismissed on the ground that it was in substance an indirect attempt to enforce the revenue laws of another country. At first instance, Kingsmill Moore J. placed some weight on the fact that the Inland Revenue was the only unpaid creditor, but this point was not touched on by the Supreme Court of Eire.

[22a] See Smart, above at n. 16, 197-211; see also Baker, in *Tolley's International Tax Planning*, above at n. 16, 33.4; and note JFAJ [1991] *BTR* 109 on an unsatisfactory case from Florida.

[22b] Smart, above at n. 16, 200 – 201, referring to *Re State of Norway's Application* [1990] 1 AC 723, [1989] 1 All ER 745, HL; and the curious case of Re Tucker [1990] 1 Ch 148, CA, on which Smart refers to Fidler 5 *Journal of International Banking and Finance Law* 19.

[23] Smart, above at n. 16, 209 – and perfect, p.v.

[24] Forsyth J. in the Alberta case of *Re Sefel Geophysical Ltd.* [1989] 1 wwr 251, 260.

[25] *Holman v Johnson* (1775) 1 Cowp 341.

[26] [1954] IR 89.

Transfer pricing methods

The issue of transfer pricing has become highly topical,[27] not least because of extreme US legislative reaction to small-scale problem. The problem arises in various contexts. In connection with the sale of goods the problems generally concern the method by which the goods are priced. In some situations there will be an actual market in which identical goods are dealt in at arm's length. Where this is not so another method must be sought. A figure may give a profit similar to that of the other companies in the same sector (the CUP, or comparable[28] uncontrolled price), or the yield on the capital involved may be employed. CUP, though attractive, requires great attention to detail in order to ensure that true comparability exists; comparability should exist in the market conditions (i.e. the levels of demand), the market level (i.e. wholesale or retail), the goods being compared, the volumes of goods ordered (a large order attracts a discount) and the contract terms (i.e. whether there are warranties, whether delivery cif, or fob, etc.).

However, both these methods make a series of assumptions which may be misplaced and the more usual methods are either cost plus or resale price, the latter being more correctly described as price minus. Cost plus involves taking the cost production and adding an appropriate percentage. This involves many problems in determining cost and the appropriate mark-up.[29] It may, however, be useful where semi-finished goods are sold or when the subsidiary is, in essence, a subcontractor. It may also be useful for services. The resale price method begins with the price at which the goods are sold on to an independent purchaser and then reduces that price by a percentage to reflect the vendor's cost's expenses and a reasonable profit.[30] Here, problems arise over the appropriate mark-up, save where the goods are sold on very quickly with little risk to the person reselling and without having been subjected to any intermediate process.

Problems also arise in connection with royalty and trademark licence payments,[31] with the allocation of research and development,[32] head office and other central administration costs.[33] There are also many problems in connection with banking enterprises.[34] However, one of the principal current problems is the

[27] See generally *Hamaekers, Rivista di Diritto Tributorario Internazionale* 3/1999 and the *International Transfer Pricing Journal* published by IBFD Amsterdam.

[28] Comparability must extend to may things – e.g. market conditions (comparable levels of demand), the market level (i.e. wholesale or retail), comparable goods, comparable volume (a large order attracts a discount) and contract terms (i.e. are there warranties, is delivery cif, or fob, etc.?)

[29] See *Transfer Pricing and Multinational Enterprises* (OECD, 1979), 63-69.

[30] Ibid., 56-62

[31] Ibid., ch. III

[32] Ibid., 102-104.

[33] Ibid..*Transfer Pricing and Multinational Enterprises: Three Taxation Issues* (OECD, 1984), 73-91.

[34] Ibid., 45-70.

effect of a loan by one company to another within the same group but usually, although not necessarily, in different jurisdictions. This is known as the thin capitalization problem.

Double taxation relief

The practice of countries taxing all income arising in the state, no matter to whom it belongs, and all income of residents, no matter where it arises, must necessarily involve the double taxation of foreign income: once in the country where the income arises and again in the country where the person entitled to such income resides. To mitigate this effect, a number of reliefs have been evolved.[35] An example of this is the Double Taxation Relief (Between The Federal Republic of Nigeria And The United Kingdom of Great Britain and Northern Ireland) Order under section 34 (i) of CITA with a commencement date of 5th July, 1988 which provides that:

> Whereas it is provided by section 34(1) of the Companies Income Tax Act, section 30(1) of the Income Tax Management Act and section 56(1) of the Petroleum Profit Tax Act that if the Minister of Finance by order declares that arrangements specified in the order have been made with the Government of any country outside Nigeria with a view to affording relief from double taxation in relation to taxes imposed under the provisions of the Companies Income Tax Act, the Income Tax Management Act 1961 and the Petroleum Profit Tax Act, and any tax of a similar character imposed by the laws of that country and that it is expedient that those arrangements were made among other things for the avoidance of double taxation:
>
> Now, therefore, the following order is hereby made:
>
> 1. It is hereby declared-
>   (a) that the arrangements specified in the agreement set out in the Schedule to this order shall apply between the Government of the Federal Republic of Nigeria and the Government of United Kingdom of Great Britain and Northern Ireland and those arrangements have been made with a view to affording relief from double taxation in relation to Income Tax, Corporation Tax, Petroleum Revenue Tax or Capital Gains Tax and taxes of a similar character imposed by the laws of the United Kingdom of Great Britain and Northern Ireland and the Federal Republic of Nigeria;
>   (b) that those arrangements include provisions with respect exchange of information necessary for carrying out the domestic laws of Nigeria and the laws of the United Kingdom concerning taxes covered by the arrangements including, in particular, provisions about the prevention of fiscal evasion with respect those taxes; and
>   (c) that is expedient that those arrangements should have effect.

[35] Eason: *Cases and Materials on Revenue Law* (1990) (Sweet & Maxwell) p.315.

Many double taxation conventions have been entered into between Nigeria and foreign government providing relief from double taxation. Each convention is different but broadly speaking the relief may take one of two forms:

(a) Certain classes of income are made taxable only in one of the countries concerned such as where the taxpayer resides.

(b) Other income is taxable in both countries but in the case of Nigerian residents the foreign tax is allowed as a credit against Nigerian taxes. Where the taxpayer is resident in both countries the relief in (a) is usually not available.

Interpretation of treaties

The correct approach to the interpretation of a treaty is controversial.[36] There are several distinct issues – thus, should treaties be interpreted in the same way as domestic tax legislation, and what materials should the court look at when interpreting a treaty? Some would like the courts simply to resolve the immediate dispute in a pragmatic fashion; others would like the courts of all countries to develop a supranational interpretation, if necessary with a supranational court.[37]

What is clear is that interpretation issues can be complex. A treaty regulates the interaction of two tax systems which are complex in themselves and the answer has to make sense in terms of the tax systems involved. There is no reason why a term should be interpreted in the same way in each system. The OECD reports on financial instruments and on software showed how divergent these views could be.[38] Even ıf the system can agree on how a particular receipt should be classified for treaty purposes, there will still be more fundamental characterization problems such as whether income can be attributed to this person or to someone else, how anti-abuse doctrines should apply or how the entity receiving the income should be classified (as a partnership or a company) as well as issues as to the source of the income or the problem of quantifying branch income.[39]

The Vienna Convention on the Law of Treaties 1969[40] requires that a treaty

---

[36] See generally, Avery Jones [1984] *BTR* 14 and 90, and the long list cited by Sandler And Li, in (1997) 45 Can. Tax Jo. 893, 898. For an interesting Australian example, see *Lamesa Holdings Ltd. BV v FCT* [1997] FCA 785, see also [1999] FCA 612, dealing with the capital gains article in the Australia-Netherlands Double Tax Treaty and whether the term "real property" could extend to shares in a company owning real property.

[37] On history of such ideas see Edwardes Ker, *Tax Treaty Interpretation* (In-Depth Publishing); and Avery Jones in *Essays for Professor Vogel* (forthcoming)

[38] *Issues in International Taxation* No. 4 (Software) (1992); and *Taxation of New Financial Instruments* (1994).

[39] See Avery et al. [1996] *BTR* 212.

[40] The leading work on the Treaty is Sinclair, *The Vienna Convention of the Law of Treaties* (Manchester University Press, 2nd ed., 168)

be interpreted in good faith in accordance with the ordinary meaning to be given to the terms of the treaty in their context and in the light of their object and purpose.[41] It then defines "context" as including any associated agreements and instruments and goes on to permit reference to subsequent agreements and practices between the parties directed to interpretation and to *travaux preparatoires.* Where the treaty is authenticated in two languages each is of equal weight unless the agreement states otherwise.[42] The English courts have authorized reference to *travaux preparatoire* and to the commentaries to the OECD Treaty.[43] *Trauvaux preparatoires* may extend to an interpretative document prepared by state A which is part of the negotiating process or which is shown to the representatives of state B before the treaty is promulgated.[44]

Authorizing reference to the commentaries is a long way from being bound by them.[45] However, the question arises whether the court should look at such materials to resolve an ambiguity or more permissively whether or not there is an ambiguity.[46] The Vienna Convention suggests the less permissive approach is likely; US practice prefers the more permissive approach, but then the United States has not ratified the Vienna Convention. It is not clear how the OECD Model Treaty can be fitted in with the words of the Vienna Convention.[47]

Nigerian tax treaties are not necessarily to be interpreted as though they have been drafted in Lincoln's inn.[48] However, it does not follow that a purposive approach is to be preferred to a textual one, and it should be noted that the Vienna Convention prefers a textual approach.[49] Moreover, the OECD commentaries do not claim too much for themselves[50] and are all too often self-serving.[51] The actual results reached are consistent with the traditional approach of strict interpretation. Looking at the result reached in *Commerzbank,* one commentator concluded that while the article was meant to mean something else, there was no admissible evidence to contradict the plain words interpretation, which all goes to show that it is what one says, rather than what

---

[41] Article 31.

[42] Article 31-33.

[43] *Sun Life Assurance Co. of Canada v Pearson* [1986] *STC 335, CA. In The Queen v Cown Forest Industries Ltd.* [1995] 2 CTC 64, (1995) 95 DTC 5389 the Canadian Supreme Court gave the OECD Model Treaty (and commentaries) high persuasive authority; for critical discussion, see Ward et al. (1996) 44 Can. *Tax Jo.* 408; but see also Vincent (1996) 44 Can. *Tax Jo.* 38.

[44] See Arnold, Edgar, Li and Sandler, *Material on Canadian Income Tax* (Carsell, 11th ed., 1996) at 207.

[45] However, for an example of UK tax law expressly incorporating OECD principles, see the new transfer pricing rules in TA 1988, Sch. 28AA, para.2.

[46] The Canadian Supreme Court took the more permissive approach in the *Crown Forest case* [1995] 2 CTC 64, 77.

[47] Arnold *et al.*

[48] Peter Gibson L.J. in *Memec v IRC* [1998] STC 754, 766; approving Mummery J. in *IRC v Commerzbank* [1990] STC 285, 297-8, (1990) 63 TC 218, 235-6.

[49] See Smith (1996) 49 *The Tax Lawyer* 845.

[50] See Avery Jones (1999) 53 *Tax Law Review* 1, 19.

[51] Sandler and Li (1997) 45 Can. *Tax Jo.* 893.

one means, that matters.[52]

One the broader question of the role of public international law Edwardes Ker concludes, depressingly:[53]

> Unfortunately even those judges who have recently focused on the applicability of the [Vienna] Convention have done little more than just cite it. Just as unfortunately some of those judges who have focused on principles of public international law have applied them with an insensitivity as inappropriate as their colleagues' lack of focus.

Treaty shopping

This practice[54] consists in a resident of a state, which is not a party to the treaty, establishing an entity within a state which is party to the treaty in order to take advantages of its provisions.[55] An OECD report concluded that the practice is consistent with treaty law but should be countered by express provisions in the treaties themselves or by the extension of over-hasty provisions of wide ambit.[56] The United States, by contrast, has been active in seeking to limit the benefits of its treaties to persons genuinely resident in the other state.[57]

---

[52] JFAJ [1990] *BTR* 388, 392.

[53] *Tax Treaty Interpretation*

[54] For an early survey, see Becker and Wurm (ed.). *Treaty Shopping* (Kluwer, 1988).

[55] Baker, *Double Taxation Agreements and International Tax Law* (Sweet & Maxwell, 1991), 52; see also Edwardes Ker, above at n. 37, chs 57-60.

[56] Brihhyon (1994) *FT World Tax Report 2.*

[57] US – Netherlands Double Tax Treaty, Art 26; on which, see Troup [1993] BTR 97; and, on compatibility with EC law, see Hinnekens (1995) 4 *EC Tax Review* 282, and Jimenez (1996) 5 *EC Tax Review 76.*

Chapter 9

Capital gains tax

Outline

Nigeria introduced a capital gains tax by the Capital Gains Tax Decree 1967 (No. 44) re-enacted in Cap 42 of the Laws of the Federation of Nigeria 1990 which catches non-exempted gains as from April 1, 1967 (s.1). The tax is administered by the Federal Board of Inland Revenue (s. 43(1)) and appeals lie through similar channels to those applicable to income tax appeals (s. 43(2)). The Capital Gains Tax Act applies as regards taxation of any company throughout the Federation. It may be remarked that many of the provisions of the Act are drafted in similar or identical terms to parallel provisions in the United Kingdom.[1]

Reasons for taxing capital gains

The main reason for taxing capital gains is that capital gains, whether or not realized, are just as much relevant to ability to pay as income liable to income tax and therefore should be taxed on grounds of equity, both vertical and horizontal.[2] Indeed for economists,[3] capital gains are just as much income as profits of a trade or a salary. Thus, an increase in wealth due to the sale of shares in a company, the increase being due to the retention and reinvestment of profits

---

[1] P.G. Willoughby & Brian W. Harvey (1969) *A Guide to Income Tax and Capital Gains Tax* (Sweet & Maxwell) Ch.10; See also Tiley (2000) Revenue Law, pp. 599-600 (Hart)

[2] The majority report of the UK Royal Commission of 1955 was against capital gains taxation – see Royal Commission on the Taxation of Profits and Income, *Final Report*, Cmnd 9474 (1955), 94-108. Their views are dissected and rejected in the Minority Report. The case for CGT is also considered (enthusiastically) in Krever and Brooks, *A Capital Gains Tax for New Zealand* (Institute of Policy Studies, Wellington, 1990), where a valuable bibliography is buried in the footnotes. A CGT was advocated for New Zealand in a consultative document issued in 1989, but not implemented. For a wide-ranging survey of US literature, see the "Report of a Colloquium on Capital Gains" 48 *Tax Law Review* 315. Among older sources, see David, *Alternative Approaches to Capital Gains Taxation* (Brookings, 1968); Report of the Royal Commission on Taxation (Ottawa, 1996) (Carter Report), Vol. 3, 325-87; Seltzer, *The Nature and Tax Treatment of Capital Gains and Losses* (New York, National Bureau of Economic Research, 1951)); Simons, *Personal Income Taxation*, Ch.7; Ilerisic, *The Taxation of Capital Gains* (1962); Australian Taxation Review Committee Preliminary Report, Ch.9; Australian Tax Forum, Vol.1, Issues No 2; Blum (1957) 35 *Taxes* 247; and Kaldor, *An Expenditure Tax* (Unwin; 1955), 54-87.

[3] For example Simons, above; Miller (1950) 59 *Yale Law Jo.* 837, 1057; and Sandford, *Taxing Personal Wealth* (George Allen & Unwin, 1971), ch. 7.

by the company, is hard to distinguish from an increase due to the receipt of a dividend. Nor, to theoreticians, is there any need for a realization; there is an increase in share value is due to the market deciding to capitalize an expected increase in company income. The development of new financial instruments has made this simple truth even clearer. If capital gains were taxed as income this would avoid the problems of distinguishing between income and capital reciepts[4] and reduce the erosion of the tax base through taking income benefits in capital form. However while everyone (or nearly everyone) in the world or theory agrees with such an approach, no tax system taxes capital gains in this way.[5] Some countries, tax on a realization basis and may even tax some accrued gains whether or not they have been realized. However, many systems, which tax-realized gains do, not do so on the same basis as income and many tax gains only partially. There seems to be an atavistic impulse which prevents the full taxation of gains; this leads to a lack of principle, with gaps in the tax base and inconsistent changes in legislation.[6] Whether that impulse is soundly based, and whether capital gains should, in the jargon, enjoy some "preference", is still unresolved.[7] Some regard the whole idea of a CGT as flawed.[8]

The nature of Capital Gains Tax is still unsettled. On the one hand, one has highly detailed legislation often interpreted by the English judges in a cautious, even mechanistic, way. On the other hand, one has decisions such as *Ramsay and Furniss* v *Dawson* where senior judges say that capital gains tax must live in "the real world". One may also cite *Marren* v *Ingles*[9] where the court adopted an imaginative construction of the legislation in defeating a technical argument on behalf of the taxpayer. As a further example of this second view, we find Lord Wilberforce in *Aberdeen Construction Group* v *IRC*[10] attempting to express the nature of capital gains tax by saying that any interpretation of the statutory provisions must have a "guiding principle", that the purpose of the legislation is to tax capital gains and make allowance for capital losses "each of which ought to be arrived at on normal business principles". In so far as this statement is intended to mean that a court should hesitate before accepting results which are paradoxical and contrary to business sense (as Lord Wilberforce also said) the statement is welcome but it has to be said that courts have always heeded this advice.

---

[4] See especially Break, (1952) 7 *Journal of Finance* 214.

[5] For the position in OECD countries in 1990, see *Taxing Profts in a Global Economy* (OCED, 1991) Table 3.4 (corporate gains) and Table 3.21 (investors in shares); and Messere, pp. 312-22.

[6] See Evans and Sandford [1999] BTR 387.

[7] See Cunningham and Schenk "Tax Law Review Symposium" 48 *Tax Law Review* 319, and comments by Halperin (p.381) and Shaviro (p.393).

[8] For a vigorous denunciation of the tax, see *A Discredited Tax: The CGT Problem and its Solution* (IEA, 1992); see also Ipaye (2002) CITN Nigerian Tax Guide & Statutes, ch. 6; see further Ola C.S. (1989), Suggested Obituary of the Capital Gains Tax in Nigeria, 2 *Gravitas Review of Business and Property Law*, No 5, pp. 81 *et seq*.

[9] [1980] STC 500. HL.; See *Simon's Tiley & Collison U.K. Tax Guide (2000-01) Ch. 14 (Tolley)*

[10] [1978] STC 127 at 131c.

Although Lord Wilberforce was anxious to establish that capital gains tax was not simply a tax on arithmetical differences, it is that simple approach which emerges from a literal examination of the statutory framework and which has often been adopted by the courts. Indeed, courts have frequently ignored any concept of a commercial gain in interpreting the legislation. So in *Bentley* v *Pike*,[11] dealing with the acquisition of a foreign asset, the court held that CGT is levied on the difference between disposal proceeds and the acquisition cost, each expressed in sterling at the relevant time and without regard to the question whether there was or was not a gain in terms of the foreign currency involved. This not to say that the decision is wrong – simply that there is a gap between the result in the case and the concept of commercial gain. Similarly in *Smith* v *Schofield*,[12] the court analysed the words of the statute without reference to the commercial measure of a gain in a time of inflation, even though Lord Jauncey in his judgment said: "I would be surprised if Parliament had intended such a result." At least, the amount of the arithmetic difference is often very different from what would be measured as a gain for commercial accounting.

What is a gain?

The scheme of the capital gain tax legislation is that for there to be a charge to tax there must be a "disposal" but the sum on which tax is charged is merely an arithmetic difference. There is little role for accountancy practice in identifying what is a "disposal"; this is largely a matter of the application of legal principles. Accountancy practice sometimes has a role in measuring the sum on which tax is charged. This sum is between that which is determined under the Act as constituting "consideration", after deduction of certain sums authorized by statute, and a sum that is specified in statute as "acquisition cost" (which is sometimes actual expenditure and sometimes market value, being treated as if it were expenditure). Indeed, from the beginning of the history of capital gains tax, the formulation has been of a charge that is independent of any concept extrinsic to the Capital Gains Tax Acts. As early as 1966, a Swedish commentator said of capital gains tax:

> Never was ...a more self-evident center of interest for tax experts around the world. I leave it to the audience to say whether the role of guinea pigs for the tax paying world is an enviable one or not.[13]

---

[11] [1981]STC 360.
[12] [1993] STC 268.
[13] Professor Leif Muten, [1966] BTR 136 at 146.

Basic elements of capital gains tax

For a liability to capital gains tax to arise:
1. there must be a disposal of a type relevant to CGT
2. of an asset of a type relevant to CGT
3. by a person chargeable to the tax;
4. on which a chargeable gain which is computed under the Act arises.

The scheme of the legislation is to distinguish a gain from a chargeable gain.[14] It is only the latter that is subjected to tax. The legislation does not specify how a gain should be computed. Rather, it specifies what costs can be deducted from the consideration.[15]

Rate of tax

The rate of tax is ten *per cent* (s. 2(1)) CGTA.

Chargeable gains and chargeable assets

The tax catches gain made on disposal of assets on or after April 1, 1967. Chargeable assets are all assets not specifically exempted and whether or not within Nigeria (though section 4 exempts disposals of non-Nigerian assets by non-resident individuals or companies or disposals of assets of "non-resident" trusts). Specifically made chargeable assets are: (section 3 C.G.T.A.)
(a) options, debts and incorporeal property generally;
(b) any currency other than Nigerian currency; and
(c) any form of property created by the person disposing of it, or otherwise coming to be owned without being acquired;

Assets

The meaning of assets was considered by the House of Lords in *O'Brien* v *Benson's Hosiery (Holdings)Ltd.*[16] It was held that the series of rights of rights of an employer under a service agreement was an asset for CGT so that a sum received to secure the release of the employee was derived from that asset and so liable to CGT. The fact that the rights could not be assigned by the employer

---

[14] Tiley & Collison (2002 – 01) *op cit* p.587.
[15] Ibid.
[16] [1979] STC 735, [1980] AC 562, [1979] 3 All ER 652, BUT CF. *Cleveleys Investment Trust Co v IRC* [1975] STC 457 (rights acquired by guarantor against debtor company on discharge of debt to third party not assets for CGT); See Tiley & Collison (2000-01) *op cit.* pp. 607, 608.

was irrelevant. It was sufficient that they could be "turned to account." This may indicate a wide view of the concept; however the right was, like the others already mentioned, legally enforceable in some way or other. It is probably the case that an unenforceable in some way or other. It is probably the case that an unenforceable promise is not an asset for the purpose of the CGT legislation. Support for this view is given in *A-G* v *Murray*[17] where proceeds of an insurance policy were held not to be part of the deceased's estate for the purpose of estate duty and the insurance policy was void. However, the attitude of the court has, in more recent years, been characterized by the maxim "where there is fruit there must be a tree." *Emmet on Title* suggests that a claim is not an asset until it is proved to be well founded. It is, however, the frequent experience of practitioners that a commercial payment is made to dispose of the nuisance value of a claim, even where it is thought that the claim would not succeed before the court. It has been argued in court proceedings[18] that such a claim, however unfounded, constitutes an asset. The view taken is that the receipt of money by the claimant is sufficient evidence of his having a right, even though that right may not have been recognized by the court.

Exemptions and gains

These are contained in sections 27 to 42 CGTA 1990.

(A) **Exempted bodies**
Assets disposed of by the following bodies do not give rise to a chargeable gain on the disposal (ss.27-28):

1. ecclesiastical, charitable or educational institutions of a public nature;
2. friendly societies;
3. co-operative societies;
4. trade unions;
5. local government councils
6. statutory companies established for certain public purposes (s.28(2))

Exemption may be lost in respect of gains arising from trading activities or not applied purely for the purposes of the Institution.

(B) **Exempted gains**
(1) Gains arising from disposal of investments of approved superannuation funds or statutory provident funs or retirement benefits schemes (s. 29).
(2) Gains arising from the disposal of decorations for gallantry acquired

---

[17] [1904] 1 KB 165.
[18] See, for example, Revenue submissions in the case stated in *O'Brien v Benson's Hosiery (Holdings) Ltd* [1978] STC 725, HL.

otherwise than for consideration in money or money's worth (s. 30).

(3) Gains accruing from a disposal "of stocks and shares or other Nigerian government securities" including treasury bonds, savings certificate and premium bonds (s. 31) (s.44 Finance (Miscellaneous Taxation Provisions) Decree No 3 of 1993)

(4) Gains accruing from the disposal of business assets if the proceeds are re-invested bona fide in other assets used for the purposes of the trade (s. 32). The exemption is lost proportionately as the proceeds of sale are not so re-invested and is lost entirely if such re-investment does not take place or is not unconditionally agreed within twelve months of the disposal (ss. (2) – (3). Section 32 specifies as assets to which the exemption may apply as (a) trade buildings and land if not owned by land developers, (b) fixed plant or machinery, (c) ships, (d) aircraft (e) goodwill (subs. (6)).

(5) Gains accruing from the disposal of, or of an interest in, life assurance policies or deferred annuity contracts other than disposal by purchasers of such policies from the original beneficial owner for value (s. 33).

(6) Gains arising from the disposal of rights under other policies of insurance (i.e., not life policies) except those effected in the course of a capital redemption business (which is, broadly, where the insured pays a capital sum under a policy not of life or industrial assurance in return for a future sum or sums) (s. 34)

(7) Sums obtained by way of damages for personal injuries and other torts, or by way of compensation for loss of office except where such compensation "exceeds ₦10, 000 in any year of assessment."

(8) Gains accruing to individuals attributable to the disposal of a principal private residence and land occupied and enjoyed therewith (s. 36). The exemption is not lost if the dwelling house has been the individual's only or main residence throughout the period of ownership except the last twelve months (s. 36(2)), but it will be lost if it can be shown that the house, or as regards any gain attributable to expenditure thereon, such expenditure, was acquired or incurred or incurred for the purpose of realizing a gain from the disposal (s. 36(4)).

Where a person disposes of a dwelling house only part of which is used as such, for example, if one room were used exclusively for business purposes, the consideration is apportioned and the exemption lost on the proportion of gain attributable to the disposal of the non-residential part (s. 36(5)). Where an individual owns more than one residence for any period he may, by giving notice to the Board within two years of the beginning of the period, elect which one shall enjoy the exemption. Otherwise the Board itself will determine the matter. (s,36(3)[19]

(9) Gains arising on the disposal of tangible movable property (excluding

[19] *Makins v Elson* [1977] 1 All E.R. 572; *Batey v Wakefield* [1980] STC 572; *Varty v Lynes* [1976] 3 All E.R. 447.

currency) at a price in a year of assessment not exceeding N1, 000 are exempted (s.37(1). If the consideration exceeds N1, 000 the capital gains tax chargeable is not to exceed half the difference between that consideration and N1, 000 (s.37(2)).

If two or more assets forming part of a set of articles (e.g. a set of valuable gold ornaments) are disposed of in parts by the owner to the same recipient (or persons connected within the meaning of section 24 of the decree) whether or not on the same occasion, the disposals are treated as a single transaction (s. 37(3)). This sub-section also states that its provisions "apply where the assets, or some of the assets, are disposed of on different occasion on the first of April, 1966, but not so as to make any gain accruing on that date a chargeable gain."

(10) Gains arising from the disposal of motor-cars are exempted unless of a type not commonly used as private vehicle and is unsuitable to be so used, e.g. a motor-car with dual controls used for tuition purposes by driving school.[20]

(11) Property disposed of by way of gift is exempted from the charge, whatever its value (s. 39). The recipient is normally deemed to have acquired the asset at the price paid by the donor or the market value at the time of the donor's acquisition if the consideration, though present, is unascertainable (s. 7(2)).

Gains chargeable

Section 6 provides that subject to the exceptions provided by the Act there is a disposal of assets by a person where any capital sum is derived from a sale, lease, transfer, assignment, a compulsory acquisition or any other disposition of assets, notwithstanding that no asset is acquired by the person paying the particular sum. Particular examples given in this section include:

(1) capital sums derived by way of compensation for loss of office
(2) capital sums received for forfeiture, surrender or non-exercise of rights,
(3) capital sums received as consideration for use or exploitation of any asset.
(4) In addition to these is specified the case "where any capital sum is received under a policy of insurance and the risk of any kind of damage or injury to, or the loss or depreciation of, assets."

It should be added that though section 6 makes chargeable sums derived from (*inter alia*) compulsory acquisitions, by section 9 such sums are exempted if the person acquiring the land did not know of the likelihood of the authority's acquiring it and had taken no steps to dispose of the land to the authority or others. An "authority" here means an authority having compulsory powers under the Land Use Act or similar legislation.

---

[20] See *Bourne (Inspector of Taxes) v Auto School of Motoring (Norwich) Ltd.*, [1964] T.R. 341.

Death

By section 8(1), on the death of an individual any assets of which he was competent to dispose are deemed to be disposed of him at the date of his death and acquired by the personal representatives for a consideration equal to –

(a) where the asset was last disposed of at ascertainable and full consideration, that amount, and
(b) in any other case the market value of the asset at that date.

Section 8(2) makes the matter quite clear by stating that gains accruing in consequence of section 8(1) are exempted form tax.

Legatees (including all beneficiaries of wills, *donationes mortis causa*[21] and under intestacies) are treated as if their acquisition of the asset had been the personal representatives' acquisition, and no chargeable gains accrues to the personal representatives (s.8(4)).

Disposal

The central concept of disposal is not defined,[22] but nor has it yet caused much reported litigation. It has been suggested that any form of transfer or alienation of the beneficial title to an asset (whether legal or equitable) from one person to another involves a disposal by the one and an acquisition by the other.[23] A disposal by a trustee of shares in the course of administration is clearly a disposal on this definition since beneficial title passes to the purchaser and the fact that the disposal on this definition since beneficial title passes to the purchaser and the fact that the disposer is not himself beneficially entitled is quite irrelevant. A disclaimer does not constitute a disposal.[24]

An exchange of assets is a disposal of each asset involved. An example is the surrender of a lease in exchange for a new one; in order to avoid CGT it is common to grant the new lease subject to the existing lease and perhaps increasing the rent under the existing lease.[25] However, where the new lease and the old lease are identical in the sense of relating to the same property and having the same terms, the Revenue by concession will not treat the surrender as

---

[21] *W.T. Ramsey Ltd v IRC* [1981] STC 174, [1981] 1 All ER 865, particularly so far as it approves dicta of Eveleigh LJ in *Floor v Davies* [1978] 2 All ER 1079.

[22] See *Turner v Follet* [1973] STC 148, 48 tc 614, where the CA made extremely heavy weather of the point if the definition in the text is right. A loan is not a disposal but a loan must be distinguished from a gift, see *Dewar* v *Dewar* [1975] 2 All ER 728. on switching between different unit trusts in a multi-portfolio see CITN *Nigerian Tax Guide* (2002).

[23] The original UK Revenue definition was "An asset is disposed of whenever its ownership changes or whenever the owner divests himself of his rights in or interest over that asset, for example, by sale, exchange or gift".

[24] See *Re Paradise Motor Co Ltd.* [1968] 2 All ER 625.

[25] On problems see *Bayley v Rogers* [1980] STC 544.

involving any disposal.[26]

There is no general exclusion for involuntary disposals.[27] The concept of disposal is extended to certain deemed disposals and by treating certain shifts of economic value as disposals even though no asset is disposed of. In deciding what is the subject matter of a disposal undertaken in steps as party of a scheme, it is permissible to look at the effect of the whole scheme.[28]

Disposals may be made either to realize a gain or to realize a loss.

Hire purchase

Where a person acquires an asset under a contract of hire purchase, the transaction is treated as if it amounted to an entire disposal of the asset to that person at the beginning.[29] If the period terminates, but the property in the asset does not pass to him, all necessary adjustments are made. The implication appears to be that the disposal and acquisition deemed to have occurred at the outset are then treated as not having taken place, so that the hirer is not treated as disposing of the asset when his interest terminates. However, he may be treated as having disposed of his rights under the contract, depending upon the circumstances.

The legislation does not say how the disposal consideration is to be valued. However, the Revenue in hire purchase cases should divide the total of the rent and purchase price into capital and interest elements, and tax only the latter as income. If this is followed, the capital element will be the purchase price rather than the sum payable under the option. In practice the asset will probably either be a car (as in *Lyon* v *Pettiggrew*[30] where the vehicle was a taxi but a chargeable gain arose in respect of consideration paid for the licence).

Disposal without acquisition

There may be a disposal of assets by their owner even though no asset is acquired by anyone else, for example, if the owner of the asset receives a capital sum, which is derived from the asset.[31] This rule is stated to apply "in particular" to four types of capital sum. It follows that these four are not exhaustive of the

---

[26] See Tiley & Collison (2000-01) p.623.

[27] But note (bankruptcy not a disposal but acts of trustee treated as acts of bankrupt) and (compulsory purchase-disposal).

[28] *W.T. Ramsay Ltd v IRC* [1981] STC 174, [1981] 1 A ER 865, particularly so far as it approves dicta of Eveleigh LJ in *Floor v Davies* [1978] STC 436, [1978] 2 All ER 1079.

[29] ibid.

[30] [1985] STC 369.

[31] Tiley & Collison (2000-01) p.624.

general principle and may have effect whether or not the general principle applies.[32] However, the rule does require that the asset should have been owned by the person treated as disposing of them. A mere hope expectation cannot be owned, and so cannot be an asset.

On sale of shares for a cash sum plus the right to receive a further sum to be computed by reference to future, unpredictable events, the right to receive the future sum is itself an asset.[33] Such a right is not a debt. When the events occur and the further sum is paid that sum is derived from the right to receive the sum and so there is a disposal of that asset. This is so whether or not the person paying the capital sum acquires any asset.[34]

Where a person received a capital sum in settlement of an action for negligence against solicitors in relation to a conveyancing matter concerning particular properties, it was held that the charge to CGT stemmed from the right to sue and not to be from properties concerned and thus was not a part disposal of those properties.[35] A sum received for entering into a restrictive covenant, in connection with the sale of shares in subsidiary companies, has been held not to be as such a capital sum derived from an asset.[36] However, on appeal, it was held that the sum in question was received in part for agreeing not to exploit the goodwill attaching to the group.[37]

Compensation for the release of an option to participate in a development has been held taxable under this head.[38] The fact that another provision[39] states that the abandonment of an option is not the disposal of an asset was irrelevant.

Forfeiture or surrender of rights

Capital sums received by a person in return for forfeiture or surrender of rights e.g. the surrender of a lease, or for refraining from exercising rights, are taxable. Thus a sum received for the release of a restrictive covenant or for an agreement not to sue on a contract would be chargeable events. It has been said that it is not

---

[32] *Davenport v Chilver* [1983] STC 426.

[33] *Marren v Ingles* [1980] STC 500, [1980] 3 All ER 95.

[34] Reversing *IRC v Montgomery* [1975] STC 182 at 189. As to "earn-out" sales where the deferred consideration takes the form of shares; *Lang v Rice* [1977] STC 172 where a sum paid as compensation for loss of trading profit was held to be an income receipt; *Davies v Powell* [1977] STC 32, [1977] 1 All ER 471; *Drummond v Austin Brown* [1984] STC 321; this distinguished at 325 a sum paid by a landlord in return for the surrender of the "fag end" of a lease. It is also important that the Landlord was entitled to possession. Quaere whether the sum was trading receipt; *Davenport v Chilver* [1983] STC 426, although in this case liability was virtually escaped because the new right was deemed to have been acquired for market value.

[35] *Zim Properties Ltd v Procter* [1985] STC 90.

[36] *Kirby v Thorn EMI Plc* [1986] STC 423; affid. [1987] STC 468, CA.

[37] [1987] STC 621.

[38] *Powlson v Welbeck Securities Ltd* [1986] STC 423; affd. [1987] STC 468, CA.

[39] Tiley & Collison (2000 – 01) *op cit* pp.624, 625.

possible to use the CGTA to widen the scope of the term "assets."[40] So, according to this view, no charge arises when a sum is received for the surrender of something which is not an asset; for example, the right to play amateur rugby, as in *Jarrold* v *Boustead*.[41] Nor does a charge arise when the asset surrendered is an exempt asset; e.g. a life interest under a settlement, or a debt. However, uncertainty has been revived as a result of the decision of Nourse J in *Davenport* v *Chilver*.[42] Following this view, it is enough to show that a sum has been derived from the forfeiture or surrender of a right and it follows that the term "right" must be defined by reference to things which can be surrendered, forfeited or not exercised, but again the failure of the draftsman to be precise causes difficulty. Thus the right to play amateur rugby is such a right and so, on this basis, the sums paid in *Jarrold* v *Boustead* could be taxable as a capital gain and, since the acquisition cost was presumably nil, the whole sum appears to be chargeable. However, the freedom to engage in business has been held not to be an asset.[43]

Date of acquisition or disposal

For the purpose of the Act, the date of any acquisition or disposal of an asset is the date of the contract to do so (s.11). Where any contract is to be performed subject to any condition under s. 11(a), the date of acquisition or disposal of asset shall be deemed to be the date when the condition is satisfied, but where a consideration of such a contract does not depend solely or mainly on the value of the asset at the time the condition is satisfied, the acquisition or disposal shall be treated as if the contract had never been conditional, in which case the date of the acquisition or disposal of asset shall be the date of the contract.

Also s.11(b) provides that where an option is conferred by virtue of any contract, the date of the acquisition or disposal of asset shall be the date when the option is exercised.

Is there a disposal under the contract?

The general rule applies only when the disposal takes place under the contract; whether this is so is a question of fact. The question can be particularly difficult if a contract is later varied and the question arises whether the disposal is under

---

[40] *O'Brien v Benson's Hosiery (Holdings) Ltd* [1978] 3 All ER 1057, [1978] STC 549, CA.
[41] (1964) 41 TC 701.
[42] [1983] STC 426.
[43] *Kirby V Thorn Emi Plc* [1986] STC 200. This judgment was overturned on appeal, [1987] STC 621, but the Court of Appeal affirmed that freedom to engage in business is not an asset for CGT purposes.

the original contract as varied or under a new contract. In *Magnavox Electronics Co Ltd* v *Hall*[44] X made a contract to sell the property to A in 1978; A later defaulted and a new purchaser, B, was found who was willing to buy but at a lower price. In July 1979 X acquired a company, S; S took an assignment of the contractual rights from A. X and A then varied the original contract so as to reflect the new lower price agreed with B; S made a separate contract to sell the property to B.

The English Court of Appeal held that these arrangements did not enable X to argue that the disposal took place under the 1978 contract – and also in 1978. The agreement between X and S did not vary the 1978 contract since A was not a party to it. The Court invoked *Furniss* v *Dawson*[45] to disregard the interposition of S.

One should note also the discussion of the phrase "in pursuance of" in *IRC* v *Mobil North Sea Ltd.*[46]

However, if the disposal is under the contract it will be treated as made when the contract is made even though the contract itself is unenforceable – *Thompson* v *Salah.*[47]

Conditional contract

If the contract is conditional then the disposal occurs when the condition is satisfied; condition here means something on which the existence of the contract depends rather than a major contractual term.

This will usually be a condition precedent. In *Pym* v *Campbell,*[48] a sale of a patent was subject to the invention being approved by a third party; the third party did not approve and so the purchaser was not liable for refusing to complete the purchase. Another example would be an agreement to grant lease of land subject to the grant of outline planning permission for the construction of a building on the land; this would be conditional until planning permission was obtained.

As is clear from *Pym* v *Campbell,* a contract which is subject to a condition precedent to its formation is not strictly a conditional contract since there can be no contract at all until the condition is satisfied.

The phraseology cannot apply to a condition subsequent. Hence, it is considered that a contract with a condition subsequent would give rise to a disposal only when it is clear that the condition cannot occur.

---

[44] [1986] STC 561, CA.
[45] [1984] STC 153, HL.
[46] [1987] STC 458.
[47] (1972) 47 TC 559.
[48] (1856) 46 TC 699, CA.

The fact that a contract to dispose of an asset is expressed to be subject to performance by the transferee of obligations imposed on him by the contract (promissory conditions precedent to performance) does not make the contract a conditional contract. Thus an agreement to grant a lease of land subject to the construction of a building on the land by the intending lessee was held to be unconditional in *Eastham* v *Leigh London & Provincial Properties Ltd.*[49] Similarly, a condition under which the contract terminates on the failure by one of the parties to perform his obligations under the contract (a promissory condition subsequent) would not make the contract a conditional contract.

Disposals under a consent order

Normally the terms of a consent order made by agreement between the parties to court proceedings derived their force and effect form the parties' agreement and so take effect when the agreement is made.[50]

In matrimonial proceedings, however, the terms embodied in the order derive their effect from the order itself and not from the agreement.[51] In *Aspden* v *Hildesley,*[52] the agreed terms were embodied in an order made before decree absolute. This was not a full consent order, but an order that the agreed terms be filed "and made a rule of court." Nevertheless it was argued that the terms had effect only by virtue of the order and that, as the order was made before decree absolute, it was conditional upon the decree *nisi* being made absolute in due course so that the disposal made under the terms in the order was not effectively provided for the immediate transfer of the taxpayer's interest in the property and that agreement could not have set aside if the decree had not been made absolute, it followed that, in these particular circumstances, the disposal was not conditional on decree absolute.

Is a contract a disposal?

The rule just stated deals with the timing of the disposal when an asset is transferred under a contract and does not answer the question whether the contract itself is the disposal. This question is or has been of importance for three reasons:

1. First, the rule applies only when the asset is conveyed or transferred and so does not expressly deal with the contract which is not completed. Where a

---

[49] (1971) 46 TC 699, CA.
[50] Tiley & Collison (2000-01) p.628.
[51] *De Lasala v De Lasala* [1979] 2 All ER 1146, PC.
[52] [1982] STC 206.

deposit is forfeited the forfeiture is not treated as the disposal of an asset,[53] a matter which presumably turns on whether equity could order specific performance of the contract. If, however, the specifically enforceable contract is itself the disposal then the Revenue may be able to ignore the subsequent ending of the contract and so charge CGT both on the original part disposal and the subsequent ending of the equitable interest. This, however, is unlikely.

2. Second, there is the problem of when the tax is due. Thus if in 2001 A made a contract to sell with completion in 2004, are the Revenue entitled to demand payment of the CGT in 2000? If the contract itself is not the disposal then presumably the Revenue may argue that they are entitled to treat the 2000 transaction as a part disposal and then when the contract is completed in 2004 relate the completion back to 2000. This, however, is only partly sound. The postponed completion date does not render the contract conditional so the postponement means that equity could not order specific performance so that there can be no part disposal in 2000; the forfeited deposit will be taxed neither on forfeiture nor on the grant of the option. If, however, the contract is itself the disposal then the Revenue can insist that there is a chargeable disposal in 2000 and so demand the tax. Generally it will be the Revenue insisting on the always be so, e.g. there might be a loss on the transaction which can therefore be rolled forward from 2000 but not back from 2004.
3. Third, there is the obsolete point that the rule is not retroactive.[54]

In view of the practical difficulties raised it seems preferable to reject the notion that the contract is itself a disposal whether or not the contract is specifically enforceable. It follows that when property is disposed of under an unconditional contract of sale, the disposition takes place under the contract and that when the contract is not followed by a disposal it is not open to anyone to treat the contract itself as a part disposal.[55]

Time of disposal when loss or destruction

Where an asset is deemed to be disposed of by reason of its entire loss or destruction, the time of the deemed disposal is the time at which the loss or destruction occurs.[56] Where the owner of the asset later receives compensation for the loss, the date of receipt is the time of disposal.[57] These statements may be reconciled by treating the right to receive compensation as a separate asset arising at the time of the loss, or at the time the claim is proved, so that the

---

[53] Tiley & Collison (2001 – 01) p.628.
[54] *Johnson v Edwards* [1981] STC 660.
[55] Cf. Forfeiture of a deposit.
[56] Tiley & Collison (200 – 01) p.628.
[57] Tiley & Collison (2000 – 02)p.629.

receipt of compensation is the disposal of that right, not the disposal of the original asset.

Computation of the capital gain

The effect of sections 12 to 16 CGTA is to base the computation of any gain on the difference between the net consideration accruing to a person on the disposal of an asset and the sum of the total consideration and expenses paid for acquiring the asset.

Any part of the disposal proceeds chargeable to income tax is excluded from the consideration (s.13) and expenditure incurred in acquiring the asset, enhancing its value, defending title to and disposing of the asset must be wholly, exclusively and necessarily incurred (s.14) and not chargeable as a deduction from profits for income tax purposes (s.15). Examples of allowable expenditure for capital gains purposes are fees for professional services or surveyors, valuers, auctioneers, accountants, agents or legal advisers, and legal conveyancing costs including stamp duties (s. 14(2)).

Incidental costs of acquisition

Incidental costs must have been incurred by the person making the disposal, wholly and exclusively for the purposes of the acquisition. This includes the costs of establishing title. Such costs are expressly limited to fees, commission or remuneration paid for the professional services of any surveyor or valuer, or auctioneer, or accountant or agent or legal adviser and the costs or transfer or conveyance (including stamp duty) together with the costs of advertising to find a seller.[58] Fees for the services on acquisition must be distinguished from the fees payable for investment advice, which are not allowable.

Other costs, such as expenses of travel to inspect property with a view to purchase, are not allowable, even if the property is in fact acquired.

Improvement expenditure

Expenditure wholly and exclusively incurred on the asset by the person making he disposal or on his behalf is allowable if it is for the purpose of enhancing the value of the asset.[59] Such expenditure must be reflected in the state or nature of

---

[58] Tiley & Collison *op cit.* CGTA 1990 S.14(2)

[59] In *Emmerson v Computer Time International Ltd* the company owed rent to its landlord. The landlord agreed to consent to an assignment of the lease on condition that the rent arrears were

the asset at the time of the disposal. If the expenditure is so reflected, no matter in how small way, it is allowable in full.

It also appears that the expenditure must make an identifiable change in the state or nature of the asset. In *Aberdeen Construction Group Ltd* v *IRC*,[60] there was expenditure on a waiver but there was a deduction for this expenditure as it did not make an identifiable change in the shares which were sold. It follows that a payment to a valuer to determine the authenticity of a painting or other work of art is not deductible - whatever his verdict. This rule also excludes an advance payment to a builder who goes bankrupt before beginning the work. When the disposal is by contract followed by conveyance it is unclear how far, if at all, the improvements must be reflected in the state or nature of the asset at the time of the conveyance.[61]

A payment may be required in order to make a disposal, but this does not, of itself, permit a deduction for this payment unless the payment makes a change to the asset, or its value. In *Emmerson* v *Computer Time International Ltd*,[62] rent was owed to landlord. The landlord agreed to consent to an assignment of the lease on condition that the rent arrears were paid. The rent arrears were not deductible in the CGT computation.

Initial repairs to let property that are. not allowable are treated as improvement expenditure allowable in computing a capital gain.[63]

Preservation of title

A further category of allowable expenditure includes the costs wholly and exclusively and necessarily incurred by the owner or on his behalf, in establishing, preserving or defending his title to, or to a right over, the asset.[64] This category must be distinguished from acquisition costs and operates narrowly. First, the word "establishing" is limited by the words "preserving" and "defending." In a case involving a settlement, a beneficiary secured the agreement of the trustees to vest the trust funds in her absolutely.[65] She was, however, required to take out a single premium policy on her life, written in favour of the trustees, to indemnify them against her predeceasing another beneficiary having a contingent interest. It was held that the payment of the premium was not to establish the beneficiary's defeasible interest in the fund, since that was not in dispute, but to acquire something greater namely the

---

paid. The Court of Appeal held that the payments of the arrears were not deductible under this rule; [1977] STC 170, 50 TC 628, [1877] 2 All ER 545.

[60] [1977] STC 302, Ct of ssess; the point was not raised in the House of Lords

[61] *Chaney v Watkis* [1986] STC 89.

[62] [1977] STC 170.

[63] *Tiley & Collison op cit*

[64] CGTA 1990, s. 14(1)(c).

[65] *Allison v Murray* [1975] STC 524, [1975] 3 All ER 561.

absolute interest. Hence, the costs could only be deducted if they came within the category of acquisition costs.[66]

The main obstacle in the way of claiming allowable expenditure under this heading is the exclusion of expenditure, which would be deductible as a revenue expense if the asset were a fixed asset in a trade, and the income tax rule that money spent on defending title to a capital asset is a revenue expense. For example, a sum paid by a liquidator in respect of arrears or rent, even if it had been spent in preserving the asset (a leasehold interest) would not have been deductible.[67] However, the incidental costs of valuing shares and securities for estate duty purposes has been held to be allowable for CGT under this category, on the grounds that the main purpose is to obtain probate of the will, which establishes the title of the executors to the assets.[69] The Revenue allows such expenses in practice on the basis of a fixed scale according to the value of the estate.

If the sum would have been deductible as a trading receipt, e.g. *Morgan v Tate & Lyle*[70] it is not allowable as a CGT deduction.

Apportionment of expenditure

The categories of allowable expenditure all require that the costs be incurred "wholly exclusively and necessarily" for acquisition, etc., although in practice this phrase is not interpreted as restrictively as for income tax. Expenditure incurred on valuing stocks and shares both for the probate and for estate duty has been held to be allowable notwithstanding the apparent dual purpose.[71] This may, however, simply be because the estate duty payment was incidental to the main purpose of obtaining probate. It is clear that where the main purpose is allowable, expenditure is deductible in full even though there is some subsidiary or incidental purpose which is not allowable. Conversely no sum is deductible at all if the allowable purpose is purely incidental.[72] This leaves open the question whether an apportionment can be made where there are two main purposes only one of which is allowable.[73]

Where a tax payer carried out a scheme designed to avoid CGT, the expenses of the scheme were deductible, even though it could be argued that one of the

---

[66] The expense did not come within the first category since it was not consideration for the acquisition of absolute title but to acquire the other beneficiary's contingent interest.

[67] *Emmerson v Computer Time International Ltd* [1976] STC 111, [1976] 2 All ER 131.

[69] *IRC v Richards Executors* [1971] 1 All ER 785, 46 TC 626; but see also *Passant v Jackson* [1986] STC 164.

[70] (1955) AC 21.

[71] *IRC v Richards' Executors* [1971] 1 All ER 785, 46 TC 626.

[72] *Cleveleys Investment Trust v IRC* [1975] STC 457.

[73] The point was not directly faced in *IRC v Richards' Executors* but compare Lord Reid, at 790, 635 with Lord Guest, at 798, 644.

purposes of the expenditure was to avoid tax.[74]

Where a sum has been spent on two or more assets the expenditure must be apportioned.[75] The issue in such cases is the correct construction of the agreement; once the parties have paid one part of the consideration for one asset and another part for another, they cannot subsequently seek to reallocate that consideration for tax purposes.

Where, under an agreement, a sum was paid for shares, the vendor was in addition to be entitled to a sum in respect of a debt due to it.[76] That sum was much the shares as reduced by the amount of the shortfall.

Market value

Where a person acquires an asset otherwise than by way of a bargain made at arm's length or the consideration given cannot be valued, market value at the time of the transaction is deemed to be the consideration for purposes of both acquisition and disposal (s.7(1)). Market value is the estimated sale price on open market assuming, if necessary, that the whole of the assets is placed on the market simultaneously (s.22).

Consideration

Any receipt is potentially liable to be treated as consideration. In *Stanton v Dryton Commercial Investment Co Ltd,*[77] the House of Lords considered an agreement whereby investments were to be purchased from an insurance company for a consideration that consisted in the taxpayer company issuing 2,461,226 ordinary shares at 160p per share. The agreement was conditional on permission being obtained for the shares to be dealt with on the Stock Exchange. Agreement was subsequently obtained and, hence, on 11th October, 1972, the agreement became unconditional. The following day, the shares were first quoted on the Stock Exchange at the price of 125p per share. The case concerned a subsequent sale of the investment acquired and an appeal against the issue by the Revenue of an assessment computed on the basis that the shares in Dryton Commercial Investment Co Ltd should be valued at 125p each. The company contended that the shares should be valued at 160p each, being the issue price noted in the agreement. The House of Lords upheld the taxpayer's computation on the basis that this was what was shown in an arm's length

---

[74] *Eilbeck v Rawling* [1980]STC 192, [1980] 2 All ER 12 not affected by [1981] STC 174, [1981] 1 All ER 865, HL.

[75] TCGA 1992, s. 52(4) (CGTA 1990, s. 20).

[76] *E V Booth (Holdings) Ltd v Buckwell* [1980] STC 578, distinguishing *Aberdeen Construction Group Ltd v IRC* [1978] STC 127, [1978] 1 All ER 962, HL.

[77] [1982] STC 585.

agreement and there was no reason for going behind this agreed value. It was accepted the market value was lower, but it was held that this was only relevant when no agreed value was available.

Where there is a complex arrangement for the disposal, such as frequently arises on commercial deals when companies are sold or reorganized, the approach to be adopted was given by Lightman J in *Spectros International Plc* v *Madden*[78] as:

> The critical issue is to identify the consideration agreed and allocated to the disposal of the shares…I must approach the question before me as a matter of construction of the composite of the three documents… I must identify and give effect to the form of transaction which the parties have entered into and which they have sought to do; and in this process I must have regard first and foremost to the terms and language of the composite documents read as a whole in their proper context, but I am also to take account business sense and reality and most particularly the value of the shares."

Where the consideration includes an asset (e.g. a right) that will be valued at the date of the first disposal. The value of the disposal consideration will then become the acquisition cost of the asset e.g. *Marren v Ingles.*[79]

The value of any consideration must be taken as at the date of disposal; hindsight is not permitted. In *Fielder v Vedlynn Ltd.,*[80] the court considered a sale by Vedlynn Ltd. of eight subsidiary companies to a third party. The subsidiary companies had incurred capital losses, which had not at that stage been agreed with the Revenue. The sale agreement provided that Vedlynn Ltd. received £19,529, but that the purchaser provided a guarantee to procure that each of the eight subsidiaries should pay Vedlynn Ltd. in addition a sum equal to 7.5% of the losses finally agreed. Two years later, the losses were agreed at £19.5m and the sums due under the payment were paid. The Revenue assessed Vedlynn Ltd. for the accounting period covering the date of the original sale on the basis that the sum subsequently paid constituted a sale consideration. The Special Commissioner upheld Vedlynn Ltd.'s appeal that the consideration was the sum of £19,529 actually received and the guarantees under which the further consideration was received were the date of the sale of no additional value.

Part disposals

Where only part of an asset is disposed of or where the transferor retains any interest therein, there is for the purposes of the Act a part disposal. According to s. 6.(2) there is a part disposal of assets:

---

[78] [1997] STC 114 at 138b.
[79] [1980] STC 500
[80] [1992] STC 553

(i) where an interest or right in or over the assets is carried by the disposal, as well as where it subsists before the disposal, and
(ii) where, on a person making a disposal, any description of property derived from the assets remains undisposed of.

The gain is then computed by apportioning the cost of acquisition according to the following formula. Where the consideration for the disposal is A and the market value of the property undisposed of is B, the fraction of the cost price allowable as a deduction is:

$$\frac{A}{A+B}$$

And the reminder of the cost price is attributable to the undisposed portion (s.17)

Thus, there is a part disposal when either: (a) there is a disposal of a physical part of an asset or (b) rights are created out of an asset. An example of (b) is the granting of a lease by the freeholder.

The definition immediately raises the question as to what is the asset. "An asset" is not defined in statute. The courts have been willing to locate an asset in many situations. The very breadth of what is encompassed in "an asset" makes it difficult to determine whether a disposal is a disposal of an entire asset or a part disposal of a larger asset.

"The general view[81] is that unless it appears from the facts at the time of acquisition that more than one asset (given its natural meaning) was acquired, a single acquisition of land (with or without buildings) whether obtained by purchase under one contract at an inclusive price or by gift or inheritance as a whole, should be regarded as a single asset (even though it comprises distinguishable elements such as a house and garden, farmhouses, buildings, woodlands, cottages, etc).

On the other hand, in the case of acquisition by purchase, there may be contemporary evidence showing that the acquisition comprised more than one asset. For example, correspondence etc, during negotiations leading up to a purchase may show that the contract price was based upon the sum rounded up or down of a number of valuation units; the land may have been offered for sale by auction in lots: or the rent roll of an estate may show separate tenants paying substantial rents for individual properties such as farms. In such cases, it may be possible to make a satisfactory apportionment of the purchase price.

Where estate of small properties (e.g. terraced urban dwelling houses) are acquired, blocks of a size convenient to hold as investments are normally regarded as single assets, but in practice no objection is taken treating individual dwelling houses as separate assets and apportioning the cost of the larger unit on the basis of such evidence as is available. As a general rule single buildings in

[81] See Tiley & Collison, *op. cit.*; Ipaye, *op. cit.*; Ola, C.S., *op. cit.*

multiple occupation such as blocks of flats or office suites are regarded as single assets, but again no objection is normally taken to treating individual flats, etc as separate assets if it appears that similar flats etc in the same ownership or in the locality have commonly been sold singly as independent dwellings.

In *Anders Utkilens Rederi A/S* v *O/Y Lovisa Stevedoring Co A/B and Keller Bryant Transport Co Ltd*,[82] the plaintiff had obtained a judgment against the second defendant for a liquidated sum. The defendant appeal but before the appeal came on for hearing, the parties reached a compromise. Under the terms of the compromise the defendant agreed to sell its premises, plant and machinery (the property) and to divide the proceeds with the plaintiff. The defendant subsequently went into creditor's voluntary liquidation and a year later the property was sold. The plaintiff contended that this constituted a disposal of an entire asset. The court held that the defendant had irrevocably dedicated the property to the purposes of the compromise and good conscience would require the defendant to realize the property exactly as agreed with the plaintiff. Accordingly, specific performance of the terms of the compromise would have been decreed by the court. The compromise therefore imposed an immediate trust for sale, making the plaintiff and the defendant co-owners of the property. It followed therefore that the compromise effected a part disposal of the property by the defendant to the plaintiff.

An extreme case is *Berry* v *Warnett.*[83] In this case, the House of Lords considered a tax avoidance scheme. Mr. Berry was the beneficial owner of shares in Rothschild Investment Trust Ltd. In March 1972 the taxpayer executed transfers of the shares in favour of a trustee in Guernsey. On 4th April 1972 the tax payer entered into a deed expressed to be a settlement made between himself, described as "the vendor", and a Jersey company, described as "the purchaser". In this deed, Mr Berry retained for himself a life interest in the shares but sold the reversion for £14,500. He claimed this was a part disposal and a part of the acquisition costs should be put against this disposal. Lord Wilberforce said on a similar U.K. Statutory provision to the Nigerian CGTA 1990 s.6 (2)(b)(ii):

> TCGA 1992, s.21(2) is not, on its face, a relieving section: it is not a section directed at cutting down what might otherwise be a total disposal to a partial disposal. It seems rather, as paragraph (a) makes clear, to be a provision of extension, enabling something, which might not be regarded as a disposal to be taxed as a part disposal. Where there is a clear total disposal, the subsection does not attach...The whole tenor and purpose of the document of 4th April 1972 was to put the shares and stock into settlement or trust – to do so was essential in order to enable the tax payer to obtain exemption on the sale of his life interest. This was only obtainable if he could be shown to have 'an interest created by or arising under a settlement'. He cannot (though

[82] [1985] STC 301.
[83] [1982] STC 396

> bravely so contended), at one and the same time asset this, and also maintain that he retained or reserved something undisposed of. I cannot, therefore, on any view accept that here there was only a part disposal."[84]

It was to be noted that the decision in *Berry* v *Warnett* is related specifically to the action of settling in trust. It is not easy to extend this decision into transactions that do not involve settlement. It is clear that there is a distinction between, on the one hand, the following disposals which are disposals of an entire asset:

(a) transfer of an asset to a company, the consideration being satisfied by the issue of new shares in the company;
(b) a sale of business for unascertained consideration;[85]
and, on the other hand, the following which are part disposals
(c) the grant of a lease out of a freehold;
(d) the sale of shares where shares of the same category in the vendor's pool remain in his ownership;
(e) the sale of land forming part of a larger holding.

It has been suggested that a possible test is that in (a) and (b) the person making the disposal is left with an item of property which did not exist before the disposal; whereas in (c), (d) and (e) there is an asset which can be identified as being undisposed of throughout. This analysis, however, does not fit comfortably with the wording of CGTA 1990, s.6(2) (b)(ii) "any description of property derived from the asset." The wording of statute would seem to indicate that it is possible to regard some disposals as part disposals even where there is not an asset remaining in the vendor's ownership throughout the transaction. Thus, a sale of land subject to a leaseback is generally treated as a part disposal, even though there is an instant during the transaction at which the person making the disposal has no interest in the land at all.

Losses

Presumably because of the limited effect of the capital gains tax it was not thought appropriate to make provision for off-setting capital losses nor, incidentally, is there any exclusion of the proportion of any gain accruing before the date of operation of the Act and in this sense its effect can be retrospective. Section 5 excludes losses by stating:

---

[84] [1982] STC 396 at 400.
[85] *Marren v Ingles* [1980] STC 500.

> In the computation of chargeable gains under this Act the amount of any loss which accrues to a person on a disposal of any asset shall not be deductible from gains accruing to any person on a disposal of such asset.

It may be remarked that the last three words appear to destroy the sense behind what is presumably the intention of the provision, namely to disallow a loss on the disposal of one asset being offset against a gain arising on the disposal of another.

Miscellaneous provisions

The following points might be noted:

1. Where the consideration on a disposal is payable by instalments there are provisions for bringing the gain into charge proportionately over the years of assessment in which such instalments fall (s.18)
2. Where an asset is lost or destroyed and compensation money is received which is expended within three years on the purchase of a replacement asset there are provisions for (a) notionally reducing the compensation to such amount as would result in neither loss or gain, and (b) notionally reducing to the same figure the sum of the amount paid for renewal of the asset and the residual value of the old one (s. 19). The effect of (a) is to negative any charge to tax on the disposal (due to the loss) of the asset, and the effect of (b) may, by reducing the notional cost price of the replacement asset, to increase eventual liability to tax on a disposal.
3. There are various anti-avoidance provisions. For instance, where a single bargain is comprised in two or more transactions there is deemed to be a single disposal (s. 20). Section 21 authorises the Board to override artificial or fictitious transactions "so as to counteract the reduction of liability to capital gains tax." Sections 23 and 24 substitute market value for the consideration expressed if the transaction giving rise to a gain is between "connected persons" – e.g. a spouse, relative, or partner of the other party.
4. There are provisions for double taxation relief on the same lines as apply to income tax and relief in respect of delayed remittance of gains arising from disposals of assets abroad (ss.41 and 42).
5. *References in the legislation to "persons" include companies and bodies corporate (s.45(2)) which are thus normally chargeable in the same way as an individual*

Chapter 10

Tax appeals

An appeal against an assessment to corporate or personal tax may be made to the Federal[1] or State[2] Body of Tax Appeal Commissioners, whose decisions are not reported, and on a point of law only, to the Federal[3] or State High Courts.[4] Appeals from the Federal[5] or state High Courts lies to the Court of Appeal[6] and then the Supreme Court.[7]

Any taxable person aggrieved by an assessment or demand notice in respect of Value Added Tax may appeal against the assessment and notice to the Zonal VAT Tribunal where the taxable person is resident.[8] An award or judgement of the Tribunal shall be enforced as if it were a judgement of the Federal High Court.[9] Appeals from the VAT Tribunal on point of law lies directly to the court of Appeal.[10]

The Minister shall make rules regulating the practice and procedure of the VAT Tribunal and, until such rules are made, the practice and procedure of the Federal High Court shall apply with such modifications as the circumstances may require. The modification is that the VAT Tribunal may operate as if it is a High Court using the Federal High Court rules although the Minister may make rules regulating the VAT Tribunal practice and procedure in a manner radically different from those of the Federal High Court. The statutory provision does not limit the VAT Tribunals to only civil matters.

Appeals against an assessment to tax to the Federal or State High Court are limited to points of law only except in the case of personal income tax where there is no such statutory limitation.

---

[1] Part X CITA 1990; See CGTA 1990 s. 43(2); See also Part VIII PPTA 1990.
[2] Part VIII PITA 1993; See CGTA 1990 s.43(2).
[3] Section 57 CITA 1990.
[4] Section 64 CITA. This section does not limit appeals to points of law only.
[5] Section 57 (7) CITA 1990.
[6] Section 63 (12) PITA 1993.
[7] NATA 1993 Second Schedule para 9.
[8] VATA 1993 Second Schedule para 12.
[9] VATA 1993 Second Schedule para 24.
[10] Para 21 VATA Second Schedule 1993.

Fact, law and the burden of proof

(A) The distinction between fact and law

The distinction between questions of fact and of law is vital,[11] since the decision of the Commissioners as to the facts is conclusive. To this end, a distinction is often made between findings of "primary facts" and "conclusions" or "inferences," which may be findings of fact, of law, or "mixed" findings of fact and law. Since the case stated by the Commissioners should set out the primary facts as found, followed by the conclusions arrived at from those facts, the question for the court on appeal is whether, given the primary facts stated, the Commissioners were justified in law in reaching the conclusions they did reach.

In *British Launderers' Research Association* v *Borough of Hendon Rating Authority*[12] Denning L.J. (as he then was) said:

> Primary facts are facts which observed by witnesses and proved by oral testimony or facts proved by the production of thing itself, such as original documents. Their determination is essentially a question of fact for the tribunal of fact, and the only question of law that can arise on them is whether there was any evidence to support the finding. The conclusions from primary facts are, however, inferences deduced by a process of reasoning from them. If, and in so far, those conclusions can as well be drawn by layman (properly instructed on the law) as by a lawyer, they are conclusions of fact for the tribunal of fact: and the only questions of law which can arise on them are whether there was a proper direction in point of law; and whether the conclusion is one which could reasonably be drawn from the primary facts: see *Bracegirdle* v *Oxley*.[13] If, and in so far, however, as the correct conclusion to be drawn from primary facts requires, for its correctness, determination by a trained lawyer as, for instance, because it involves the interpretation of documents or because the law and the facts cannot be separated, or because the law on the point cannot properly be understood or applied except by a trained lawyer-the conclusion is a conclusion of law on which an appellate tribunal is as competent to form an opinion as the tribunal of first instance...

Also in *Griffiths* v *J.P. Harrison (Watford) Ltd*[14] Lord Denning said,

> Now the powers of the High Court on an appeal are very limited. The judge cannot reverse the commissioners on their findings of fact. He can only reverse their decision if it is "erroneous" in point of law." Now here the primary facts were all found by the commissioners. They were stated in the

---

[11] Salter & Ker (1990) *Easson: Cases & Materials on Revenue Law* (Sweet & Maxwell) pp. 30-35.
[12] CA [1949] I KB 462; [1949] 1 All ER 21.
[13] [1947] KB 349
[14] [1962] 1 All ER 909

> case. They cannot be disputed. What is disputed is their conclusion from them. And it is now settled, as well as anything can be, that their conclusion cannot be challenged unless it was unreasonable, so unreasonable that it can be dismissed as one which could not reasonably be entertained by them. It is not sufficient that the judge would himself have come to a different conclusion...

(B) *The findings of the Commissioners as to the facts are final*

The court is restricted to considering whether, on the facts found as set out in the case stated, the Commissioners have erred in law. The facts themselves are not open to challenge.

In *Levene* v *Inland Revenue Commissioners* Viscount, Sumner stated that:[15]

> In substance persons are chargeable or exempt, as the case may be, according as they are deemed by this body of Commissioners or that to be resident or the reverse, whatever resident may mean in the particular circumstances of each case. The tribunal thus provided is neither bound by the findings of other similar tribunals in other cases nor is it open to review, so long as it commits no palpable error of law, and the Legislature practically transfers to it the function of imposing taxes on individuals, since it empowers them in terms so general, that no one can be certainly advised in advance, whether he must pay or can escape payment. The way of taxpayers is hard, and the Legislature does not go out of its way to make it any easier. If it had been possible in the case to apply the principle that a taxing statute must impose a charge in clear terms or fail, since it is to be construed *contra proferrentem*, our duty would have been plain, but since the words are plain and it is only their application that is haphazard and beyond all forecast, Mr. Levene has no remedy in your Lordships' House...

(C) *Appeals from the conclusions of the Commissioners*

The position is explained in *IRC* v *Lysaght*[16] where Viscount Sumner said that:

> It is well settled that, when the Commissioners have thus ascertained the facts of the case and then have found the conclusion of fact which the facts prove, their decision is not open to review, provided (a) that they had before them evidence, from which such conclusion could properly be drawn, and (b) that they did not misdirect themselves in law in any of the forms of legal error, which amount to misdirection...

---

[15] [1928] A.C 217
[16] [1928] A.C. 234

(i) The "only reasonable conclusion"

In *Edwards* v *Bairstow and Harrison*,[17] Lord Radcliffe stated that:

> If a party to a hearing before commissioners expresses dissatisfaction with their determination as being erroneous in point of law, it is for them to state a case and in the body of it to set out the facts they have found as well as their determination. I do not think that inferences drawn other facts are incapable of being themselves findings of facts, although there is value in the distinction between primary facts and inferences drawn from them. When the case comes before the court it is its duty to examine the determination having regard to its knowledge of the relevant law. If the case contains anything *ex facie* which is bad law and which bears upon the determination, it is, obviously, erroneous in point of law. But, without any such misconception appearing *ex facie*, it may be that the facts found are such that no person acting judicially and properly instructed as to the relevant law could have come to the determination under appeal. In those circumstances, too, the court must intervene. It has no option but to assume that there has been some misconception of the law and that this has been responsible for the determination. So there, too, there has been error in point of law. I do not think that it much matters whether this state of affairs is described as one in which the evidence is inconsistent with and contradictory of the determination, or as one in which the true and only reasonable conclusion contradicts the determination. Rightly understood, each phrase propounds the same test. For my part, I prefer the last of the three, since I think that it is rather misleading to speak of there being no evidence to support a conclusion when themselves and only to take their colour from the combination of circumstances in cases such as these many of the facts are likely to be neutral in which they are found to occur…

(ii) Where the conclusions of the Commissioners are not erroneous in law and can be supported on the facts, the court may not substitute its own conclusion.

Salmon, L.J. in *Pilkington* v·*Randall*,[18] said:

> Now, as was restated by the House of Lords in *Edwards* v *Bairstow* and *Harrison*,[19] the decision of the Commissioners on any question of this sort must be accepted and cannot be overruled unless it is plain from the primary facts found that "no person acting judicially and properly instructed as to the relevant law could have come to the determination under appeal," or unless one comes to the conclusion that no reasonable person could have arrived at the same conclusion as the Commissioner. I agree that this case is very close to the borderline, and I am by no means certain that if I had been sitting as a Commissioner and had had to draw inferences of fact, I should have come to the same conclusion as the Commissioners. But it is important to guard oneself against the temptation, to which I suppose we are all prone, and

[17] [1955] 3 All E.R. 48

[18] CA (1966) 42 T.C. 662

[19] [1956] A.C. 14.

> which is happily put by Cross J., in *Lucy & Sunderland Ltd.* v *Hunt.*[20] When we think a conclusion of fact is one at which we would not have arrived ourselves, we are tempted to say that it follows that no reasonable person could have come to that conclusion. I think the facts here were evenly balanced. On the whole I think I would have come down the other way, but I cannot say that the view at which the Commissioners arrived is not a possible view for a reasonable man to take...

(D) The burden of proof

In *John Ihekwoaba* v *Commissioner of Internal Revenue,*[21] the appellant who was a member of the Eastern House of Assembly had an income which was small and ascertainable. He also had other business income as a produce dealer on which there was no information. The appellant appealed to the High Court and then to the Supreme Court but failed to prove that the assessment was excessive. The Supreme Court of Nigeria held that the onus of proving that an assessment was excessive is on the taxpayer, and the appellant had failed to discharge the onus.

(E) Tax deposit as condition precedent for appeal

In *The Queen v Port Harcourt Tax Collection Authority,*[22] the High Court of Eastern Nigeria held that the tax to be paid as condition precedent for appeal is the tax chargeable that is in dispute and so it is the difference between the tax assessed and the tax chargeable on one's income that should be deposited.

It was further held in *The Queen* v *Western Urhobo Rating Authority,*[23] that granting a stay of action on tax collection pending appeal is discretionary and that if it was found that too much tax had been paid, the amount over paid shall be refunded with interest.

(F) Appeal made out of time

The Supreme Court held in *Aboud* v *Regional Tax Board*[24] that where no appeal had been lodged against an assessment within the statutory time permitted by the law, the assessment should be final and conclusive for all purposes of the law as regards the amount of the chargeable income. It was also held in *Anosike* v *Tax Assessment Authority (Abakaliki)*[25] that where notice of appeal is made within

[20] (1961) 40 T.C. 132 at 138.
[21] 1 NTC 60
[22] 1 NTC 45
[23] 1 NTC 76
[24] 1 NTC 124
[25] 1 NTC 71

time, but to a wrong tribunal contrary to law, the effect is the same as if no notice had been made.

Appeals procedure

(A) Personal income tax

Under Section 60 PITA 1993 a taxable person being aggrieved by an assessment to income tax made upon him, having failed to agree with relevant tax authority in the manner provided in subsection (3) of section 57 of this Decree, may appeal against the assessment on giving notice as provided in section 61 of this Act within thirty days after the date of service of notice of the refusal of the relevant tax authority to amend the assessment as desired.

Section 61(1) A notice of appeal to be given under the provisions of section 60 of this Decree shall be given in writing to the relevant tax authority and shall set out–

(a) the name and address of the applicant;

(b) the official number and the date of the relevant notice of assessment;

(c) the amount of the assessable, total chargeable income and the tax charged as shown by that notice and the year of assessment concerned;

(d) the precise grounds of appeal against assessment;

(e) the address for service of any notice of other documents to be given to the application;

(f) the date on which the applicant was served with notice of refusal by the relevant tax authority to amend the assessment as desired.

(2) As soon as may be after receipt of notice of appeal, the secretary to the Appeal Commissioners, shall having regard to the grounds of appeal therein disclosed and to any relevant provisions of this Decree deliver a copy thereof to the relevant tax authority and the appeal shall thereupon be listed by the secretary for hearing accordingly.

(3) A notice or other document to be given to the Appeal Commissioners shall be addressed to the secretary and be delivered at or sent by registered post to his official address.

(4) A tax payer may discontinue an appeal by him under this section on giving notice to the secretary to the Appeal Commissioners in writing at any time before the hearing of the appeal.

(5) Notwithstanding that notice of appeal against an assessment has been given by a tax payer under this section the relevant tax authority may revise the assessment in agreement with the tax payer, and on notice of the agreement being given in writing by the relevant tax authority to the secretary to the Appeal Commissioners at any time before the hearing of the appeal, the appeal shall be treated as being discontinued.

(6) On the discontinuance of an appeal under the provisions of this section, the amount or revised amount of the assessment, as the case may be, shall be deemed to have been agreed between the tax authority and the tax payer under the provisions of subsection (3) of section 57 of this Act.

Section 62 (1) The appeal Commissioners shall, as often as may be necessary, meet to hear appeals in any town in which is situation an office of the relevant tax authority and, subject to the provisions of the next following subsection, at any such meeting –

(a) any three or more Appeal Commissioners may hear and decide an appeal; and

(b) the Appeal Commissioners present shall elect one of their number to be the chairman for the meeting.

(2) An Appeal Commissioner who has a direct or indirect financial interest in a tax payer or being a relative of a person having such an interest, and having knowledge thereof, shall, when any appeal by such tax payer is pending before the body of Appeal Commissioners, declare such interest to the other Appeal Commissioners and give notice to the relevant tax authority in writing of such interest or relationship and interest, and he shall not sit at any meeting for the hearing of that appeal.

(3) The provisions of subsection (2) of this section shall also apply where an Appeal Commissioner is a legal practitioner or an accountant, and the tax payer is or has been a client of that Appeal Commissioner.

(4) The secretary to the Appeal Commissioners shall give seven clear days notice to the relevant tax authority and to the applicant of the date and place fixed for the hearing of an appeal except in respect of an adjourned hearing for which the Appeal Commissioners have fixed a date at their previous hearing.

(5) All notices, precepts and documents, other than decisions of the Appeal Commissioners may be signified under the hand of the secretary.

(6) All appeals before the Appeal Commissioners shall be held in camera.

(7) A tax payer who appeals against an assessment shall be entitled to be represented at the hearing of the appeal:

Provided that, if the person intended by the tax payer to be its representative in an appeal is unable for good cause to attend the hearing thereof, the Appeal Commissioner may adjourn the hearing for such reasonable time as they think fit, or admit the appeal to be made by some other person or by way or written statement.

(8) The onus of proving that the assessment complained of is excessive shall be on the appellant.

(9) At the hearing of an appeal, if the representative of the relevant tax authority proves to the satisfaction of the Appeal Commissioners or the court hearing the appeal in the first instance that -

the appellant has, contrary to subsection (1) of section 41 of this Act, for the year of assessment concerned, failed to prepare and deliver to the relevant tax authority the statement mentioned in that subsection; or

the appeal is frivolous or vexatious or is an abuse of appeal process; or it is expedient to require the appellant to pay an amount as security for processing the appeal, the Appeal Commissioners or, as the case may be, the court may adjourn the hearing of the appeal to any subsequent day and order the appellant to deposit with the relevant tax authority before the day of the adjourned hearing an amount, on account of the tax charged by the assessment under appeal, equal to the tax charged on the appellant for the preceding year of assessment, or one half of the tax charged by the assessment under appeal, whichever is the lesser.

(10) If the appellant fails to comply with an order under subsection (9) of this, the assessment against which he has appealed shall be confirmed and the appellant shall have no further right of appeal whatsoever with respect to that assessment.

(11) The Appeal Commissioner may confirm, reduce, increase or annul the assessment or make such order thereon as they see fit.

(12) A decision of the Appeal Commissioners shall be recorded in writing by their Chairman and a certified copy of the decision shall be supplied to the appellant or the relevant tax authority by the secretary, on a request made within three months of the decision.

(13) Where on the hearing of an appeal -

- (a) no accounts, books or records relating to profits were produced by or on behalf of the appellant; or
- (b) those accounts, books or records were so produced but the Appeal Commissioners reject the same on the ground that it has been shown to their satisfaction that they were incomplete or unsatisfactory; or
- (c) the appellant or his representative, at the hearing of the appeal has neglected or refused to comply with a precept delivered or sent to him by the secretary to the Appeal Commissioners without showing any reasonable excuse; or
- (d) the appellant or a person employed, whether confidentially or otherwise, by the appellant or his agent (other than his legal practitioner or accountant acting for him in connection with his liability to tax) has refused to answer any question put to him by the Appeal Commissioners, without showing any reasonable cause, the chairman of the Appeal Commissions shall record particulars of the same in his written decision.

(14) The State Commissioner may make rules prescribing the procedure to be followed in the conduct of appeal before the Appeal Commissioners.

(B) Companies Income Tax

Under Section 54 CITA 1990:

(1) any company which being aggrieved by an assessment made upon it, has failed to agree with the Board in the manner provided in subsection (3) of section 51 of this Act, may appeal against the assessment of the Appeal Commissioners upon giving notice in writing to the Board and to the secretary to such Appeal Commissioners within thirty days after the date of service upon such company of notice of the refusal of the Board to amend the assessment as desired.

(2) A notice of an appeal against an assessment, to be given under subsection (1) of this section shall specify the following particulars –

- (a) the official number of the assessment and the year of assessment for which it was made;
- (b) the amount of the tax charged by such assessment;

(c) the amount of the total profits upon which such tax was charged as appearing in the notice of assessment; as desired.
(d) the date upon which the appellant was served with notice of refusal by the Board to amend the assessment as desired;
(e) the precise grounds of appeal against the assessment but such grounds shall be limited to the grounds stated by the appellant in its notice of objection; and
(f) an address for service of any notice, precepts or other documents to be given to the appellant by the secretary to the Appeal Commissioners.
Provided that at anytime, the appellant may give notice to such secretary and to the Board by delivering the same or by registered post, of a change of such address but any such notice shall not be valid until delivered or received.

(3) All notices or documents to be given to the Appeal Commissioners shall be addressed to the Secretary to the Appeal Commissioners in writing at any time before the hearing of such appeal.

(4) A company may discontinue any appeal by it under this section,, on giving notice to the Secretary to the Appeal Commissioners in writing at any time before the hearing of such appeal.

Notwithstanding the notice of appeal against an assessment has been given by a company under this section, the Board may revise the assessment in agreement with the company, and upon notice of such assessment being given in writing by the Board to the secretary of the appeal Commissioners at any time before the hearing of the appeal, such appeal shall be treated as being discontinued.

Upon the discontinuance of any appeal under the provisions of this Section, the amount or revised amount of the assessment, as the case may be, shall be deemed to have agreed between the Board and the company under the provisions of subsection (3) of section 51 of this Act.

Section 55:

(1) As often as may be necessary, the body of appeal commissioners shall meet to hear appeal in any town in which is situated an office of the Federal Inland Revenue Services (FIRS) and, subject to the provisions of the next following subsection, at any such meeting –
(a) any three or more Appeal Commissioners may hear and decide an appeal; and
(b) the chairman of the body of Appeal Commissioner shall preside and where the Chairman is absent, the Appeal Commissioners present shall select one of their number to be the Chairman for the meeting.

(2) An Appeal Commissioner having a direct or indirect financial interest in any company (including the holding of or the beneficial interest in any shares, stock or debentures issued by such company) or being a relative of any person having an interest, and having such knowledge thereof, shall when an appeal of such company is pending before the body of Appeal Commissioners declare such interest to the other commissioner and give notice to the Board in writing of such interest or relationship and interest and he shall not sit at any meeting for the hearing of the appeal, the like provisions shall apply when the Appeal Commissioner is legal practitioners or an accountant, and the company is or has been a client of that Appeal Commissioner.

(3) The Secretary to the Appeal Commissioner shall give seven clear days notice to the Board and the appellant of the date and place fixed for the hearing of each appeal except in respect of any adjourned hearing for which the Appeal Commissioners have fixed a date at their previous hearing.

(4) All notices, precepts and documents, other than the decisions of the Appeal Commissioners, may be signified under the hand of the secretary.

(5) All appeals before the Appeal Commissioners shall be held in camera.

(6) Every company so appealing shall be entitled to be represented at the hearing of the appeal.

Provided if the person intended by the company to be its representative in any appeal is unable for good cause shown to attend the hearing thereof, the Appeal Commissioners may adjourn the hearing for such reasonable time as they fit, or admit the appeal to be made by some other person or by way of written statement.

(7) The onus of proving that the assessment complained of is excessive shall be on the appellant.

(8) At the hearing of any appeal if the representative of the Board proves to the satisfaction of the Appeal Commissioners or the court hearing the appeal in the first instance that -

(a) the appellant has (contrary to subsection 1 of section 41 of this Act), for the year of assessment concerned, failed to prepare and deliver to the Board the statement mentioned in that subsection;

(b) the appeal is frivolous or vexatious or is an abuse of the appeal process; or

(c) it is expedient to require the appellant to pay an amount as security for prosecuting the appeal, the Appeal Commissioners or, as the case may be, the court may adjourn the hearing of the appeal to any subsequent date and order the appellant to deposit with the Board before the date of the adjourned hearing an amount, on account of the tax charged by the assessment under appeal, equal to the tax charged upon the appellant for the proceeding year of assessment or half the tax charged by the appellant under appeal, which ever is lesser plus a sum equal to ten per cent of the said deposit, and if the appellant fail to comply with the order, the assessment shall have no further right of appeal whatsoever with respect to the assessment.

(9) The Appeal Commissioners may confirm, reduce, increase, or annul the assessment or make such order thereon as they see fit.

(10) Every decision of the Appeal Commissioners shall be recorded in writing by the Chairman and a certified copy of such decision shall be supplied to the appellant or the Board by the Secretary, upon a request made within three months of such decision.

(11) Where, upon the hearing of an appeal –

(a) no accounts, books or records relating to the profits were produced by or on behalf or the appellant, or

(b) such accounts, books or records were so produced but Appeal Commissioners rejected the same on the ground that it had been shown to their satisfaction that they were incomplete or unsatisfactory; or

(c) the appellant or his representative, at the hearing of the appeal, has neglected or refused to comply with a precept delivered or sent to him by the secretary to the Appeal Commissioners without showing any reasonable excuse; or

(d) the appellant or any person employed, whether confidentially or otherwise, by the appellant or his agent (other than his legal practitioner or account acting for him in connection with his ability to tax) has refused to answer any question put to him by the Appeal Commissioners, without showing any reasonable cause, the Chairman of the Appeal Commissioners shall record particulars of the same in his written decision.

(12) The Minister may make rules prescribing the procedure to be followed in the conduct of appeals before the Appeal Commissioners.

(d) Value Added Tax

Under the second schedule of Value Added Tax Act of 1993:

(1) The Ministry may, by notice in the Federal Gazette, establish a Value Added Tax Tribunal in each zone of the Federal Inland Revenue Service.

(2) Each of the Zonal VAT Tribunal shall consist of not more than eight persons, none of whom shall be a serving public officer and one of whom shall be designated as Chairman by minister.

(3) The Chairman of each of the Zonal VAT Tribunal;

shall be a legal practitioner of not more than 15 years post call experiences;
shall preside over the proceedings of the Tribunal.

(4) Members of each of the Zonal VAT Tribunal-

shall be appointed by notice in the Federal Gazette by the Minister from among persons appearing to him to have wide and adequate practical experience, professional knowledge, skills and integrity in the profession of law, accountancy or taxation in Nigeria as well as persons that have shown capacity in the management of trade, business and retired senior public servant in tax administration;

shall hold office for a period of three years from the date of appointment and may resign at any time by a notice in writing addressed to the Minister;

shall cause to be a member upon the minister determining that his office be vacated upon notice of such determination.

(5) Where the Minister is satisfied that a member:

has been absent for two consecutive meeting without the written permission of the chairman of the Board; or

is incapacitated by illness; or

has failed to made any declaration to give notice of his direct or financial interest in a case when any appeal by such case is pending before the Tribunal; or

has been convicted of any felony or of any offence under any enactment imposing tax on income or profit;

The Minister shall make a determination that has his office as a member is vacant.

(6) Where for some reason there is insufficient number of members to here an appeal, the Minister may make an ad-hoc appointment in writing for the purpose of hearing such appeal.

(7) The Minister shall designate a serving public officer to be Secretary to a Zonal VAT Tribunal and the official address of the Secretary shall be published in the Federal Gazette.

(8) The members of the VAT Tribunal shall remain in office until new ones are sworn in.

(9) Any taxable person who being a person aggrieved by an assessment or demand notice made upon him, may appeal against assessment and notice to the Zonal VAT Tribunal where the taxable person is resident giving notice in writing through the Secretary to the Zonal VAT Tribunal within fifteen days after the date of service upon such taxable person of the assessment or demand notice and the appeal shall be heard by the Tribunal.

(10) The Board, if aggrieved by the non-compliance of a taxable person to any provision of this Act, may appeal to the Zonal Tribunal where the table person is resident giving notice in writing through the secretary to the Zonal VAT Tribunal

(11) Where a notice of appeal is not given within the period specified, the assessment or demand notices shall become final and conclusive and the Board may recover tax, interest and penalty which remain unpaid form any taxable person through the proceeding at the Zonal Tribunal.

(12) An award or judgement of the VAT Tribunal shall be enforced as if it were a judgement of the Federal High Court on registration of a copy of the award or judgement in the Registry of the Federal Court by the party seeking to enforce the award or judgement.

(13) Notice of appeal against assessment shall contain;

the name and address of the taxable person;

the total amount of goods and service chargeable to tax in respect of each month;

an input tax

net amount of tax payable;

the copy of assessment notice;

the precise grounds of appeal against the assessment; and

an address for service of any notice, precept or other documents to be given to the appellant by the Secretary to the Zonal VAT Tribunal.

(14) The Board or a taxable person may discontinue an appeal at any time before the hearing of the appeal by giving notice in writing through the Secretariat to the Zonal Tribunal.

(15) The Zonal Tribunal shall meet as often as may be necessary to hear appeal in any town and place in which the office of the Tribunal is situated.

(16) At least five members may hear and determine an appeal.

(17) The Secretary to the Zonal Tribunal shall give seven days notice to the parties to an appeal of the date and place fixed for the hearing of the appeal.

(18) All notice and documents, other than the decisions of the Tribunal may be signed the hand of the secretary. All appeals before the Tribunal shall be held in camera. Every taxable person so appealing shall be entitled to be represented at the hearing of the appeal by a legal practitioner, a qualified chartered accountant, or tax consultant.

(19) The onus of proving the basis of grievance against an assessment or non-compliance with the provisions of the law shall be on the appellant.

(20) The Zonal Tribunal may upon hearing the appeal, confirm, reduce, increase or amend the assessment or make such orders thereon as it deems fit.

(21) The Minister shall make rules regulating the practice and procedures of the VAT Tribunal and, until such rules are made, the practice and procedure of the Federal High Court shall apply with such modifications (whether by way of addition, alteration or omission) as the circumstances may require.

(22) Any case or proceeding relating to a matter for which the VAT Tribunal has jurisdiction pending before the Federal High Court on the commencement of this paragraph shall be continued and completed as if this Act had not been made.

(23)(1) Following the decision of the VAT Tribunal, notice of the amount of the tax chargeable under the assessment as determined by the VAT Tribunal shall be served by the Board on the company or person in whose name the tax is chargeable.

(2) Notwithstanding that an appeal is pending, tax shall be paid in accordance with the decision of the VAT Tribunal within one month of notification of the amount of the tax payable in pursuance of sub-paragraph (10) of this paragraph.

(24)(1) Any party aggrieved by the decision of the VAT Tribunal may appeal against the decision on point of law to the Court of Appeal on giving notice in writing to the Secretary to the VAT Tribunal within thirty days after the date on which the decision was given setting out the grounds on which the decision is being challenged.

(2) On receipt of a notice of appeal under sub-paragraph (1) of this paragraph, the Secretary to the VAT Tribunal shall compile the record or proceedings and judgement before the VAT Tribunal and shall cause them to be transmitted to the Chief Registrar of the Court of Appeal together with all the exhibits tendered at the hearing before the VAT Tribunal within thirty days after the date on which the decision was made.

(25) The President of the Court of Appeal may make rules providing for the procedure in respect of appeals made under this Act and until such rules are made, the Court of Appeal Rules relating to the hearing of appeals shall apply to the hearing and determination of an appeal under this Act.

Hearing

(A) Preparation

The axiom as far as preparation of a case for presenting to the commissioners is concerned is that it always takes a good deal longer than expected; for the amount of effort involved is virtually open-ended. All the fact and arguments which are to form the basis of the contention before the commissioners must be clearly and specifically brought out at the hearing. This is of the utmost importance in any event but vital if the client is determined to take the issue further since the courts are generally circumscribed by the primary facts found by the commissioners. The success of a case begins with its proper preparation of lawful evidence: contrary to the corpus of stories, mainly apocryphal, about meetings, victory can rarely be attributed to any dramatic piece of advocacy.[26]

It is convenient to divide the preparation of the normal case into four sections, which may be categorised as materials, documentation, examination and final address. All cases may not fit into this specification but this has been found to suit the majority. The quarry for each of these sections is, in the first stage is to work through the notes, the interviews and the correspondence from the beginning and try, if possible, to take a dispassionate view of it. The preparation of an appeal case is an academic exercise in the final analysis and must be approached without prejudice.

The opening statement to the commissioners is obviously of great significance and, after making a careful resume of the information on file, it should be possible to narrate the facts of the case in a simple and logical form. But, unless the appellant's advocate is unable to present a case without a word for word statement (in which situation he might seriously consider whether he will make the best of it) the ideal form is a brief consisting of a detailed framework which is clearly and flexible. Commissioners do not like scripts being read to them; so the facts presented much more naturally if they are in note form.

Having dealt with the facts of the case, the second stage is to consider the sections or section of the Taxes Acts which are relevant to these facts and which are to be brought to the attention of the commissioners. It is a matter both of courtesy and good strategy to have copies of those parts which are to be quoted available for the use of all parties not just the commissioners; and care should be taken to see they are good copies, clearly legible.

After the exposition of the statute law comes the discussion of gloss which has been put upon it by case law. Here again, if possible, copies should be made of the relevant judgments. But if this is not going to prove manageable owing perhaps to the number of cases, the clerk to the commissioners should be informed of the references of the tax cases which are to be quoted so that he can flag the respective volumes for the use of his commissioners and himself.

While researching the file for the raw material of the opening statement, a note should also be made of any documents which need to be put in as evidence. This covers accounts and returns as well as correspondence, agreed notes of interview and so on. Here again it is essential to ensure that all the copies are clearly legible, and contain all the information required. Such documentation should be agreed with the inspector beforehand so that no proof of them is necessary; but it is often a sensible precaution to see that the originals are on hand case the commissioners wish to inspect them.

All this is very time-consuming and some of it, for instance making extract form returns or abstracts form accounts, is semi-routine. It is as well, therefore, to enlist the aid of an assistant from the outset who can become familiar with the

---

[26] Basil Sabine, *Tax Appeals Handbook* (London Butterworths 1983) p.72-76.

case from its initial preparation and who can be responsible for much of the hard labour in getting the case together. It may seem a counsel of perfection but it is a great help in presentation, besides being a feature which will assist, and possibly even impress the commissioners, if all this documentation, statute of reference, case references, copies of letters and so on, is bound up in a booklet. The pages have to be securely fastened and numbered in any case; it is very little extra trouble, and well worth it, to add a cover and a plastic spine. This can well be a task for the assistant and the end product is far more satisfactory and manageable than a bunch of papers however carefully marshalled and tagged.

That covers the first two stages of the preparation, the collection of the material for the opening address and the arrangement of the requisite documentation. But before passing to the witness or witnesses, it is prudent at this juncture to pause. It is fatally easy, when preparing a case, with a conviction that the facts and law both support the appellant's contention, to be carried away with an enthusiasm which owes more perhaps to emotion than reason. This is the time to consider the inspector's case for it is vital to master both the appellant's and the inspector's case in detail.

For the inspector will have made himself thoroughly familiar with all aspects of the case. He too will have carefully prepared his line of argument in reply to that of the appellant, being well aware that a full appreciation of the case for the appellant is essential to the proper presentation of the case for the Revenue. He also has the advantage of being able to spend almost unlimited time on his assessment of the case. All this should be taken into account when reviewing the opening address to be made to the commissioners.

The third stage involves a question of nice judgment. The appellant will almost certainly be giving evidence and the first point to decide is how the appellant is to give his evidence. This depends on the type of evidence to be given and the ability of the appellant to present it. In the very simplest case it may be advisable mainly to let the appellant tell his own story, in which case the preparation of the examination will be minimized, consisting mainly of some judicious questions designed to bring out the particular points to which the commissioners' attention should be drawn. On the other hand, the appellant's evidence may be of a complex nature suitable only for bringing out in a series of questions and answers: or he may find difficulty in giving his evidence in narrative form even when the facts are reasonable straightforward when again the question and answer formula will have to be resorted to. There is obviously no rule of thumb here and the examination will have to be tailored to fit the peculiar circumstances of the appeal. It is certainly advisable to iron out any possible weakness of the case for it is on those that the inspector will focus his attention: the appellant should be appraised accordingly and such points can then be suitably rehearsed.

In an appeal hearing which is being formally conducted, for instance before the Appeal Commissioners, it will be for the appellant's solicitor ultimately to prepare the co-called 'proof of evidence' which tells counsel precisely what the witness may be expected to say. It may be that he delivers this reasonably well, but he is certainly not expected to read it or the commissioners will discount it as lacking the spontaneity which they feel justified in looking for. If, in dispute but of which the witness has first-hand knowledge then all parties may agree that this proof should be handed to the commissioners and that the witness should be allowed simply to read it over.

The Revenue is now well aware that it did not in the past play its ace of trumps often enough, the ace being the devious appellant who is likely to make a poor showing before the commissioners if he has to tell them his dubious story in person and be cross examined on it. These days the accountant is rarely permitted to come and tell his client's story for him which he can probably do much more convincingly. The Revenue is almost certainly going to try and persuade the commissioners to discount the representative's hearsay evidence and to say that the appellant himself must appear before them if he is to have any change of displacing the onus of proving that the assessment under appeal is excessive.

As far as the other witnesses are concerned the same pattern should be followed. If, before the Commissioners, the witness can deliver a 'plain unvarnished tale' then this is probably the best way of presenting the evidence with the necessary judicious prompting where important points need emphasis and with a review to cover the queries which will be raised in cross examination.

With regard to expert witnesses, it is permissible to ask leading questions with the commissioners' consent, to establish the credentials of the witness. Then it is essential to be precise about the questions which are to be put to the experts since they have a fatal facility, if not kept firmly to the relevant points at issue, of expatiating on their speciality generally. On this subject expert witness tends to breed expert witness in that it may be necessary to prepare to cross-examine an expert witness on the other side (it is unlikely, as has been noted, that the Revenue will call any other type of witness). This can become a difficult process and it is often a sensible move to enlist the aid of the expert on the appellant's side at least to monitor the questions that suitable. It should also be remembered that leading questions are allowed in cross-examination.

After sifting of the file, the drafting in extended note form of the opening observations to the commissioners and the preparation of examination and cross-examination of witness, there remains only final address, which has basically two features: it is a reply to the inspector's case and a brief re-statement of the appellant's case. It is usually suggested that this should not be prepared; indeed that it cannot. It has been found very effective, however, to plan the conclusion, preceding it by the inspector's arguments (which may be amended during the hearing) using one side of a ring binder: the purpose of the other side is for adaptations during the hearing which made the final address more spontaneous: but it is essential to have had a trying few hours and are probably looking forward to the conclusion: it is counter productive to delay it too long however telling some of the final comments seem to be.

(B) Appellant's case

It is possible,[27] in a minor contentious case, that at the discretion of the commissioners, the general order of procedure in the High Court which is usually followed, may be varied somewhat, and, since the Revenue does not object to this, it would certainly be inadvisable for the appellant to do so. In important appeals, however, and certainly when counsel is present on behalf of the appellant, and before the Commissioners the formal order is as follows:

(i) Adviser/counsel opens the case for the appellant
Adviser/counsel examines the appellant for the purpose of eliciting the facts relevant to his case. This is known technically as the examination-in-chief
The inspector cross-examines the appellant with a view to bringing out facts and evidence bearing on the Revenue side
Adviser/counsel re-examines the appellant on points arising from the inspector's cross-examination
Witness for the appellant, if any, are called and examined by the adviser/council, cross-examined by the inspector, then re-examined if necessary
Inspector states the case for the Revenue
Inspector calls any witnesses for the Revenue who are examined by the inspector, cross-examined by adviser/counsel and re-examined where necessary by the inspector
The inspector may sum up his case
Adviser/counsel has the right of making a final reply

Documents are generally referred to and relevant extracts read in the opening speeches on both sides.

When all the preparatory work has been done and the procedures thoroughly studied, there still remains one useful piece of familiarization for the newcomer to the appeal arena. Before the actual day of the hearing, it is suggested that any professional inexperienced in appeals should spend a few hours in a magistrates' court to observe the ritual of examination and cross-examination of witnesses: for it is unlikely that there will be another commissioners' meeting which he would be entitled to attend immediately before.

On the day, it is advisable to arrive in good time; and the appellant should be advised accordingly; there is nothing more unnerving than appearing at the

---

[27] Basil Sabine, *Tax Appeals Handbook* (London Butterworths 1983) p. 76–84

last minute or wondering when the appellant will present himself: of course it is always possible to be kept waiting and to have to suffer a strained period of interchange of courtesies with the inspector; it is politic to try and ensure that this does not upset the appellant. It is at this juncture that the inspector may well say that he has brought with him one or possibly more of his colleagues for experience and that he hopes there will be no objection (he will already have obtained the secretary's permission). Naturally, no opposition would be raised, but it can prove somewhat demoralizing to be faced by three experts even if only one is actually leading the Revenue side. All the witnesses, as previously stated enter with the principals and may stay for all the hearing.

In order to avoid breaking what is hoped will be a smoothly continuous flow of fact, law and submission, the first step should be to distribute copies of the documentation in booklet for if that has been found possible, which it is proposed to use. This should be done as informally as possible. The secretary to the commissioners may perhaps ask if there are any papers, which the principal should have and hand them out himself. That does not matter: the main point is that there should be a brief explanation of how the documentation has been made up. This breaks the ice and gives the speaker the chance to get used to the room and his audience before he actually opens. All he needs to say is something to the effect that as the commissioners will see pages 1 & 2 contain the agreed facts, pages 3-4 copies of the various sections of the Act which will be quoted and pages 5-8 summaries of the tax cases and relevant quotations: the pages numbered 10-16 are extracts from correspondence in chronological order which the inspector is aware are being used in evidence. No more need be said: but it is a comforting feeling to know that the Commissioners have before them a handy reference to all that is going to be said over the period of the appeal.

As emphasized more than once, the proceedings are informal but there is a wide distinction between informality and the merely casual: so when in doubt it is prudent to err on the side of formality. For instance, only the chairman should be addressed, and invariably as 'Sir': it is, however, permissible to reply directly to the clerk if asked a direct question: this may often be procedural. The inspector, as previously mentioned, may be referred to by his name.

The opening should always be slow and as clear as possible. The sort of oral submissions which comprise the conduct of an appeal are a form of public speaking and previous practice in that most difficult of arts can be a great help. There is, in addition, a certain nervous tension arising from some unfamiliar procedures: cross-examination and re-examination can be daunting: concentration on the inspector's case can be almost as trying as opening: and it may be necessary to challenge points made which could be out of order or rulings by the commissioners themselves. It is, incidentally, essential to read over the notes before they are delivered, since the spoken word can turn out to be very different from what has been written down.

The actual words of the introduction might well be 'Good morning/afternoon, gentlemen (rather than 'May it please the commissioners' which is a trifle legalistic). My client, Mr. X is the appellant and I am Y, a tax consultant: (there is no need to introduce the inspector: the commissioners will find him a familiar presence). My client's appeal is against an assessment for 20-/20- on him to income tax under PITA 1993 in respect of his profits as a haulage contractor. As you will see from the form in front of you, the amounts of his profits have been estimated at ₦40,000. Accounts have been submitted which would enable the appeal to be determined but in those accounts a deduction has been claimed under the Personal Income Tax Act 1993, Section 20, which you will hear more of later form both sides, of ₦6,748 expended on the hard-standing at my clients' premises. The inspector seeks to disallow a part of this sum.' This is all, by and large, which needs to be said. It should be taken deliberately to enable the commissioners to get used to the speaker's voice, to look at the immediate references to assessment and amount in their papers and, in fact to settle down.

Then follows the final stage of the opening; the presentation of the facts of the case. They should be marshalled into a coherent and readily intelligible story, together with as much background information as considered necessary. If the case, for instance, concerns the purchase and sale of land, the narrative will clearly lend itself to chronological treatment which is very helpful since it is more easily prepared and gives the commissioners a clear framework for the notes. A back duty case is a more difficult subject where background can be almost as important as the story of the negotiations and the explanations put forward. It is easy to forget, after long and protracted discussion with Revenue, when both sides are familiar with the finer points of the story and the nice balance of the argument, that the commissioners are hearing it for the first time so that its relation should not be so pared down that it assumes the commissioners know more than they do, or so elaborate that they cannot distinguish the thread of the story from the detail. They should be given plenty of time to make their own notes: the fact they have finished writing should be noted before embarking on another section of the address even if progress is lower. The expression of any opinion even by inference should be carefully avoided at this stage. This factual exposition should be concluded by a factual summary if possible, that is, the story in a nutshell.

Having presented the facts, it is now necessary to move on to the second stage of the opening statement, that is to draw attention to and explain if necessary the relevant statute law and its to draw attention to and explain if necessary the relevant statute law and its interpretation, where this is relevant, by the courts as recorded in the reports of tax cases. This is always the most difficult part of the opening address. Facts can always be made interesting and even when they are not especially dramatic, they are at least readily comprehensible. But the law is a more tenuous matter altogether and its vocabulary and phraseology not easy to grasp. It is vital, therefore, to try and explain it as simply as possible while retaining the exact sense, and to put it in the proper context. As far as the relevant section or sections of the Taxes Acts are concerned, it may well be that the quotations will not need to be lengthy. They should be read slowly with the correct emphasis on the implication of the particular part to which the commissioners' attention is being drawn. The commissioners will, as suggested, have been provided with copies of the sections, which they can, follow as the wording is being read. It may be found convenient briefly to relate the facts of the case to the law simply to highlight the relevance of various parts being quoted to the particular circumstances, but that may well be left to the third stage.

If reliance is going to be placed on case law there are two considerations, which must be borne in mind. The first is that although commissioners will readily accept that valid comparisons may only be made between like and like, they may, when it comes to looking at tax cases, have some difficulty in picking up where the precise resemblance lies. After all a case about a factory chimney is not obviously on all fours, to the layman with one about repairs to a cellar although the principles involved may be identical. Therefore, when inviting comparisons between one of the decided cases and the issue before the commissioners, it is essential to ensure that all the commissioners understand that the comparisons which are being made relate to similar points of law notwithstanding the apparent disparity of the facts, and that it is this question of law which is under discussion. If this point can be underlined by quoting two relevant decided cases with widely differing facts, that is, a bonus.

The second consideration is to use simplicity as a guiding principle. It is a far more effective technique before the commissioners to concentrate on explaining the basic points of the law as they refer to the issue in question than to try and buttress those points with comparatively minor illustrations. While these may be significant and possibly in sum clinching an expert, they often simply serve to cloud the issue to non-lawyer commissioners. Before the Commissioners however a display of expertise and erudition is, to an extent, expected and is, on that account, more desirable.

The decision on how much of a case should be read can often present problems. If reliance is being placed on only one case, the commissioner will merely need to hear enough to understand the issue, the facts of the case and the reasoning behind the judgment. If reliance is being placed on a series of cases, the decision to be faced is whether to begin with the leading case, or lead up to it historically from the earlier judgement. No hard and fast rule can be laid down: the most that can be said that the historical approach is perhaps the simpler and it can be put across to the commissioners more easily. But, whichever method is selected, the leading, the leading case must be developed in sufficient detail to help in formulating a convincing argument and to establish that it constitutes the main base of the contentions which are being mounted. To be effective in the field of decided cases an argument based on judicial findings may either display a logical progression of decisions up to that principal and final case, or it must show how that particular decisions up to that principal and final case, or it must show how that particular decision has been a trap of producing a series of quotations out of context no matter how telling they may appear to be: it is also very tempting. But it is superficial strategy for the appellant's advocate to say airily: 'As Mr. Justice X said in the case of Y v Z....' For one thing the commissioners will not necessarily be able to relate the quotation to the facts of the issue before them: and for another, the inspector will certainly be on the look-out for such misuse and would certainly counter, if given the chance, that the quotation related to a case where an entirely different set of facts were being considered. In any event, a diet of gobbets has no nutritional value as food for thought.

There is one further point in this context. The art of reading aloud with style and intelligibility is one, which few people are naturally endowed with but, with practice, it can be mastered. It is essential to get to know the relevant passage or passages in the first place, that is to say not only what is being said but how it is being said. For instance, the head note of a tax case is in summary note form and takes a great deal of reading or it becomes a meaningless jumble: it may be desirable, although it is not easy, to prepare a simpler alternative. The styles of the judges, in delivery of their judgements, differ greatly, ranging from terse to verbose: each type equally requires a different style of rendering. It may seem rather academic to lay so much emphasis on this aspect of the presentation, but if a series of paragraphs needs to be read to the commissioners as an integral part of the argument being developed then it impairs the desired effect if the judicial comment upon which reliance is being placed is not heard to the best advantage. It can even be worth while to have a trial reading before the hearing takes place. The whole of the text should be read slowly: reading too quickly is the most common of faults. For it is the slowest commissioners who determine the pace of the address. Here again the commissioners should have copies as these are read through.

The commissioners will now have before them the facts, the statute law, and the gloss which has been put upon it by the decided cases. These ingredients have now to be amalgamated and the commissioners have to be led to understand how the facts fit in with the statute and case law, which has been expounded. It may be compared with doing two halves of a jigsaw puzzle, then slotting those two halves together to give the desired picture to the commissioners. The facts and the law should combine to create the desired pattern of non-assessability, if that is the issue.

The conclusion should simply be to maintain that, as has been demonstrated, the law supports the interpretation of the facts which the appellant has put upon them and that the assessment for 20-/20- should accordingly be determined in the sum of ₦X-Y capital allowance as shown in the copy of the computation which they have before them. A vague determination that the expenditure should be allowed is not altogether satisfactory. It will pass as a preamble, but an actual determination of the figures is the real outcome, which is needed.

Then follows the examination of the appellant which should have been prepared according to whether he is to be allowed to tell his own story as being the most effective way of presenting his case or where the exercise is to be more formally structured, which latter is the more likely procedure if the hearing is before the Federal Tax Appeal Commissioners. In either case he should have been well rehearsed but not too elaborately so that his responses seem natural and not mechanical. He should be taken through his evidence slowly, more attention being paid, of course, to any facts, which may be in dispute and to any important parts of the evidence, which he may not have made clear to the satisfaction of the commissioners. Leading questions, that is, questions, which suggest the answers the person putting the questions wishes or expects to receive, or suggesting disputed facts to which the witness is to testify are not allowed. The phraseology to be avoided is for example, 'And then you did so and so?' 'It would then be correct to say that such and such was the position?' The inspector knows very well that leading a witness, particularly an appellant, is a very obvious way of putting the most favourable construction on a dubious set of facts and he is no objection to leading questions in the case of an expert witness to establish his credentials or to say precisely what his function is as far as the lawful evidence to be presented to the commissioners is something to the effect that in the interests of time he will lead until he comes to some debatable point, in a case where there is a great deal which is not in dispute.

As well as avoiding leading questions, the interrogation should not be too detailed if there are no essential features in dispute, as the commissioners can become impatient at hearing a repetition of what they have been told in the opening summary of facts. This is especially true in the case of other witnesses whose function tend to be mainly corroborative. Normally, the evidence of supporting witnesses may be given as a brief narrative or in the form of an equally brief question and answers session unless the evidence is of such importance that the witness ranks as a principal witness to the appellant: an accountant, for instance, in a back duty case, would clearly come into that category.

To discuss the evidence of supplementary witnesses is to move ahead slightly in the strict order since the cross-examination of the appellant take place, of course, before the other witnesses appear on the scene, and their cross-examination follows their examination in chief as with the appellant. The cross-examination of the appellant is the first occasion when the inspector has been able to speak and from the outset he will be anxious to make a good impression: and the general experience of interviews with the Revenue would endorse the opinion that the average inspector is a practiced and skilful questioner.

In addition he is instructed that the cross-examination of the appellant can be the most important feature in the presentation of his case. It is also the most difficult part since, although he will have prepared his questions in advance, he may well have had to modify them in the course of the examination-in-chief. His function, if he carries it out as he should (and inspectors generally do), particularly in relation to disputed facts, is not to destroy the credibility of the appellant, or indeed any of his witnesses for that is far too dramatic a word, but to shake the weight of his testimony and force the commissioners to weigh the degree of belief to be attached to his evidence. He will without doubt question the appellant on the whole of that part of the Revenue case which relates to matters within his knowledge: for the secondary purpose of the cross-examination is to prepare the way for the Revenue arguments and contentions. He can also put leading questions.

After cross-examination, the re-examination of the appellant (and subsequently his witnesses) follows immediately on its conclusion. The purpose of this is to seek to undo the effect in the minds of the commissioners of the cross-examination and to emphasis again the main facts in favour of the appellant. It should be noted that the scope of the re-examination is confined to those points, which had arisen on cross-examination. If exceptionally it seems necessary to raise new issues it can only be with the consent of the commissioners: and then the inspector has a renewed right to cross-examine on such issues.

(C) Revenue case

It is fair to assume that the inspector will have made the same preparation for his address to the commissioners as the appellant's adviser did for his opening, more especially as he does not have a second chance.[28] He also will have reviewed his file and arranged his evidence in a comprehensive and orderly fashion, and to an extent the pattern of his statement will be very like the opening of the case for the appellant. He will start with a review of the material facts and he would be less than human if he did not tend to emphasis those he thought more favourable to his argument, or which he could contend had not been fully or properly dealt with in the opening. He is likely to end this part of his statement with a short account of the logical progression by which his counter-argument has been reached. His next step is likely to be a dissection of his case, to demonstrate how each part is supported, first by the facts he has cited in his opening remarks and then by the statute and case law; the whole, where necessary, being underpinned by the relevant documents and correspondence. Then should come what may well be the most significant part of his statement, his reply to the arguments used on behalf of the appellant for

---

[28] Basil Sabine, *Tax Appeals Handbook* (London Butterworths 1983) p.84, 85.

that will form the basis of the closing remarks for the appellant. Finally, he will summarize the main heads of his contentions and try, as the appellant's representative has done, to guide the commissioners to consider the broad principles involved and not be diverted by matters of detailed.

It may happen that the inspector considers the appellant's case as presented differs materially form the tenor of the correspondence and the discussions before the hearing. This is likely if the normal course of exchanging facts, cases and opinions and of agreeing documents has been followed: but if the inspector does take that view he may request an adjournment and it will be for the commissioner to decide whether he has justification in so doing and whether they would be prepared to grant it. The issue can well be argued there and then: and the case could proceed.

If the inspector has any witnesses, however, his procedure may differ slightly. He will open for the Revenue and proceed only as far as countering the arguments of the appellant. He may then call his witnesses. They are examined, cross-examined and re-examined, as were those of the appellant. As previously stated, the Revenue's witnesses tend to be expert and a similar expert should, have carefully vetted any cross-examination. When those witnesses have been disposed of, the inspector may then proceed to his final summary.

This account of the appeal proceedings generally, unless they are before the VAT Tribunal, presupposes a degree of formality and orderly progression which may not in fact be the case. For one thing, the commissioners may interrupt the proceedings at any time, either during the address or during the various examinations of witnesses. This may be disconcerting, and possibly less so to the inspector who is more used to it. The best policy is to try and take advantage of such interventions because they indicate what the commissioners are thinking or, if the interruption is in any phase of the examinations, what line they think the questions should be taking. If they seem to be getting the wrong impression from their particular queries it may be necessary to re-examine. As far as interruptions from either party are concerned, the appellant should be instructed never to interrupt and his representative should set him the example. It is most unlikely the inspector will: he knows that, whatever the provocation, it will only alienate the commissioners.

(D) Final reply

The penultimate act of a hearing consists of the right of reply exercisable by the appellant.[29] It should not be long, but that brevity bears no relation to its importance: for cases have been won (and lost) on this final statement. By this time the commissioners may have made up their minds: and if not in the appellant's favour, this is the last chance of influencing them. The summary can

---

[29] Basil Sabine, *Tax Appeals Handbook* (London Butterworths 1983) p.85, 86.

be broken down into three parts. The first should be a resume of the inspector's argument and the reasons for rejecting it: this can be prepared to an extent but should be left very flexible and capable of being adapted to the way the inspector has presented his case. The second part should be a short but comprehensive summary of the appellant's case: and the winding-up should simply be 'I submit therefore that the assessment for 20-/20- should be adjusted to ₦X – ₦Y capital allowances in accordance with my computation.' It is possible to add that there is no dispute about the figures if the appellant's argument is accepted.

The commissioners may then withdraw or the parties may do so: it is then a matter of awaiting the final stage of what has probably been a somewhat gruelling experience that is the determination.

It is not easy to summarize the progress of a hearing since different techniques are required at different stages. The opening is a type of speech: but effective examination and cross-examination are almost arts in themselves and real faculty only comes with ling experience. The most important point to remember from the beginning is that an appeal meeting is not an extension of the argument which has previously been conducted by correspondence: it is what is popularly referred to as a whole new ball game, where, to prolong the metaphor, the stationary ball of ordinary speech has to be abandoned for the moving ball of advocacy. The second essential is that of thorough preparation, in the certain knowledge that opposition will be equally thorough. The final requisite is something that no amount of advice, however exhaustive, can teach, and that is a certain feel for this type of hearing, especially when it is before an quasi-tribunal, a sense of knowing when the commissioners' attention is being held, or equally when that attention is slipping away. It can be a rewarding exercise: it is certainly always exhausting.

Decision

The decisions of the Commissioners are usually given orally and the secretary would usually provide a formal record of the proceedings upon request.

(A) Personal income tax

Under Section 63 PITA 1993:

(1) Notice of the amount of the tax chargeable under the assessment as determined by the Appeal Commissioners shall be served by the relevant tax authority on the tax payer or on the person in whose name the tax payer is chargeable.

(2) Where the tax chargeable on a taxpayer or a year of assessment in accordance with a decision of the Appeal Commissioners does not exceed two hundred Naira no

further appeal by the tax payer shall lie form that decision except with the concept of the Board.

(3) Notwithstanding that a further appeal is pending, tax shall be paid, in accordance with the decision of the Appeal Commissioners, within one month of notification of the amount of the tax payable pursuant to subsection (1) of this section, and if it is not so paid, with or without applying the provisions of section 55 of this Decree as the relevant tax authority thinks fit, proceedings may be taken for its recovery in accordance with section 54 of this Decree.

(B) Companies income tax

Under Section 56 of CITA 1990:

(1) Notice of the amount of the tax chargeable under the assessment as determined by the body of Appeal Commissioners shall be served upon the company by the Board or person in whose name such company is chargeable.
(2) Where the tax chargeable upon a company for a year of assessment in accordance with the decision of the Appeal Commissioners does not exceed ₦400.00 no further appeal by the company shall lie from that decision except with the consent of the Board.
(3) An award or judgement of the Body of Appeal Commissioners shall be enforced as if it were a judgement of the Federal High Court upon registration of a copy of such award or judgement with Chief Registrar of the Federal High Court by the party seeking to enforce the award of judgement.
(4) Notwithstanding that an appeal is pending, tax shall be paid in accordance with the decision of the Appeal Commissioners within one month of notification of the amount of the tax payable in pursuance of subsection (1) of this section.

(C) Value added tax

The Zonal Tribunal under section 20 of VATA may upon hearing the appeal confirm, reduce, increase or amend the assessment or make such orders thereon as it deems fit.

Under section 23 of VATA:

1) following the decision of the VAT Tribunal, notice of the amount of the tax chargeable under the assessment as determined by the VAT Tribunal shall be deemed by the Board or the company or person in whose name the tax is chargeable;
2) Notwithstanding that an appeal is pending, tax shall be paid in accordance with the decision of the VAT Tribunal within one month of notification of the amount of the tax payable.

Appeals to court

(A) Personal income tax

Under section 64 PITA 1993 and subject to provisions of subsection (2) of section 63 of this Decree:

(1) A tax payer who, having appealed against an assessment made on him to the Appeal Commissioners under the provisions of section 60 of this Decree is aggrieved by the decision of the Appeal Commissioners may appeal against the assessment and the decision to the High Court of the State on giving notice in writing to the relevant tax authority within thirty days of after the date on which the decision was given.

(2) Where no body of Appeal Commissioners has been appointed with jurisdiction to hear an appeal against an assessment made on a tax payer, the relevant tax authority in the manner provided in subsection (3) of section 57 of this Decree, may appeal against the assessment to the High Court of the State on giving notice in writing to the relevant tax authority within thirty days after the date of service of notice of the refusal by the relevant tax authority to amend the assessment as desired.

If the relevant tax authority is dissatisfied with a decision of the Appeal Commissioners, it may appeal against that decision to the High Court of the State on giving notice in writing to the other party to the appeal within thirty days after the date on which decision was given.

Seven clear days notice of the date fixed for the hearing of the appeal shall, unless rule made hereunder otherwise provide, be given to all parties thereto.

The provisions to subsections (7), (8) and (9) of section 62 of this Decree and of subsection (1) of section 63 of this Decree shall apply to an appeal under this section with any necessary modifications.

All appeals shall be heard in camera unless the judge shall, on the application of the taxpayer, otherwise direct.

If on the hearing of an appeal from a decision of the Appeal Commissioners given under the provisions of section 62 of this Decree a certified copy of that decision is produced before the high Court and the decision contains a record by reference to- (a) paragraph (a) of subsection (13) of section 62 of this Decree, the High Court may dismiss the appeal on prima facie evidence, with respect of the accounts, books or records having been incomplete or unsatisfactory, as the court may seem sufficient; or (c) paragraph (c) or (d) or subsection (13) of section 62 of this Decree, the High Court shall dismiss the appeal unless it considers that the cause of the neglect or refusal was reasonable.

Notwithstanding anything contained in section 67 of this Decree, if in a particular case the judge, from information given at the hearing of the appeal, is of the opinion that the tax may not be recovered, he may, on application being made by or on behalf of the relevant tax authority, require the appellant to furnish within such time as may be specified security for payment of the tax and if the security is not given within the time specified by the tax assessed shall become payable and recoverable forthwith.

The cost of the appeal shall be in the discretion of the Judge hearing the appeal and shall be a sum fixed by the Judged.

The Chief Judge of the State may make rules providing for the method of tendering evidence before a Judge on appeal, the conduct of the procedure to be followed by a judge.

An appeal against the decision of a Judge shall lie to the Court of Appeal and thereafter to the Supreme Court-

at the instance of the tax payer, where the decision of the Judge is to the effect that the tax chargeable on the tax payer for the relevant year of assessment exceeds four hundred Naira; and

at the instance of or with the consent of the relevant tax authority, in any other case:

Provided that no costs shall be awarded against the tax payer in an appeal instituted by the relevant tax authority under this subsection unless the decision of the judge was to the effect mentioned in paragraph (a) of this subsection.

(B) Companies income tax

Under section 57 subject to section 56(2) of this Act:

(1) Any company which, having appealed against an assessment made it to the Appeal Commissioners under section 61 of this Act, is aggrieved by the decision on such body may appeal against such decision on point of law to the Federal High Court upon giving such decision on point of law to the Federal High Court, upon giving notice in writing to the secretary to the Appeal Commissioners within thirty days after the date on which such decision was given. Such notice shall set out all the grounds of law on which the decision is being challenged.

(2) If the Board is dissatisfied with the decision of the Appeal Commissioners it may appeal against such decision to the Federal High Court on a point of law by giving notice in writing as in subsection (1) of this section to the Secretary to the Appeal Commissioners within thirty days after the date on which such decision was given.

(3) Upon receipt of a notice of appeal under subsection (1) or (2) of this section, the secretary to the Appeal Commissioners shall comply the records of proceedings and judgement before the Appeal Commissioners and shall cause the same to be transmitted to Chief Registrar of the Federal High Court along with all the exhibit tendered at the hearing before the Appeal Commissioners within 30 days after the date on which such decision was made.

(4) The provisions of subsection (6),(7), and (9) of section 55 of this Act and subsection (1) of section 56 of this Act shall apply to an appeal under this section with any necessary modifications.

(5) If upon the hearing of an appeal from a decision of the Appeal Commissioners given under provisions of section 55 of this Act, a certified copy of the decision is produced before the Federal High Court and such decision contain a record by reference to-

(a) paragraph (a) of subsection (11) of that section, the Federal High Court shall dismiss such appeal; or

(b) paragraph (b) of subsection (11) of that section, the Federal High Court may dismiss such appeal upon such prima facie evidence, with respect to the accounts, books or records having been incomplete or unsatisfactory as the Federal High Court may seem sufficient; or

(c) paragraph (c) or (d) of subsection (11) of that section, the Federal high Court shall dismiss such appeal unless it considers that the cause of the neglect or refusal was reasonable.

(6) The cost of appeal shall be in the discretion of the judge hearing the appeal and shall be a sum fixed by the judge.

(7) An appeal against the decision of a judge shall lie to the Court of Appeal-

(a) at the instance of the company, where the decision of the judges is to the effect that tax chargeable upon the company for the relevant year of assessment exceeds N1,000; and

(b) at the instance of or with the consent of the Board, in any case:

Provided that no cost shall be awarded against the company in any appeal instituted by the Board under this subsection unless such decision of the judge was to the effect mention in paragraph (a) of this subsection.

(8) The Chief Judge of the Federal High Court may make rules providing for the procedure in respect of appeals made under this section and until such rules are made the rules applicable in civil cases from Magistrates courts to the High Court of Lagos State shall apply with such modifications as the Chief Judge of the Federal High Court may direct.

(c) Petroleum Profit Tax Act

Under section 38:

(1) Any person (being a company or person in whose name a company is assessed) being aggrieved by an assessment made upon him, who has failed to agree with the Board as referred to in section 36(6) of this Act, may appeal against the assessment to the appropriate Appeal Commissioners upon giving notice in writing to the Board and to the secretary to such commissioners within thirty days after the date of service upon him of notice of the refusal of the Board to amend the assessment as desired:

Provided that notwithstanding the lapse of such period of thirty days, by not more than a further period of sixty days, such person may appeal against the said assessment if he gives such Commissioners the particulars mentioned in paragraph (a) to inclusive of subsection (2) of this section and if he shows to their satisfaction that, owing to absence from Nigeria, sickness or other reasonable cause he was prevented from giving notice of appeal within such period of thirty days, and that there has been no unreasonable delay on his part; and upon the Commissioners being so satisfied, such person shall give such notice in writing to the Board and such secretary within seven days thereof.

(2) A notice of an appeal against an assessment, to be given under subsection (1) of this section, shall specify the following particulars-

the official number of the assessment and the accounting period for which it was made;

the amount of tax charged by the assessment;

the date upon which an appellant was served with notice of refusal of the board to amend the assessment as desired;

the precise ground of his appeal against the assessment; and

an address for service of any notice, precepts or other documents to be given, by the secretary to the appropriate appeal commissioners, to the appellant.

Provided that at any time the appellant may give notice to such secretary and the Board, by delivering the same or by registered post, of a change of such address but any such notices shall not be valid until delivered or received.

For the purpose of this section, the appropriate Appeal Commissioners and their secretary to whom an appellant may give notice of appeal against an assessment under subsection (1) of this section shall be the Body of Appeal Commissioners, if any, established, under the provisions of section 53(1) of the Companies Income Tax Act, for the area in which the notice of that assessment was issued.

For the purposes of this Act, the provision of section 54 and 55 of the Companies Income Tax Act shall apply in like manners as they apply to the provisions of the last mentioned Act.

The provisions of subsection (5), (7), (8), and (9) of section 39 of this Act shall apply to an appeal under this section with any necessary modifications.

All appeals shall be heard in camera.

(a) The Minister may make rules prescribing the procedure to be followed with respect to precepts and other like documents to be issued on behalf of Appeal Commissioners, for the examination of witnesses and in the conduct of appeals before them.

(b) Pending the making of nay rules under this subsection, any rules made or to be made (or any rules replacing any such rules) under section 55(12) of the Companies Income Tax Act shall apply to any appeal or to any such procedure for the purpose of this section and Act with any necessary modifications.

Under section 39:

(1) Any person (being a company or person in whose name a company is assessed) who, having appealed against an assessment made upon him to the appropriate Appeal Commissioners under the provisions of section 38 of this Act, is aggrieved by the decision of such Commissioners may appeal against the assessment and such decision to the Federal High Court upon giving notice in writing to the Board within thirty days after the date upon which such decision was given.

(2) Notwithstanding the lapse of such period of thirty days but not more than a further period of sixty days, such person may appeal against the said assessment and decision if he shows to the satisfaction of the judge that, owing to absence from Nigeria, sickness or other reasonable cause, he was prevented from giving notice of appeal within such period of thirty days, and that there has been no unreasonable delay on his part; and upon the judge being so satisfied such person shall give such notice in writing to the Board within seven days thereof.

(3) Where no appropriate Body of Appeal Commissioners has been appointed with jurisdiction to hear an appeal, against an assessment made upon any person, under

the provisions referred to in subsection (3) of section 38 of this Act, such person being aggrieved by the assessment and having failed to agree with the Board as referred to in subsection (6) of section 36, shall appeal against the assessment to the Federal High Court upon giving notice in writing to the Board within thirty days after the date of service upon him of notice of the refusal of the Board to amend the assessment as desired and the provisions of subsection (2) of this section, so far as they are applicable, shall apply.

(4) If the Board is dissatisfied with a decision of the Appeal Commissioners, it may appeal against the decision to the Federal High Court upon giving notice in writing to the other party to the appeal under section 38 of this Act upon which such decision was given, within thirty days after the date upon which such decision was given, within thirty days after the date upon which such decision was given and the provisions of this section, so far as they are applicable, shall apply to any such appeal to the Federal High Court by the Board.

(5) Every company appealing shall appoint an authorized representative who shall attend before the court in person on the day and at the time fixed for the hearing of the appeal, but if it be proved to the satisfaction of the judge that owing to absence from Nigeria, sickness or other reasonable cause any duly appointed representative is prevented from attending in person at the hearing of the company's appeal on the day and fixed for that purpose, the judge may postpone the hearing of the appeal for such reasonable time as he thinks necessary for the attendance of the appellant's representative, or he may admit the appeal to be made by any other agent, clerk or servant of the appellant, on its behalf or by way of written statement.

(6) Twenty-one clear days notice shall, unless rules made hereunder otherwise provide, be given to the Board of the date fixed for the hearing of the appeal.

(7) The onus of proving that the assessment complained of is excessive shall be on the appellant.

(8) The judge may confirm, reduce, increase or annul the assessment or make such order thereon as to him may seem fit.

(9) Notice of the amount of tax payable under the assessment as determined by the judge shall be served by a duly authorized representative of the Board either personally on, or by registered post to, the appellant.

(10) Notwithstanding anything contained in section 44 of this Act, if an any particular case, the judge from information given at the hearing of the appeal, is of the opinion that the tax may not be recovered, he may on application being made by or on behalf of the Board require the appellant to furnish within such time as may be specified security for the payment of the tax and if such security is not given within the time specified the tax assessed shall become payable and recoverable forthwith.

(11) All appeals shall be heard in camera, unless the judge shall, on the application of the appellant, otherwise direct.

(12) The costs of the appeal shall be in the discretion of the judge hearing the appeal and shall be sum fixed by the judge.

(13) (a) The Chief Judge of the Federal High Court may make rules providing for the method of tendering evidence before a judge on appeal, the conduct of such appeal and the procedure to be followed by a judge upon stating a case for the opinion of the Court of Appeal.

(b) Notwithstanding that an appeal is pending tax shall be paid in accordance with the decision of the Federal High Court within one month of notification of the amount of the tax payable in pursuance to subsection (9) of this section.

(14) An appeal against the decision of the judge shall lie to the Court of Appeal-

(a) at the instance of the appellant where the decision of the judge is to the effect that the correct assessment of tax is in the sum of ₦1,000 or upwards, and

(b) at the instance of the Board where the decision of the judge is in respect of a matter in which the Board claimed that the correct assessment of the tax was in the sum of ₦1,000 or upwards.

Under section 40:

(1) Where no valid objection or appeal has been lodged within the time limited by section 36, 38, or 39 of this Act, as the case may be, against an assessment as regards the amount of the tax assessed thereby, or where the amount of tax has been agreed to under subsection (5) of section 36 of this Act, or where the amount of the tax has been determined on objection or revision under subsection (6) of section 36 of this act, or an appeal, as the case may be, shall be final and conclusive for all purpose of this Act as regards the amount of such tax, and if the full amount of the tax in respect of any such final and conclusive assessment is not paid within the appropriate period or periods prescribed in this Act, the provisions thereof relating to the recovery of tax, and to any penalty under section 43 of this Act, shall apply to the collection and recovery thereof subject only to the set-off of the amount of any tax repayable under any claim, made under any provisions of this Act, which has been agreed to by the Board or determined on any appeal against a refusal to admit any such claim.

(2) Where an assessment has become final and conclusive, any tax overpaid shall be repaid.

(3) Nothing in section 36 of this Act or in this Part shall prevent the Board from making any assessment or additional assessment to tax for any for any accounting period which does not involve re-opening any issue on the same facts which has been determined for that accounting period, under subsection (5) or (6) of section 36 of this Act by agreement or otherwise or on appeal.

Public law challenges

(A) Judicial review

This remedy is applicable to the decisions of the Bodies of Appeal Commissioners at both the Federal and State levels. In the words of Megarry J in *IRC* v *Sneath*,[30] "the commissioners discharge functions which are essentially judicial in nature. They hear evidence and argument, and decide questions of fact and law impartially and without regard to so-called considerations of

[30] (1932) 17 TC 149 at 420

policy." It is therefore apposite that their decision should be subject to judicial review once the applicants are shown to have sufficient interest or *locus standi.*

Judicial review is not new in Nigeria, indeed in a line of cases[31] such as *Aboud* v *R.T.B*,[32] *Williams* v *Adelaja*,[33] *Rev. Shodipo* v *F.B.I.R*[34] and *Offshore International* v *F.B.I.R*,[35] declaratory actions as to non-liability to tax has been brought before the courts. Also, an order of *certiorari* and prohibition to quash assessment and prohibit payment of taxes was canvassed in the cases of *Alitalia Airlines Ltd* v *F.B.I.R*[36] and *Okupe* v *F.B.I.R.*[37]

An order of mandamus to compel the tax authority to stay action on tax collection was sought in *The Queen* v *Urhobo Rating Authority.*[38]

(B) Public law defence

The second remedy is to establish a public law defence to a Revenue enforcement action,[39] e.g. by arguing that the original assessment is *ultra vires* and therefore void. In *IRC v Aken*,[40] this line of argument was used – unsuccessfully – to argue that the profits of prostitution could not be taxable since, as a matter of law, the profits of an illegal activity cannot be subject to tax. The English Court of Appeal rejected this argument. Judges will no doubt keep this use of the *ultra vires* doctrine under very tight control to prevent if from becoming another avenue of appeal tax. Inspectors do not act *ultra vires* merely by making a mistake of law. Since *IRC v Aken* was decided the courts have developed the law on collateral challenge. The English House of Lords has held that it is open to citizens charged with a criminal offence to argue that the law under which they are charged is invalid.[41] That case concerned a prosecution for breach of a byelaw against smoking. The House had to distinguish a recent case,[42] which had not allowed a person to challenge the validity of an enforcement notice in the planning notice enforcement proceedings, and did so by treating the matter as one of statutory

[31] M.T. Abdulrazaq, *Judicial Review in Nigerian Taxation* (Maples & Temples Associates) p.16.

[32] 1 NTC 124

[33] 1 NTC 141

[34] 1 NTC 273

[35] 1 NTC 384

[36] 1 NTC 222

[37] 1 NTC 321

[38] 1 NTC 76

[39] *Pawlowski* v *Dunnington* [1999] STC 550 (taxpayer allowed to argue legality of condition for Revenue action under PAYE regulations allowing action against employee for recovery of tax following deduction by employee). On differences between public law defence and judicial review, see ibid. *557*, per Simon Brown L.J.

[40] *IRC* v *Aken* [1990] STC 497, CA.

[41] *Boddington* v *British Transport Police* [1999] 2 AC 143; see Elliott 3 *Judicial Review* 144, Forsyth (1998) *Public Law* 364 and Hare [1998] CLJ 429; see also the Supreme Court of Nigeria decision in *Abacha v State.*

[42] *R. v Wicks* [1998] AC 92.

construction. In planning law the English Parliament had provided a complex system of appeal and the decision was addressed to the defendant; the exercise of the right of appeal and judicial review was enough. These might have had weight in matters but were swept aside by the Court of Appeal in *Pawlowski v Dunnington.*[43]

(C) Damages

The third remedy is the altogether more ingenious suggestion that a cause of action lies against the Revenue for damages, perhaps even exemplary damages, on the unlawful collection of or demand for tax.[44] This argument may gain credibility as a result of the incorporation of the African Charter of Human Rights into Nigerian law. However, a credible argument is not necessarily a successful one.

(D) Constitutionalism

The requirements under section 55(5) CITA 1990 and section 62(6) PITA 1993 that all appeals before the Appeal Commissioners shall be held in camera raises issues of constitutionalism. The fact that publicity would be embarrassing or even economically damaging is not sufficient grounds to hear tax appeals in camera.

This issue was explained *in In re-*[45] where it was held that:

> it is, of course, a fundamental and extremely important requirement of our administration of justice that it should take place in public, he said..... 'I have not the slightest doubt that in this case, as the only consideration in favour of preserving the respondent's anonymity is his own convenience, including possible loss of repute in his own neighborhood and of income from his profession, there is by no means strong enough reason to over-ride the extremely important and fundamental requirement of publicity in our administration of justice.'

It has often been somewhat cynically suggested[46] that the courts can always unearth a question of law when they consider a case should be reviewed and equally they can always take refuge in the proposition that they have been called upon to pronounce on a question of pure fact if they do not wish to interfere. Certainly it is very difficult to discern any consistent pattern in the long line of judicial decisions where it has been thought necessary to draw a distinction

---

43 See above at n.39.

44 Wilde [1995] BTR 137. The argument may be weakened (but not destroyed) by the decision of the House of Lords in *O'Rourke* v *Camden B.C.* [1998] AC 188; on which see Camwarth [1998] *Public Law 407.*

45 (1964) 42 TC 14

46 Basil Sabine, *Tax Appeals Handbook* (Butterworths) p.135, 136

between questions of fact, which cannot be appealed against, and questions of law, which can. Possibly the position is still most aptly summarized in words of Scott L.J. in *Bean v Doncaster Amalgamated Collieries Ltd.*[47]

> Between pure white on the one side and jet black on the other side is a penumbra of grey, shading off into black and white respectively. Within this penumbra there must, of course, often lie cases where the decision is one of fact for the commissioners: but in others it will depend on the correct appreciation of the true character in law of some one or more of the facts. Where it is clear to the court that the commissioners have misread that character, the decision in law rests with the courts.

It would seem that the courts have deliberately, perhaps wisely, refrained from trying to lay down any general principles.

Finally, it must always be remembered that there should in the minds of both the appellant and the Revenue, be no such thing as trying to categorise any decision as a victory or a defeat. What both parties should strive for is an elucidation of the contentious points, which means a result in which justice is seen to be done and a decision arrived at which is both legally correct and as fair as current Nigerian tax law, practice and procedure will allow.

[47] (1946) 27 TC 310.

Selected bibliography

Abdulrazaq, *Nigerian Tax Offences and Penalties*
Allan, *Theory of Taxation*
Diamond, *Public Expenditure in Practice*, 1975
Tiley, *Revenue Law*, 1981
Tiley, *Revenue Law*, 2000
Willoughby & Harvey, *A Guide to Income Tax and Capital Gains Tax in Nigeria*, 1969

Index

www.ingramcontent.com/pod-product-compliance
Lightning Source LLC
Chambersburg PA
CBHW031322230926
51848CB00001B/51